Microsoft® SQL Server™ 2005
New Features

Michael Otey

McGraw-Hill/Osborne

New York   Chicago   San Francisco
Lisbon   London   Madrid   Mexico City   Milan
New Delhi   San Juan   Seoul   Singapore   Sydney   Toronto

The McGraw·Hill Companies

McGraw-Hill/Osborne
2100 Powell Street, 10th Floor
Emeryville, California 94608
U.S.A.

To arrange bulk purchase discounts for sales promotions, premiums, or fund-raisers, please contact **McGraw-Hill**/Osborne at the above address. For information on translations or book distributors outside the U.S.A., please see the International Contact Information page immediately following the index of this book.

Microsoft® SQL Server™ 2005 New Features

234567890 FGR FGR 019876

ISBN 0-07-222776-1

Vice President & Group Publisher	Mike Hays
Vice President & Publisher	Scott Grillo
Acquisitions Editor	Wendy Rinaldi
Project Editor	Julie M. Smith
Acquisitions Coordinator	Alex McDonald
Technical Editor	Tom Rizzo
Copy Editor	Bob Campbell
Proofreader	Susie Elkind
Indexer	Valerie Perry
Composition	Elizabeth Jang, Dick Schwartz
Illustrators	Kathleen Edwards, Melinda Lytle
Series Design	Peter F. Hancik
Cover Series Designer	Pattie Lee

This book was composed with Corel VENTURA™ Publisher.

Contents

Acknowledgments

I'd like to acknowledge all of the help from the great people at Osborne who made this book possible. Wendy Rinaldi planted the seed for this book on SQL Server 2005's new features and gave me the encouragement to grow it from an idea into a full fledged book. Julie Smith, the book's project editor, juggled a hectic schedule and a stream of new material, revisions, and edits as she managed the tough task of bringing all of the material for the book together. I'm also thankful for the efforts of copy editor Bob Campbell, proofreader Susie Elkind, indexer Valerie Perry, and Elizabeth Jang and Dick Schwartz for page composition.

I also got substantial help from Tom Rizzo and Eric Brown who provided essential technical reviews. Their efforts helped me to keep up with the rapidly evolving product as it moved through its prerelease and beta cycles. To the degree this book meets my goals of technical excellence; I owe a lot to Tom and Eric. Of course, I take responsibility for any errors that may remain in the final version.

And I'd also like to give a special thanks to my wife, and not-so-silent partner, Denielle Otey, one of the book's technical editors. She rigorously tested and retested all of the code samples used in the book as well as giving me advice and support throughout the project.

Michael Otey

About the Author

Michael Otey is the Technical Director for *Windows ITPro Magazine* and Senior Technical Editor for *SQL Server Magazine*. He is also President of TECA, Inc (www.teca.com), a software development and consulting company that specializes in networking and database applications. Michael is the co-author of the *SQL Server 2000 Developer's Guide* and the *ADO.NET: The Complete Reference* published by McGraw Hill/Osborne.

Dedication

This book is dedicated to my Mom who planted
in me the faith to tackle life's challenges and problems.

Michael Otey

Introduction

SQL Server 2005 is a feature-rich release, providing a host of new tools for the database administrator as well as the database developer. This book is written to help the IT manager, database administrator, database developer, systems integrator, and consultant to quickly get up to speed on the most important new features found in the SQL Server 2005 release. This book will help you to understand how SQL Server 2005 is different from its predecessors and will provide you with information that you can use to evaluate the benefits of adopting the new release.

In order to get this book out in a timely manner, I needed to make choices about which features to cover and the level of detail to give to each feature. This is both a good news and bad news story. The good news is that Microsoft SQL Server 2005 is packed with new features—more features than any release of SQL Server since its inception. The bad news is that there just isn't enough space in this book to provide comprehensive coverage of all these features. When deciding between features I leaned toward selecting those features that I felt would be the most significant for the enterprise and those features that embodied the biggest changes from the prior release. Hopefully, you'll agree that I made the right choices in most regards.

Likewise, to make this new features guide available in a timely fashion, the information presented here is based on the beta 2 version of Microsoft SQL Server 2005. This means that in some cases there will be minor differences in the screens and some of the implementation details that are found in the final RTM (Release to Manufacturing) version and the coverage provided in this book. However, Microsoft has stated that they expected beta 2 to be feature complete and this book is intended mainly as a guide to introduce you to those new features. While I do provide numerous examples showing how to make use of these features, the goal of those examples is to help you to better understand the purpose of the new features and get an idea of their implementation. Moreover, in my experience I've found that Microsoft is very disciplined with regard to their beta programs and I expect that all of the major new features presented in this book will be consistent with the final release and that any differences between what is presented here and the final released product will be minor. Every effort has been made to make sure that the information presented here is as up-to-date as possible.

As an additional note I should stress that this book is not intended as a general tutorial on using Microsoft SQL Server. It is written with the assumption that the reader has a basic familiarly with SQL Server. I've split this book into three parts—reflecting the three general areas of Microsoft SQL Server 2005 itself. Part I of this book covers the database administration features. Here you'll learn about the features that are most important to the database administrator. In this section you'll get an introduction to the new SQL Workbench, which gives the SQL Server database administrator a whole new management experience. In addition in Part I you'll also learn about the new important security, architectural, high availability, and disaster recovery features the Microsoft has provided in SQL Server 2005.

Part II covers the new features found in the database development area. As you would expect if you've read anything about Yukon (the codename for the SQL Server 2005 release), in the press, then you've certainly heard that the biggest change found in SQL Server 2005 is the integration of the Microsoft .NET Common Language Runtime (CLR) with the SQL Server 2005 database engine. SQL Server's CLR integration allows any of the .NET languages like C#, Visual Basic.NET or managed VC++ to be used to write stored procedures, triggers, and user-defined functions. Part II of this book provides thorough coverage of these new features showing both how you write CLR-based database objects as well as how you incorporate them into the database and where they are best utilized. Additionally, the chapters in Part II will go on to cover the new SQL Notification Services, the SQL Broker Service and the improved XML integration features.

Part III hits the last big area of enhancements found in Microsoft SQL Server 2005. In Part III you can learn about the new Business Intelligence (BI) features. The BI area for SQL Server 2005 has some of the richest new features found in the new release. For instance, with SQL Server 2005, the new SQL Service Reporting Services feature is included as an integral part of the base SQL Server package and one of the chapters in this section will guide you through the use of its graphical report designer as well as exploring SQL Server Reporting Service's rich report formatting and deployment features. Integration Services, the replacement for Data Transformation Services (DTS) has also been totally revamped in SQL Server 2005. First introduced with SQL Server 7, DTS has become a cornerstone of both the data warehousing extraction-transformation-load (ETL) function as well as the primary vehicle for moving data between SQL Server and other platforms. With the SQL Server 2005 release Integration Services has been rewritten from the ground up all in managed code and one of the chapters in Part III goes into to detail about the new changes that you'll find in the new Integration Services. If that weren't enough, Part III will also introduce you the new feature found in SQL Server's Analysis Services and data mining features.

As you can see there's a lot to cover and the SQL Server 2005 has more new features that any previous release of SQL Server.

Database Administration
Features

Database Architecture and Storage Engine Features

IN THIS CHAPTER:

New Hardware Support

SQL Server Engine

Security

Building on the same essential architecture that was established with the SQL Server 7 release, Microsoft has continued to make evolutionary improvements in the SQL Server engine. Following Moore's Law, hardware has continued to double in capacity every 18 months, while at the same time hardware costs have continued to decline. However, while hardware has been getting cheaper, people costs have risen. In the SQL Server 2005 release, Microsoft has made enhancements that enable SQL Server to take advantage of the newest generations of high-performance hardware, providing it with the capability to scale to the utmost peak of the enterprise. At the same time, the company has added features that make SQL Server easier to manage and also provided new capabilities that enable you to get more value out of SQL Server for your organization. In this chapter, I'll introduce you to some of the most important architectural improvements that Microsoft has made to SQL Server 2005, with the goal of helping you to see how these features can improve your productivity and the reliability of your database environment.

New Hardware Support

One of the key new features that enables SQL Server 2005 as a database engine to achieve the same performance levels as the biggest UNIX databases is its improved hardware support. Memory has always been one of the most critical factors that contribute to database performance, and the large UNIX databases that topped the non-clustered TPC-C performance rankings all attained that level of performance using a 64-bit hardware and operating system platform. When a comparable 64-bit platform became available for SQL Server in the form of the 64-bit Intel Itanium2 processor and Windows Server 2003's native 64-bit support, SQL Server immediately jumped to the top of TPC-C benchmarks. SQL Server 2005 inherits that native 64-bit support from Windows Server 2003 along with the capability to support Non-Uniform Memory Architecture (NUMA). Building on the Windows Server 2003 platform, SQL Server 2005 provides 64-bit support for both the Itanium IA-64 architecture and the AMD x64 architecture.

Native 64-Bit Support

When running on Windows Server 2003 for 64-bit Itanium systems, SQL Server 2005 supports Intel's Itanium and Itanium2 processors. When running on Windows Server 2003 for 64-bit Extended Systems, SQL Server 2005 supports AMD's 64-bit

Opteron and Athlon 64 processors as well as Intel's Xeon with Intel Extended Memory 64 Technology (EMT64). SQL Server 2005 fully supports both 32-bit and 64-bit hardware platforms for all of its major services, including the SQL Server Engine, Analysis Services, SQL Agent, and Reporting Services. The real advantage in moving a database to the 64-bit platform isn't faster processing power. Rather, the real advantage lies in the vastly increased addressable memory. Figure 1-1 shows a comparison of the maximum addressable memory for the 32-bit SQL Server and the 64-bit version of SQL Server 2005.

The native 32-bit architecture is limited to a maximum of 4GB of addressable memory. Under Windows, this 4GB limit is divided evenly between the operating system and the applications. In other words, 2GB is reserved for the Windows operating system, leaving the remaining 2GB for applications. Using the Advanced Windowing Extensions (AWE) support found in the 32-bit version of Windows, the 32-bit version of SQL Server can address a maximum of 32GB of RAM. While this increase is substantial, there was still the overhead of paging to get to the appropriate memory pages. The native 64-bit implementation virtually eliminates the memory constraint by raising the maximum addressable memory to 32TB. Currently no production system supports anywhere near this amount of physical RAM. The maximum amount of physical RAM on which SQL Server 2005 has been tested at the time of release is 512GB. With the upcoming release of the next service pack for Windows Server 2003, the maximum supported memory is expected to jump to 1TB.

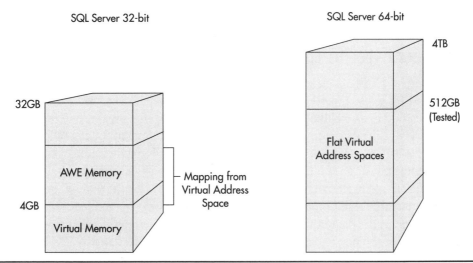

Figure 1-1   *Comparing 32-bit and 64-bit memory addressing*

NUMA Support

Another new feature that leverages the Windows Server 2003 operating system is Non-Uniform Memory Architecture (NUMA) support. NUMA is a system architecture used by some system manufacturers such as IBM and Unisys that manages CPU and memory usage in multiprocessor systems more efficiently than the typical SMP architecture. In standard SMP systems, as the speed and number of processors increase, the competition between the processors for access to memory creates bus contention. This injects delays in the processing and hinders the capability of a system to scale. The result of this is that SMP systems don't scale linearly as the number of processors increases. The NUMA architecture is designed to solve this problem found in SMP systems, in which the processors are able to access the data in RAM faster than the RAM and system bus can provide it. The NUMA architecture groups the CPU and memory into local pods of multiple processors. These pods are connected to each other via an external bus that transports cross-pod data traffic. This pod arrangement addresses the contention issue by limiting the number of CPUs competing for access to memory. To realize the maximum benefits from this architecture, both the operating system and the applications must be designed to minimize cross-pod data traffic and maximize the faster intra-pod memory access. If the operating system and the application are designed correctly, the NUMA architecture enables nearly linear scaling as more processors are added. Windows Server 2003 and SQL Server 2005 incorporate architecture improvements to increase the degree to which threads and the memory they use are located in the same pod.

Support for Hyper-Threading

SQL Server 2005 can also take advantage of hyper-threading, thanks in part to the new support for hyper-threading that Microsoft has added to Windows Server 2003. Hyper-threading is a CPU technology developed by Intel that creates two logical processors for each physical processor in a system. Each logical processor is capable of simultaneously executing separate threads. The goal of hyper-threading is to provide better resource consumption for multithreaded applications or multiple applications running on a single machine. While hyper-threading provides the potential of increasing the throughput on a server, the logical processors do compete for system resources such as the data in the processor's cache. This competition for resources prevents a hyper-threaded CPU from performing as well as a comparable system that is using two physical CPUs.

SQL Server 2005 gets two main benefits from Windows Server 2003's support for hyper-threading. First, unlike Windows 2000, Windows Server 2003 counts only physical processors for licensing purposes. Thus, a single processor using hyper-threading is licensed as a single processor rather than a dual processor, as it would be under Windows 2000. Next, Windows Server 2003 provides improved thread scheduling for hyper-threaded systems. These changes result in better performance for multithreaded applications like SQL Server.

SQL Server Engine

While the first section of this chapter looked at the bigger picture of new hardware support provided in SQL Server 2005, this next section will drill down into some the most important improvements that Microsoft has made to the SQL Server engine itself.

.NET Framework Integration

The most significant SQL Server engine enhancement in SQL Server 2005 is the integration of the Microsoft .NET Framework. The integration of the .NET Framework with SQL Server extends the capability of SQL Server 2005 by enabling the development of stored procedures, user-defined functions, triggers, aggregates, and user-defined types using any of the .NET languages, such as VB.NET, C#, or J#. The integration of the .NET CLR with SQL Server 2005 is more than just skin deep, as the SQL Server database engine hosts the CLR in-process. You can learn more about the integration of the .NET Framework with SQL Server 2005 in Chapter 4.

Enhanced Multiple Instance Support

Another important enhancement found in the Enterprise Edition of SQL Server 2005 is support for up to 50 instances. This is up from the maximum of 16 instances that was supported in SQL Server 2000. This is a particularly significant improvement for hosting vendors who lease out multiple SQL Server services as part of their web services offerings.

New Data Types

SQL Server 2005 also supports several new data types. While the integration of the .NET Framework enables support for user-defined types, SQL Server 2005 also provides a couple of other new native data types: the varbinary(max) and XML data types. The varbinary(max) data type provides a new method for using LOBs with SQL Server. Unlike the older Image and Text data types, the new varbinary(max) data type can be used as a variable, and programmatically it can be treated like the smaller data types, allowing for easier and more consistent usage scenarios.

The new XML data type, based on the varbinary(max) data type, enables you to store XML documents in the database. However, unlike the varbinary(max) data type, which is essentially data agnostic, the new XML data type is designed expressly for XML data and supports schema verification of XML documents. You can learn more about the new data types supported by SQL Server 2005 in Chapter 7.

Database Snapshots and Mirroring

Database Mirroring protects against database failure by giving SQL Server 2005 an instant database standby capability. Database Mirroring is a database-level availability technology that works with all of the standard hardware supported by SQL Server. There's no need for any shared storage between the primary server and the mirrored server, and there are no distance limitations. Database Mirroring works by sending transaction logs between the primary server and the mirroring server, basically making the new Database Mirroring feature a real-time log shipping application. Database Mirroring can be set up with a single database, or it can be set up for multiple databases.

Database Snapshots provide a read-only snapshot of a database at a specific point in time. Database Snapshots are best suited for creating copies of a database for reporting or for creating backup copies of a database that you can use to roll back a production database to a prior state. Database Snapshots can be combined with Database Mirroring to create a reporting server based on the data that's on the mirrored server. The data on the mirrored server can't be accessed directly because the mirroring server is always in recovery mode. However, you can create a Database Snapshot on the mirrored database and then access the database view for reporting. You can learn more about database views and mirroring in Chapter 3.

Native HTTP Support

One of the other significant improvements to the SQL Server database engine is the addition of native HTTP support to the engine itself. The capability of SQL Server to process incoming HTTP requests enables SQL Server to provide SQL statement execution and stored procedure invocation via the SOAP protocol. This means that SQL Server 2005 is able to process incoming web service requests without the presence of IIS or another web server. The new HTTP support gives SQL Server native HTTP listening capabilities, including the capability to support HTTP endpoints specifying the URL, port, and requests that will be supported. SQL Server is also able to publish web services as Web Services Description Language

(WSDL) for endpoints. SQL Server's HTTP support is standards-compliant, supporting SOAP 1.0 and 1.2, as well as WSDL 1.1. The new native HTTP support feature also supports both Windows and SQL Server authentication, as well as SSL. To enable this new feature to have greater compatibility with middle-tier programming, stored procedures can return result sets as an ADO.NET DataSet.

Server Events and DDL Triggers

SQL Server 2005's new Server Event and DDL Triggers features enable you to programmatically respond to changes in the system. While both of these new features can accomplish similar functions, they are implemented quite differently. Like standard DML triggers, DDL triggers are synchronous events that execute stored procedures. You learn more about DDL triggers in Chapter 4.

In contrast, server events are asynchronous. In the server event model, the server posts an event to a SQL Broker Service, and then a consumer can independently retrieve that event. The event itself is recorded as XML data. There is no way to roll back an event, and an event can be ignored if no consumer retrieves it. When the event occurs, the system event is fired, which can notify you of the event or optionally execute a code routine. The following example illustrates the syntax used to set up an event notification:

```
CREATE EVENT NOTIFICATION MyDDLEvents
ON SERVER FOR DDL_STATEMENTS TO SERVICE MyDDL_log
```

This example creates a new event, names the event notification MyDDLEvents, and attaches the event to the DDL statement. The TO SERVICE clause specifies that the SQL Broker Service named MyDLL_log will be the recipient of the events. You can find out more about the SQL Service Broker in Chapter 6.

Database Data File Enhancements

SQL Server 2005 now supports the ability to change the path of a database's data and log files using the ALTER DATABASE command. SQL Server 2000 provided the ability to move the files for the tempdb database, but this wasn't allowed for any other database. As you might expect, SQL Server 2005 supports moving the files only as an offline operation. The following example illustrates the new ALTER DATABASE statements syntax:

```
ALTER DATABASE <database_name>
  MODIFY FILE(name=<'data_file_name'>, filename=<'new path'>)
```

Data Partitioning

Another new enhancement that's found in SQL Server 2005 is the ability to perform data partitioning. *Data partitioning* allows you to break a single database object such as a table or an index into multiple pieces. The new data partitioning feature facilitates the management of very large tables and indexes. The partitioning is transparent to the applications, which see only the database object itself and are unaware of multipart underlying storage, which is managed by SQL Server. Partitions can be created and dropped without affecting the availability of the database object itself. Essentially, partitioning enables you to split the underlying data store into multiple objects while still presenting a unified view of the object and all its partitions to an application. Figure 1-2 presents a basic overview of partitioning.

SQL Server 2005 supports data partitioning for tables, indexes, and indexed views. The row is the basic unit of partitioning. The partitions can be created according to values found in the columns in a row. This is known as *horizontal partitioning*. For instance, a table might be partitioned by date, where a different partition is created for each year. This type of partitioning by date enables you to perform a sliding date window type of processing, where you can drop the partition containing data from last year and not affect access to data contained in the current year's partition.

Data partitioning provides a couple of important benefits for very large databases (VLDBs). Data partitions can facilitate data management, enabling you to selectively back up only specified partitions. For example, in the case of a large table that is partitioned by date you may want to back up only the current year, not last year's partition. Another advantage is that in multiprocessor systems, you can devote a CPU to processing its own partition for improved throughput.

There are two basic steps to implementing data partitioning. First, you need to determine exactly how you want to partition a given object. Second, you need to assign each partition to a physical storage location. The different partitions can all be assigned to a single filegroup or different partitions can be mapped to multiple filegroups.

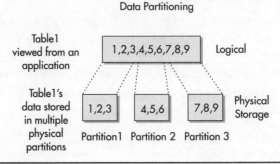

Figure 1-2   *Data partitioning*

The following example shows the syntax for creating a simple partition function and scheme that will partition a table using a Range partition:

```
CREATE PARTITION FUNCTION MyPF
(int) AS RANGE LEFT FOR VALUES (50, 100)
GO
CREATE PARTITION SCHEME MyPS
 AS PARTITION MyPF TO (FileGroup1)
GO
CREATE TABLE MyTable (col1 int, col2 varchar(50))
  ON MyPS(col1)
GO
```

The first line creates a partition function named MyPF. The (int) shows that the partitioning will be performed on a column that's defined using the int data type. The keyword RANGE specifies that Range partitioning will be used. The LEFT keyword controls which partition will receive borderline values. The value of LEFT indicates that any row that has a value that matches the partition boundary will be moved to the partition immediately to the left. The VALUES clause is used to define the boundary points of the partitions. It's important to note that these values are boundary points and not the partitions themselves. This will actually result in the creation of three partitions: the first will contain negative values to 50; the second partition will contain the values 51–100; the third partition will contain all values of 101 and over.

The second line creates a partition scheme named MyPS. The AS PARTITION clause is used to specify the partition function that will be used by this scheme. This example uses the MyPF partition function. The TO clause identifies the filegroup or filegroups that will store the partitions. This example uses a single filegroup, named FileGroup1.

Next, the partition scheme needs to be attached to the table that will be partitioned. This example shows the extended CREATE TABLE syntax that enables the table to be partitioned. The first part of the CREATE TABLE statement is unchanged. It specifies the table name, MyTable in this example, and the table's columns. This simple table uses two columns, named col1 and col2. The new ON keyword is then used to specify the partition scheme that will be used. This example uses the MyPS partition scheme that was just created. And the column that contains the partition's key data is supplied in parentheses. This example uses the column col1 for the partitioning key. This column is an int data type, which must match the data type specified in the partition function.

There are a few restrictions on the types of columns that can be used for the partitioning key. These restrictions are very similar to the limitation of columns that can be used in an index. The text, ntext, and image data types cannot be used.

Likewise, timestamp columns are also restricted. Only native "T-SQL" data types can be used. You can't use a user-defined type as a partitioning key. However, you can use the new varchar(max) data type. There is also a limitation of 1000 partitions per table, and all partitions must exist on a single node.

Index Enhancements

There are many new enhancements to indexes in SQL Server 2005. First, rebuilding a clustered index no longer forces all of the non-clustered index to be rebuilt. In SQL Server 2000, when you rebuilt a clustered index all of the related non-clustered indexes were rebuilt as well. That's no longer the case, as SQL Server 2005 keeps the non-clustered indexes intact during the rebuild of the clustered index.

Next, there's a new included columns feature that enables you to add non-key columns to an index. This new feature enables more queries to be covered by the index, thereby enhancing the performance of the queries by minimizing the need for the SQL Server engine to go to the underlying table to complete the query. Instead, the engine can satisfy the query requirements by using just the data in the covering index. One of the really nice aspects of the new included columns feature is the fact that the included columns that are not part of the key are not included in the maximum size of the index, which is still 900 bytes.

Another new index enhancement that Microsoft added to SQL Server 2005 is the ability to disable an index. Disabling an index stops that index from being maintained by the SQL Server engine and also prevents the index from being used. When an index is disabled, SQL Server deallocates the storage space used by the index but keeps the index's metadata. Before a disabled index can be enabled again, it needs to be rebuilt using the ALTER INDEX command.

Online Index Operations

Prior versions of SQL Server didn't allow any access to an index while that index was being rebuilt. You needed to wait until the rebuild process completed until the table could be updated again. SQL Server 2005's new online index operations feature enables applications to access the index as well as perform update, insert, and delete operations on a table while the index rebuilding operation is running. You can find more information about SQL Server 2005's online index operations in Chapter 3.

System Catalog and Metadata Enhancements

In SQL Server 2000 and earlier versions, the system catalog and metadata were stored as part of every database in the master database. With SQL Server 2005, this has changed and the metadata now resides in the resource database, which the system stores as a sys object. SQL Server 2005 no longer allows any direct access to system tables. This change has enabled better security and faster system upgrades by consolidating the system's metadata. The catalog metadata is secured using row-level filters. You can learn more about SQL Server 2005's row-level security in the later section "Security" in this chapter.

The new metadata is completely backward compatible as long as you haven't used the undocumented system tables that Microsoft has repeatedly warned everyone not to use. The systems metadata in SQL Server 2005 is exposed through a set of catalog views. Catalog views, as well as ANSI INFORMATION_SCHEMA views, Property functions, and Built-in functions, replace the need to use system tables like you may have done in SQL Server 2000 . In all, there are over 250 new catalog views in SQL Server 2005, and they can be viewed from the sys schema of every user database. You can find the new system views by using the Microsoft SQL Server Manager Studio to open the Object Browser and then navigating to the Databases | <database> | Views | System Views node. You can also open a new query window and enter the following query:

```
select * from sys.system_views
```

Multiple Active Results Sets (MARS)

Previous versions of SQL Server were limited to one active result set per connection. SQL Server 2005 is now capable of supporting multiple active result sets on a single connection. This new feature enables you to open a single connection to the database, execute a query and process some results, and then later begin another query and process its results. Your applications can freely go back and forth between the multiple open results sets. Examples showing how you use the new MARS feature are presented in Chapter 4.

Bulk Data Loading

SQL Server 2005 provides some great improvements as well as performance increases in bulk data loading. The bulk data loading process now uses an XML-based format file that provides all of the functionality found in previous versions of the Bulk Copy Program's (BCP) format file and more. Plus, the XML format makes the BCP format file easier to read and understand. For backward compatibility with existing applications, the old BCP format file can still be used.

SQL Server 2005's bulk data loading process now supports logging of bad rows. This enables the bulk data loading process to continue even if invalid rows or data are encountered. Incorrectly formatted rows are written to an error file along with a description of the error condition. Rows that violate constraints are redirected to an error table along with their specific error condition.

Full-Text Search

Support for Full-Text search has also been enhanced in SQL Server 2005. Earlier versions of SQL Server required the use of stored procedures to create Full-Text search catalogs. With SQL Server 2005, several new DDL statements have been introduced to enable you to work with SQL Server's Full-Text search features. For instance, two of the new T-SQL Full-Text search DDL statements are: CREATE FULLTEXT CATALOG and CREATE FULLTEXT INDEX.

Other enhancements to Full-Text search in SQL Server 2005 include the ability to back up and restore Full-Text search catalogs and indexes along with your database data. Likewise, Full-Text catalogs and indexes can be attached and detached with their corresponding databases. Another interesting enhancement in SQL Server 2005's Full-Text search support is the ability to use a thesaurus to find synonyms of search words.

T-SQL Query Processor Enhancements

There are several enhancements to the query processor in SQL Server 2005, including Common Tables Expressions (CTE), an enhanced TOP clause, an enhanced WAITFOR statement, and a new OUTPUT clause for DML statements. Examples of using these enhancements in T-SQL are presented in Chapter 4.

Security

Security has been a big push for Microsoft ever since the company kicked off its Trustworthy Computing Initiative. The goal of Microsoft's Trustworthy Computing Initiative is to make all Microsoft products more secure and more reliable. As you would expect, being a part of the Trustworthy Computing Initiative, SQL Server 2005 is the recipient of a number of very significant security enhancements. Microsoft's security push for SQL Server is focused on making the product more secure and more robust from its design through its deployment. When designing the security enhancements for SQL Server 2005, Microsoft followed some basic security tenets. First, it wanted to make the system secure right out of the box by gearing all of the default installation settings toward creating a secure environment. While it left options open for users to select less secure settings, selecting these options required deliberate choices. Next, Microsoft followed the principle of least privileges in their system design. The system is designed so that an individual should have only the require privileges to perform a given function and no more. Finally, Microsoft wanted to reduce the potential exposure surface area by providing the ability to install only those components that are needed.

All of the new security features found in SQL Server 2005 were deeply influenced by the things Microsoft discovered during its security push in early 2002 and were carried into the SQL Server 2005 design and implementation. Some of the core security feature enhancements found in SQL Server 2005 that you'll read about in this section include the separation of users from schemas, the new stored procedure execution context, more granular control of permissions, new password policy enforcement, changes to row-level security, and enhanced security for catalogs.

User-Schema Separation

The most significant new security-related change found in SQL Server 2005 is user-schema separation. A user, or perhaps more accurately, a principal, is any entity against whom database objects are secured. A principal can be a Windows user, a SQL Server user, a role, or an application role. With SQL Server 2000, directly owned by users database objects and the users themselves were found in the sys_users system table. That's all changed with SQL Server 2005. Now database objects are owned by schemas. Users no longer directly own database objects; instead they own schemas. With SQL Server 2005, users and other security principals can be found in the new sys.database_principals view. SQL Server 2005's list of schemas can be found in the new sys.schemas view.

A *schema* is a container of objects. The schema is identified by the third part of the four-part object naming syntax used by SQL Server. The following example illustrates SQL Server 2005's naming syntax, where each part of the name gets increasingly more specific.

```
Server_name.Database_name.Schema_name.Object_name
```

In all of the previous releases of SQL Server, the schema name and the owner name were essentially the same thing. With SQL Server 2005, the owner has been separated from the schema. When SQL Server 2000 and earlier releases resolved object names, SQL Server first looked for Database_name.User_name.Object_name, and if that failed, it then looked for Database_name.dbo.Object_name.

The main reason for this separation of user and schema in SQL Server 2005 is to address the problem of needing to change the ownership of multiple database objects if a given user (aka the old object owner) leaves the organization. In addition, the action of changing a database object's ownership also resulted in a name change. For instance, if the owner of Table1 in database MyDB is changed from UserA to UserB, then the qualified name of Table1 will be changed from MyDB.UserA.Table1 to MyDB.UserB.Table1. To help prevent this problem, many organizations adopted the standard of having all database objects owned by dbo, but there was nothing in the server that forced this practice.

SQL Server 2005's implementation of the concept of a database schema introduces a level of abstraction in the chain of database object ownership. You can see SQL Server 2005's database object ownership chain in Figure 1-3.

With SQL Server 2005, database objects are contained in schemas, and the schemas are in turn owned by users. This new level of abstraction makes the problem of changing database object ownership much more manageable. Dropping a user that owns database objects in SQL Server 2005 means that the DBA now needs to change only the ownership of the schema and not all of the individual database objects. This vastly reduces the number of objects that the DBA needs to touch in order to change the ownership of the objects in a database. To change the ownership of all the objects in a SQL Server 2005 database, you simply change the owner of the schema, and then you can drop the old user. Changing the owner of database object doesn't change an object's name because the schema name doesn't change, just its ownership.

As you might expect, the new schema object changes the way that SQL Server performs database object name resolution. Each user now has a default schema associated with that user, and SQL Server 2005 will first look for an unqualified object name using the user's default schema. If that fails, SQL Server will look for the object using the schema name of dbo. For instance, if UserA has a default schema of MySchema1 and that user performs a query looking for Table1, then

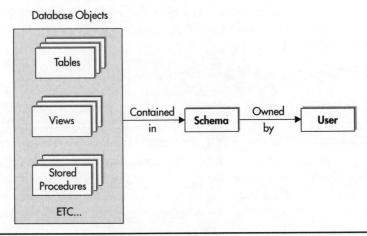

Figure 1-3   *SQL Server 2005's object ownership chain*

the server will first attempt to resolve the name using MySchema1.Table1 and then fall back to dbo.Table1.

Just as SQL Server 2000 databases could contain multiple users and roles, SQL Server 2005 databases can contain multiple schemas. Each schema has an owning principal, which is typically either a user or a role. For name resolution purposes, each user has a default schema. The actual database objects are then contained in a schema. To create new database objects inside a schema, you must have CREATE permission for the database object itself and ALTER or CONTROL permission for the schema. Ownership chaining is still based on actual owners, not schemas.

SQL Server 2005 introduces several DDL changes for dealing with the new user and schema separation, including a CREATE/DROP/ALTER statement for USER, ROLE, and SCHEMA objects. The following listing demonstrates how a database schema is created and assigned:

```
/* Create a login */
CREATE LOGIN UserA WITH PASSWORD = 'ABC123#$'
GO
/* Create a user for that login - the schema doesn't need to exist*/
CREATE USER UserA FOR LOGIN UserA
   WITH DEFAULT_SCHEMA = MySchema
GO
/* Create the schema and assign its owner */
CREATE SCHEMA MySchema AUTHORIZATION UserA
GO
/* Create a Table in the new schema */
CREATE TABLE MySchema.Table1 (col1 char (20))
GO
```

The first line in this listing creates a new login named UserA and sets a password for that login. The next line creates a new user named UserA for the login and sets the default schema for UserA to MySchema. The actual schema does not need to exist at the time it is specified in the CREATE USER statement. If you don't specify a default schema when you create a new user, then the default schema will be set to dbo. Next, the CREATE SCHEMA statement is used to create a new schema named MySchema. The AUTHORIZATION clause sets the owner of the schema to be UserA. Finally, a table named Table1 is created in the schema named MySchema. The owner for MySchema and its objects such as Table1 is UserA.

Stored Procedure Execution Context

While Microsoft has referred to one new feature as a stored procedure execution context, it really applies to modules rather than just stored procedures. A module can be a stored procedure, a function, or an assembly. Setting the execution context for a module causes all statements that are contained in that module to be checked for permissions against the specified execution context. In other words, by setting the execution context of a given module, you cause all the statements that are contained in that module to be executed using the authority of the user that you specify rather than the actual caller of the module. This new feature enables you to get advantages similar to those realized through SQL Server 2000's ownership chaining, but it is more flexible, as it doesn't have the same limitations. For example, unlike SQL Server 2000's ownership chaining, which didn't allow you to alter the execution context for dynamic SQL, SQL Server 2005's module execution context applies to dynamic SQL just as it does to static SQL. To better understand this, take a look at Figure 1-4, which demonstrates SQL Server 2000's ownership chaining.

For UserA to execute dbo.Proc1, UserA must have execute permission for that object. However, when dbo.Proc1 accesses dbo.Table1, no permissions are checked, because dbo is the owner of both objects. This is an example of an intact ownership chain. In the next scenario, for UserA to execute UserB.Proc2, UserA must have Execute permissions for that object. Then, when UserB.Proc2 attempts to access UserC.Table2, Select permissions from UserA must be checked. In this case, because UserB.Proc2 and UserC.Table2 have different owners, the ownership chain is broken.

SQL Server 2005's execution simplifies this scenario, as shown in Figure 1-5. In this scenario, when UserA attempts to execute UserB.Proc2, SQL Server checks to ensure that UserA has Execute permissions for the UserB.Proc1. If the object UserB.Proc1 is created with an execution context that specifies that a stored procedure will be executed as UserZ, then when the UserB.Proc1 stored procedure attempts to access UserC.Table1, SQL Server will check for Select permissions only on the user specified in the execution context, which in this case is UserZ. No Select permissions are required for UserA, who is the actual caller.

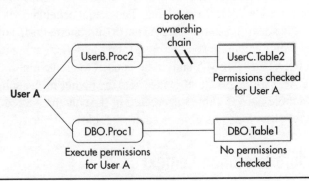

Figure 1-4   *SQL Server 2000's ownership chains*

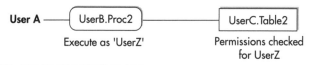

Figure 1-5   *SQL Server 2005's execution context*

The following listing shows how you change the execution context of a stored procedure named MyProc1:

```
ALTER PROC MySchema.Proc1 WITH EXECUTE AS USER UserB
```

This statement shows the new WITH EXECUTE clause. Here, the stored procedure named Proc1 that's contained in MySchema is set to execute under the context of UserB. You must specify a user name for the execution content. You cannot specify the name of a role. Changes in execution context are stored in the new sys.sql_modules view.

More Granular Permissions Control

SQL Server 2005 also provides more granular control over permissions. With SQL Server 2005, Microsoft added more permissions at different scopes. The scopes to permissions that can be applied are: server, database, schema, object, and principal. The design idea behind SQL Server 2005's enhanced permissions is the principle of least privileges, giving the DBA the ability to control exactly what permissions are assigned. The new granular permissions do not do away with SQL Server's existing fixed roles. All of the older roles are still present and can coexist with no problems alongside the new permissions. One specific scenario that these new granular permissions are meant to address is the case of auditing. On SQL Server 2000, you needed to be a member of the sysadmins group in order to perform auditing. However, membership in this group also enables many other, more far-reaching capabilities. Some of the new permissions available in SQL Server 2005 enable auditing functions to be performed without requiring that the user be a part of the sysadmins group.

The same basic permission states of GRANT, DENY, and REVOKE that were used in previous versions of SQL Server still apply. One thing that's different about the way that SQL Server 2005 uses permissions is that the same permission can be applied at multiple scopes. For example, if you apply a permission to the database scope, it applies to all objects in the database. If you apply a permission to the schema level, it applies to just those objects contained in the schema. With the exception of the DENY permission, the higher-scope permission is always used. However, a DENY at any level always takes precedence. Table 1-1 lists some of the

Permission	Description
ALTER	Grants the ability to change the properties of an object. Also grants the ability to execute CREATE/DROP/ALTER statements.
ALTER ANY 'X'	Grants the ability to alter any object of type X. For instance, if you substituted TABLE for X, this would grant the ability to alter any table in the database.
ALTER TRACE	Grants the ability to perform auditing and run Profiler.
CONTROL	Grants a principal owner-like permissions.
SELECT	Grants the ability to access an object. Now applies to the schema and database levels rather than just the object level.
EXECUTE	Grants the ability to execute a procedure, assembly, or function. Now applies to the schema and database levels rather than just the object level.
IMPERSONATE	Grants a login or a user the ability to impersonate another user.
TAKE OWNERSHIP	Grants the ability to assume the ownership of an object.
VIEW DEFINITION	Grants the ability to view an object's metadata.

Table 1-1   *Some New Permissions in SQL Server 2005*

most important new SQL Server 2005 permissions. The server permissions are found in the sys.server_permissions view, while the database permissions are found in the sys.database_permissions view.

Password Policy Enforcement

Another important new security feature found in SQL Server 2005 is support for password policies. This new policy enforcement feature follows local Windows password policies and enables you to implement a consistent enterprise-wide security policy, not just for your Windows server systems but also for your SQL Server database systems. SQL Server 2005 now has the capability to enforce password strength, password expiration, and account lockout policies. As you would expect, the password strength policy forces passwords to consist of a given complexity. The password expiration policy ensures that passwords expire and must be reset at a given interval. And the account lockout policy enables an account to be locked out after a given number of bad password attempts. All of these new password policies are supported on Windows Server 2003. However, only the password complexity policy is supported on Windows 2000 Server. Following Microsoft's security push, all of the policies are enabled in the default installation, but they can also be reconfigured on a per-login basis. SQL Server 2005 stores the new password policies in the sys.sql_logins catalog view.

Catalog Security

The final security-related enhancement that I'll cover in this section is the new catalog security provided by SQL Server 2005. The system tables that were used by SQL Server 2000 in the individual databases and in the master database are now implemented as catalog views in SQL Server 2005. The server's metadata exposed in these views is secured by default, and there are minimal public permissions. SQL Server 2005's catalog views employ row-level security, limiting access to the data contained in those views to only those objects that you own or have permissions to. Naturally, sa is an exception to this. The sa account still has access to all of the objects in the server.

To enable a user or role to access the metadata, the DBA needs to use the new VIEW DEFINITION permission. The VIEW DEFINITION permission can be used to grant a user who is not the owner and doesn't have permissions to access an object the ability to view the object's metadata. The VIEW DEFINITION permission can be applied at the server, database, schema, and object scopes.

CHAPTER 2

Database Administration and Development Tools

IN THIS CHAPTER:
Management and Development Tools
Performance Tools
New Management Frameworks

A lot has changed for the DBA in SQL Server 2005. There are several new subsystems that need to be managed, and in addition, the entire management tool set has been upgraded. Several of the administrative tools that were used to manage the previous versions of SQL Server have been replaced with new tools. In addition, a number of new management tools have been added as well. In this chapter, I'll guide you through the new administrative features that Microsoft has added to the SQL Server 2005 release.

Management and Development Tools

SQL Server 2005 uses an entirely new set of management tools from any of the previous versions of SQL Server. In the next part of this chapter, you'll get a closer look at the new management tools found in SQL Server 2005.

SQL Computer Manager

One of the first things that the experienced SQL Server DBA will notice about the new set of SQL Server 2005 management tools is that the Server Manager is missing. In the previous versions of SQL Server, the Server Manager was located in the System Tray. The Server Manager provided a graphic representation of the status of the different SQL Server Services, including the SQL Server service, the SQL Agent service, and the Distributed Transaction Coordinator service. You could also use the Server Manager to start and stop those services. While it was a handy tool, the Server Manager was not Windows Logo–compliant, and that was the main reason Microsoft removed it from SQL Server 2005. For SQL Server 2005, you can view and control the SQL Server services using the new SQL Computer Manager. The SQL Computer Manager is an MMC snap-in and can be accessed using the My Computer | Manage option. You can see the new SQL Computer Manager in Figure 2-1.

Using the SQL Computer Manager, you can see all of the SQL Server services that are running on the system listed underneath the main Services node. You use the Computer Management window to manage the following services: SQL Server, SQL Agent, ReportServer, MSSearch, MSDTC, Microsoft SQL Server Analysis Services, and Full Text.

You can control any service by first selecting it in the tree pane shown on the left side of the screen. This displays the status of the service in the details pane shown on the right side. To manage the service, you right-click the service in the details pane and then select the option to Start, Stop, Pause, Resume, or Restart the service from the pop-up context menu.

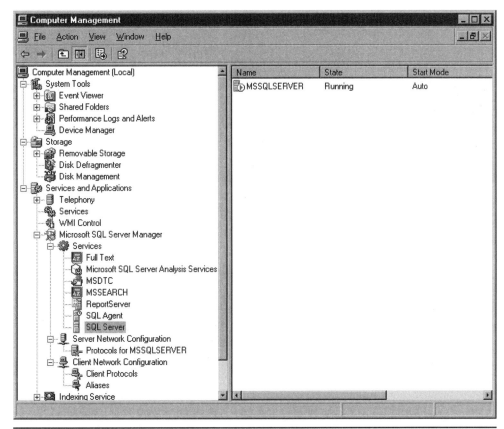

Figure 2-1   *SQL Computer Manager*

SQL Server Management Studio

The Server Manager isn't the only familiar management tool that's been changed in SQL Server 2005. The SQL Server Enterprise Manager, which was the primary management tool for SQL Server versions 7 and 2000, has been replaced by the new SQL Server Management Studio. Likewise, the Query Analyzer, which was the core T-SQL development tool in SQL Server versions 7 and 2000, has also been replaced by the new SQL Server Management Studio. SQL Server 2005 also provides a number of other administrative tools to the DBA, including the new Administrative Console, the Database Tuning Advisor, and a new Profiler.

The new SQL Server Management Studio is a radical departure from the administrative tools that were provided in the earlier releases of SQL Server.

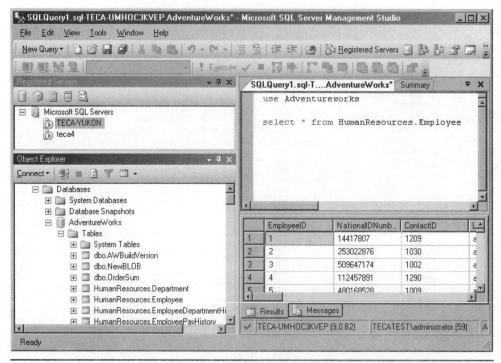

Figure 2-2 *SQL Server Management Studio*

The new SQL Server Management Studio incorporates most of the functionality that used to be provided by SQL Server Enterprise Manager and Query Analyzer. The SQL Server Management Studio is accessed using the Start | Programs | Microsoft SQL Server | SQL Server Management Studio menu option. You can see the SQL Server Management Studio in Figure 2-2.

The SQL Server Management Studio can be used to manage SQL Server 2005 systems as well as SQL Server 2000 and SQL Server 7 systems. It cannot be used on SQL Server 6.5 or older systems. You can use the older SQL Server 7 or SQL Server 2000 Enterprise Manager to manage a new SQL Server 2005 system, but because of some architectural changes between the two releases, this isn't supported or recommended. And the older management tools cannot access any of the new features that have been added to SQL Server 2005. While you can perform basic database and table browsing, many other actions will result in errors. SQL Server Management Studio is the tool of choice for managing mixed SQL Server 2005 and SQL Server 2000 systems.

The SQL Server Management Studio is built using a specialized version of the Visual Studio 2005 IDE (interactive development environment). Like Visual Studio 2005, the SQL Server Management Studio supports the creation of software projects. It allows you to write, edit, run, and debug code. It is also integrated with Visual SourceSafe for source code version control. However, unlike Visual Studio 2005, it doesn't allow you to compile VB.NET, C#, J#, or VC++. Instead, the SQL Server Management Studio works with T-SQL, MDX, MX, and XMLA.

The SQL Server Management Studio offers a number of important improvements over the SQL Server Enterprise Manager and the Query Analyzer combination. First, all of the dialog boxes displayed by the SQL Server Management Studio are non-modal, which means that you don't have to respond to the dialog before you can do anything else. The dialog boxes that were used by the old SQL Server Enterprise were all modal, and if you opened a dialog, you couldn't do anything else until the dialog was closed. The new non-modal dialogs used by the SQL Server Management Studio solve that problem and make it possible for the DBA to perform other management tasks while one of the dialogs is displayed.

In addition, the SQL Server Management Studio deals with large numbers of database objects much better than the old SQL Server Enterprise Manager. In the previous versions of SQL Server, the SQL Server Enterprise Manager always enumerated all of the database objects when it connected to a registered server. For most small and medium-sized businesses, this wasn't a problem. However, for organizations with very large databases containing thousands of database objects, the SQL Server Enterprise Manager could take a very long time listing all of the database objects and their properties—essentially rendering the SQL Server Enterprise Manager unusable until all of the objects were listed. With SQL Server 2005, the SQL Server Management Studio is much smarter in the way it handles database objects in that it doesn't enumerate the database objects until the user chooses to expand a database item display in the Object Browser. This enables the SQL Server Management Studio to provide much better responsiveness when it's used to manage very large databases.

The SQL Server Management Studio serves as the host for the majority of the SQL Server management and development tools. The Registered Servers window allows you to select the SQL Server systems that you will manage. The Object Explorer window enables you to work with the database objects in each server. And the Solutions Explorer window enables you to group your database source code into logical collections. You can find out more about the Registered Servers, Object Explorer, Query Editor, and Solution Explorer in the following sections in this chapter. More information about the Report Designer is presented in Chapter 8. The DTS Designer is covered in Chapter 9.

Registered Servers

Very much as when using the SQL Server Enterprise Manager, you must register servers in the SQL Server Management Studio before you can use it to manage them. You use the SQL Server Management Studio's Registered Servers window (shown in the upper left-hand portion of Figure 2-2) to register new SQL Server systems. Also as in the SQL Server Enterprise Manager, the SQL Server Management Studio's Registered Servers window enables you to group common servers together into logical server groups. To register a new SQL Server system in the Registered Servers window, you right-click in the window and select the New | Server Registration option from the context menu. Similarly, to create a new server group, you right-click in the Registered Servers window and select the New | Server Group option from the context menu. One nice feature in the Registered Servers window is the ability to export and import all of the registered servers. This enables you to quickly populate the Registered Servers windows of other SQL Server Management Studios without having to manually reregister all of the managed servers.

After a server is registered, you can manage its services by right-clicking the server in the Registered Servers window. This displays a context menu that enables you to connect to the server as well as start, stop, pause, resume, or restart the SQL Server service. You can work with a server's database objects by double-clicking the server name. This will connect you to the registered SQL server and will automatically open the Object Explorer window.

Object Explorer

The SQL Server Management Studio Object Explorer window enables you to perform the same management functions that were possible using the SQL Server Enterprise Manager. You can see the Object Explorer window in the lower left-hand corner of Figure 2-2. Using the Object Explorer, you can

- ▶ Start and stop a server
- ▶ Configure a server's properties
- ▶ Create databases
- ▶ Attach or detach databases
- ▶ Create database objects such as tables, views, or stored procedures
- ▶ Generate T-SQL object creation scripts
- ▶ Set up server logins
- ▶ Manage database object permissions

- ▶ Configure and manage replication
- ▶ Configure and manage linked servers
- ▶ Monitor server activity
- ▶ View system logs

To work with the database objects displayed in the Object Explorer, you right-click the desired object in the Object Explorer tree to display the object's context menu. The context menu provides a unique set of options for each of the different database objects. For instance, the database context menu allows you to delete, rename, attach, detach, shrink, back up, and restore databases, while the table context menu allows you to create a new table, modify a table, open the table view dependencies, and set permissions.

Another cool feature of the new Object Explorer is its ability to easily generate scripts to create any of the database objects shown in the Object Explorer list. The Script Wizard can be used to document a database's schema, to create a backup of a database, or to create a test copy of a database or selected database objects. You can choose to create a single script for all of the selected objects or to create multiple scripts—one for each object. The T-SQL scripts can be output to a file, to the clipboard, or to the SQL Server Management Studio Query Editor.

Query Editor

The Query Editor is the replacement for Query Analyzer. It enables you to write and run T-SQL scripts. You can see the Query Editor in the upper-middle portion of Figure 2-2. You start the Query Editor from the SQL Server Management Studio by either selecting the New Query option on the Start page or selecting the File | New | SQL Server Query | SQL Server Query option. The Query Editor supports developing queries in T-SQL, MDX, DMX, XMLA, and SQL Mobile Queries. Unlike the Query Analyzer, which always worked in connected mode, the new Query Editor has the option of working either connected or disconnected from the server. By default, it automatically connects to the server as soon as you opt to create a new query.

Like its Visual Studio 2005 counterpart, the Query Editor supports color-coded keywords, visually shows syntax errors, and enables the developer to both run and debug code. In addition, unlike the old Query Analyzer, the Query Editor supports the concept of projects, where groups of related files can be grouped together to form a solution. The new Query Editor also offers full support for source control using Visual SourceSafe. The Query Editor also adds in the elements that were present in Query Analyzer. It is able to display query results in a grid or as text, and it is able to graphically show a query's execution plans. There's also an option to save your T-SQL scripts using the built-in SourceSafe version control. Version control facilitates group development by preventing multiple developers from simultaneously changing the same module. Source code must be checked out of the code repository before it can be modified and then checked back in, giving you a central location to store your database code. Using version control with your T-SQL database creation scripts provides a valuable method for isolating the source code associated with each release of your database schema. This can also act as a basis for comparing the schema of a deployed database to the expected schema that's been saved using version control. Plus, as you'll see in "Performance Tools" later in this chapter, Query Editor also has the capability to graphically represent a query's execution plan.

Results Window

The SQL Server Management Studio's Results window displays the results of the queries that were executed in the Query Editor. You can see the Results window in the lower-right section of Figure 2-2. The Results window can be set up to display query results either in text format or in a grid.

Solution Explorer

Another important management tool that's provided as part of the SQL Server Management Studio is the Solution Explorer. You can see the Solution Explorer in the upper right-hand corner of Figure 2-3. The Solution Explorer is used to provide a hierarchical tree view of the different projects and files in a solution. The top item listed in the Solution Explorer is the name of the SQL Server Management Studio solution. By default, this name is Solution 1, but you can change this to whatever name you want by selecting the solution and then changing its name in the Properties window.

Under the solution, you can have one or more project items or one or more files. The files that are listed in the Solution Explorer can be associated with a project, or else they can be associated with the SQL Server Management Studio solution itself without an intermediate project. The files can include all of the different file types that can be modified using the SQL Server Management Studio, including T-SQL Queries, Analysis Server Queries, and XMLA Queries.

The SQL Server Management Studio Solution Explorer supports a number of different project types, including SQL Server Scripts, Analysis Server Scripts, and SQL Mobile Scripts. You can see the SQL Server Management Studio's New Project dialog in Figure 2-4.

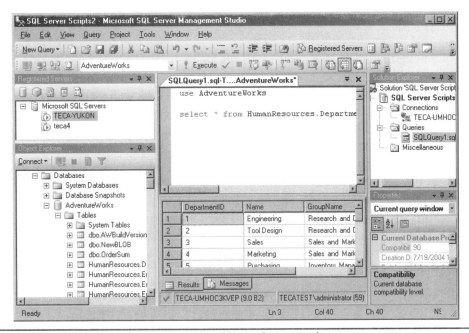

Figure 2-3   *SQL Server Management Studio—Solution Explorer*

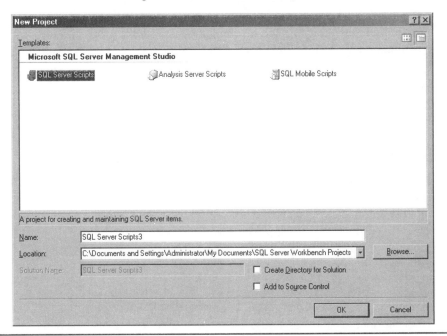

Figure 2-4   *SQL Server Management Studio—New Project*

SQL Server Scripts The SQL Server Scripts projects are used to group together related SQL Server connections and T-SQL scripts. One common use for this type of project is to group together all of your database's Data Definition Language (DDL) scripts.

Analysis Server Scripts Much as SQL Server Scripts are used for T-SQL-based files, Analysis Server Scripts projects are intended to contain Analysis Server connections as well as MDX and XMLA scripts. Again, one way you might take advantage of this type of project is to have the project contain all of the scripts that create your data warehouse and another project might contain the scripts to load your data warehouse.

SQL Mobile Scripts SQL Mobile Scripts projects are used to group together the connections and queries for a SQL Server CE database. For a SQL Server CE project, a connection object represents the connection to the CE database.

Properties

The Properties window shown in the lower right-hand corner of Figure 2-3 is used at design time to set the properties of the objects selected in the Solution Explorer. You can use the Properties window for a number of different tasks, including setting the names of your solutions, projects, and files, as well as controlling the time-out for DTS packages. One nice feature about the Properties window that's not immediately obvious is the fact that you can use it to simultaneously set the properties for multiple items. To do this, you select multiple items in the Solution Explorer window by holding down the CTRL key and then clicking the items. Then when you change a value in the Properties window, it will be changed for all of the selected items. As you might expect, the selected items in the Solution Explorer window must share common properties for this to work.

Dynamic Help

Like the Visual Studio 2005 IDE that it's based on, the SQL Server Management Studio also provides a new Dynamic Help window. The contents of the Dynamic Help window automatically change according to the position of the current cursor or mouse pointer in the SQL Server Management Studio.

Source Control

Integrated source control is another new feature that's provided by the SQL Server Management Studio. Source control facilitates team development by providing a central control mechanism that manages access to source files. In order to use the SQL Server Management Studio source control feature, you must have previously installed Visual

SourceSafe, which comes with Microsoft's Visual Studio 2005 product. The SQL Server Management Studio source control feature provides a check-in and check-out process to ensure that two developers cannot simultaneously change the same source file (and potentially wipe out one another's modifications). The source control system is also able to archive past versions of each project. You can add solutions projects and files to the Visual SourceSafe source control system by using the File | Source Control option from the SQL Server Management Studio menu.

Current Activity Window

As if it didn't encompass enough functionality already, SQL Server 2005's new SQL Server Management Studio also provides an integrated process monitoring feature called the Current Activity window. You can run the Current Activity Monitor from the Object Explorer by selecting the Database | Management | Activity Monitor node. The Current Activity window gives you an overview of the current processes running on your SQL Server system. It shows

► Process information
► Blocked processes
► User connections
► Locks
► User locks

Business Intelligence Development Studio

Just as the SQL Server Management Studio is used to develop relational database projects, the new Business Intelligence Development Studio is used to create Business Intelligence solutions. Unlike the SQL Server Management Studio, the Business Intelligence Development Studio is not really designed to be an administrative tool. You use the Business Intelligence Development Studio to work with Analysis Services projects, to develop and deploy Reporting Services reports, and to design Data Transformation Services packages.

Since the Business Intelligence Development Studio has a different purpose from the SQL Server Management Studio, it also has a different look and feel. In addition, while the SQL Server Management Studio utilized a connected mode by default, the Business Intelligence Development Studio starts off in a disconnected mode. The Business Intelligence Development Studio is accessed using the Start | Programs | Microsoft SQL Server | Business Intelligence Development Studio menu option. You can see a picture of the Business Intelligence Development Studio in Figure 2-5.

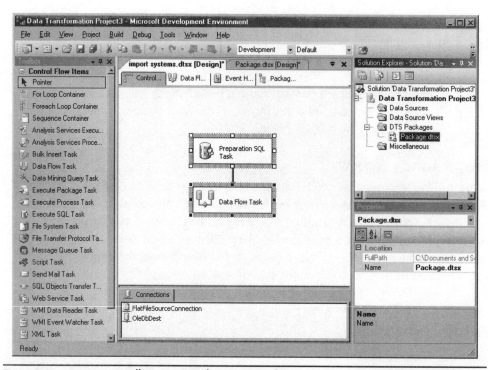

Figure 2-5 *Business Intelligence Development Studio*

Like the SQL Server Management Studio, the Business Intelligence Development Studio is built on top of the Visual Studio 2005 IDE. It provides a solution-oriented development environment where one or more projects are contained in a solution. Each project consists of the types of objects that are suitable for that project. For example, a Reporting Services project will contain Report definitions, while a DTS project contains DTS package objects. Like the SQL Server Management Studio, the Business Intelligence Development Studio doesn't allow you to compile VB.NET, C#, J#, or VC++. Instead, the Business Intelligence Development Studio is designed expressly for working with BI projects like DTS and Reporting Services. The Business Intelligence Development Studio is also integrated with Visual SourceSafe for source code version control.

Toolbox

The Toolbox window in the Business Intelligence Development Studio is shown on the left side of the screen in Figure 2-5. The Toolbox is used by the DTS Designer and the Reporting Services Designer to drag and drop components onto their respective design surfaces.

Solution Explorer

Like the SQL Server Development Studio, the Business Intelligence Development Studio also has a Solution Explorer window. You can see the Solution Explorer at the upper right-hand corner of the screen shown in Figure 2-5. The Solution Explorer provides a hierarchical tree view of the different projects and files that compose a Business Intelligence Development Studio solution. The top item in the Solution Explorer hierarchy is the solution name. Under the solution, you can have one or more project items and/or multiple items. The Business Intelligence Development Studio Solution Explorer provides the following project templates: Analysis Services Project, Data Transformation Project, Import Analysis Services 9.0 Database, Report Project, and Report Project Wizard. As in the SQL Server Management Studio, Business Intelligence Development Studio solutions are not restricted to one project. You can create multi-project solutions that are made up of any of the supported project types. You can see the Business Intelligence Development Studio's New Project dialog in Figure 2-6.

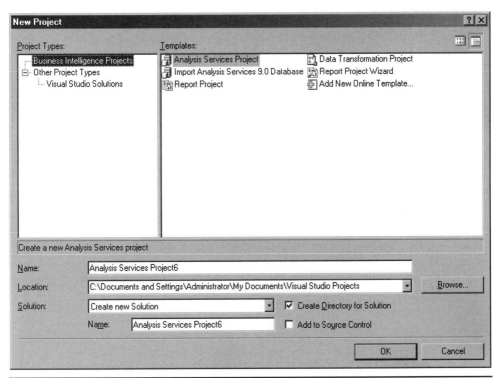

Figure 2-6 *Business Intelligence Development Studio—New Project*

Analysis Services Project   Analysis Services projects contain the definitions for the objects in an Analysis Services database. These include the definitions for data sources, data source views, cubes, dimensions, mining models, roles, and assemblies. One of the primary tools in the Analysis Services projects is the Cube Designer.

The Cube Designer is a visual tool for building OLAP cubes. It is started by double-clicking the Cube node shown under an Analysis Services project or by right-clicking the Cube node and selecting View Designer. More detailed information about the cube designer is presented in Chapter 10.

Data Transformation Project   The project definition for Data Transformation projects enables you to create the objects used in a DTS solution. These definitions include the creation of data sources, data source views, and DTS packages.

The DTS Designer, shown in the middle of the screen in Figure 2-5, enables you to visually create DTS packages by selecting the DTS components from the toolbar and dragging and dropping them onto the DTS design surface. Using the DTS Designer, you can specify the data sources, select the types of transformations that will be used, as well as set up the DTS package's data flow. You can find out more about DTS in Chapter 9.

Import Analysis Services 9.0 Database   The Import Analysis Service 9.0 project type enables you to create a new SQL Server 2005 Analysis Services project by importing the definitions for an existing SQL Server 2000 Analysis Services or SQL Server 7 OLAP Server database.

Report Project   You use the Report Project template to create Reporting Services projects. This project template starts the Reporting Services Designer, where you select data sources and visually lay out reports.

The Reporting Services Designer enables you to visually design reports as well as control their deployment. Using the Reporting Services Designer, you create a Dataset and then use the visual design surface along with controls from the Report Items toolbox to lay out reports. These reports can run against a SQL Server 2005 database as well as any OLE DB- and ODBC-compliant database sources. Reporting Services and the Report Designer are covered in more detail in Chapter 8.

Report Project Wizard   The Report Project Wizard project template starts the Report Wizard, which guides you through a series of easy-to-use screens that enable you to define a basic report. The integrated Query Builder is included in the Report Wizard to help you construct your SQL queries. Once you've created a report using the

Report Wizard, you can go back and fine-tune it using the Report Designer.
The Report Wizard is also covered in more detail in Chapter 8.

Properties

The Properties window shown in the bottom-right corner of Figure 2-5 is used at
design time to set the properties of the objects selected in the Solution Explorer.

Dynamic Help

Like the SQL Server Management Studio, the Business Intelligence Development
Studio also has a new Dynamic Help window. The help contents shown in the
Dynamic Help window change according to the position of the current cursor or
mouse pointer in the Business Intelligence Development Studio.

Source Control

The Business Intelligence Development Studio also provides completely integrated
source control using Visual SourceSafe. Source control facilitates team development
by providing a central control mechanism that manages access to source files. To use
the source control feature with the Business Intelligence Development Studio, you
need to have previously installed Visual SourceSafe, which is distributed with Visual
Studio 2005. Source control provides a check-in and check-out process to ensure that
two developers cannot simultaneously change the same source file, and it is also able
to archive past versions of each project. You can add solutions, projects, and files to
the source control system by using the File | Source Control option from the
Business Intelligence Development Studio.

When to Use the SQL Server Management Studio and the Business Intelligence Development Studio

While they may seem similar at first, the SQL Server Management Studio and
Business Intelligence Development Studio are designed to fulfill different purposes.
Both the SQL Server Management Studio and the Business Intelligence Development
Studio are based on the Visual Studio 2005 IDE, and since SQL Server 2005 ships
with both a SQL Server relational database server and an Analysis Services OLAP
server, you might be tempted to think that the SQL Server Management Studio is used
to manage SQL Server while the Business Intelligence Development Studio is used to
manage Analysis Services. That's not the case. The SQL Server Management Studio
is used to manage both SQL Server and Analysis Services as well as to develop T-SQL
and MDX queries. The SQL Server Management Studio can connect to instances of

SQL Server, Analysis Services, and Reporting Services. You can use it to start and stop those services, as well as to manage them using the SQL Server Management Studio GUI or by running scripts.

The Business Intelligence Development Studio is not an administrative tool. Instead, the Business Intelligence Development Studio is designed to enable you to develop and deploy business intelligence solutions. It can be used to design DTS packages and Reporting Services reports as well as create and run MXD and XMLA queries, but it's not used to manage Analysis Services.

Sqlcmd

Another important new management tool found in SQL Server 2005 is the new Sqlcmd utility. The Sqlcmd utility is essentially a replacement for the older osql and isql utilities found in the earlier releases of SQL Server. The old isql program used the deprecated SQL Server DB-library to connect to SQL Server, while the osql program uses ODBC. The new Sqlcmd utility connects to SQL Server using OLE DB. For backward compatibility, the osql utility is still shipped with SQL Server 2005. However, isql has been dropped from the SQL Server 2005 release. Like those tools, the Sqlcmd utility is run from the command prompt and enables you to enter and execute T-SQL statements, stored procedures, and T-SQL batches.

One important feature that the Sqlcmd utility has in addition to the ability to execute commands is the fact that it can connect to the database with a Dedicated Administrative Connection (DAC). The DAC permits you to connect and run at a higher priority than any other SQL Server process, enabling you to terminate any runaway process. To use the DAC, you must start the Sqlcmd utility using the –A switch. You can find more information about Sqlcmd's DAC capability in Chapter 4. In addition to the –A switch, the Sqlcmd utility supports a number of other useful command-line switches. For example, you can use the –L switch to list all of the registered SQL Server systems, as shown here:

```
Sqlcmd -L
```

Another useful switch is the –p switch, which outputs the performance statistics for the result set. You can get a full listing of the supported command-line switches by entering **Sqlcmd /?** at the command prompt.

Sqlcmd Scripting

In addition to supporting the execution of standard T-SQL statements, the Sqlcmd utility also supports a number of scripting extensions that enable you to include flow control and variables in your scripts. You can define scripting variables implicitly using the –v switch, or you can set them using the command-shell setvar command. The following example illustrates how you can combine the Sqlcmd command-line switches with variables used in scripts:

```
sqlcmd -S MySQLServer -d AdventureWorks -v CUSTOMERID="ALFKI" -i MyScript.sql
```

NOTE

The Sqlcmd utility uses a trusted connection by default.

This example uses the –S switch to specify the SQL Server system name. The –d switch specifies the database that it will be connected to. The –v switch is used to define a variable named VENDORNAME and supply that variable with the value of International. The –I switch is used to tell the Sqlcmd utility that the T-SQL command will come out of the file MyScript.sql. You can see the contents of the MyScript.sql file in this listing:

```
select * from Purchasing.Vendor where Name = '$(VENDORNAME)'
```

In addition to providing for user-defined variables, Microsoft has also provided a set of predefined variables that can be used with Sqlcmd scripts. Table 2-1 lists the extended variables that Microsoft has added to the Sqlcmd utility and the command-line switches that can be used to supply values for those variables.

Variable	Command–Line Switch
SQLCMDUSER	–U
SQLCMDPASSWORD	–P
SQLCMDSERVER	–S
SQLCMDWORKSTATION	–H
SQLCMDDBNAME	–d
SQLCMDLOGINTIMEOUT	–l
SQLCMDSTATTIMEOUT	–t
SQLCMDHEADERS	–h
SQLCMDCOLSEP	–s
SQLCMDCOLWIDTH	–w
SQLCMDPACKETSIZE	–a
SQLCMDERRORLEVEL	–m

Table 2-1   *Sqlcmd Extended Variables*

Command	Description
[:]GO [count]	Signals the end of a batch and executes the cached statements. Adding an optional count value executes the statements a given number of times.
[:]RESET	Clears the statement cache.
[:]ED	Starts the next edit for the current statement cache.
[:]!!	Executes operating system commands.
[:]QUIT	Ends the Sqlcmd utility.
[:]EXIT (results)	Uses the value of a result set as a return value.
[:]r <filename>	Includes additional Sqlcmd statements from the specified file.
:ServerList	Lists the configured SQL Server systems.
:List	Lists the contents of the statement cache.
:Error <filename>	Redirects error output to the specified file.
:Out	Redirects query results to the specified file.
:Perftrace <filename>	Redirects performance statistics to the specified file.
:Connect [timeout]	Connects to a SQL Server instance.
:On Error [exit |retry	ignore]	Specifies the action to be performed when an error is encountered.
:XML [ON	OFF]	Specifies whether XML results will be output as a continuous stream.

Table 2-2   *Sqlcmd Extended Utilities*

In addition to providing a set of predefined variables, the Sqlcmd utility also provides a list of extended commands. The extended Sqlcmd utilities commands are listed in Table 2-2.

The following listing gives you an idea of how the Sqlcmd utilities' extended commands can be used. This example connects to the server and then uses the :EXIT command to return the row count from the customers table:

```
C:\>sqlcmd
1> use adventureworks
2> :EXIT(select count(*) from sales.customer)
Changed database context to 'AdventureWorks'.
-----------
         91
(1 rows affected)
```

Performance Tools

In addition to a full set of new management tools, SQL Server 2005 also provides an updated set of tools for analyzing and improving server performance. In the five years since the last release of SQL Server, Microsoft has been able to add a lot of functionality to the management tools provided with SQL Server, and as you'll see in this section, the performance tools are no exception. In this section, you'll get a look at four of the most important new performance management tools included in SQL Server 2005: the SQL Server Management Studio Query Editor's graphical Showplan, the Database Tuning Advisor, and last but not least, Profiler.

SQL Server Management Studio Query Editor: Execution Plans

Like the old Query Analyzer, the new Query Editor has the capability to graphically display the execution plan for a query. The new SQL Server Management Studio Query Editor also extends this capability by enabling you to display an estimated execution plan as well as the actual execution plan. You can see a sample execution plan in Figure 2-7.

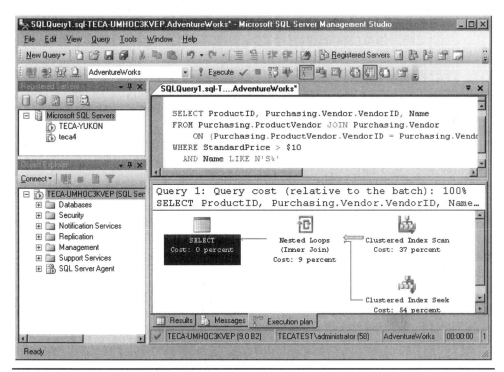

Figure 2-7   *Query Editor Showplan*

Some of the new features that have been added to the Query Editor's graphical Showplan include a new set of redesigned icons that are more intuitive. The new color coding follows a set pattern. All iterators are blue, cursors are yellow, and SQL language constructs are green. Parameter values that were used for parameterized queries will be displayed in the Showplan. There's improved information for queries that were executed in parallel where the Showplan can show how many rows were produced by each thread. In addition, the new Showplan information will also show when CLR user-defined extensions (UDX) are used as part of a query.

Exportable XML Showplan   Unlike the old Query analyzer, the Query Editor also has the ability to export the Showplan results as an XML document. This Showplan XML document can then be imported by Microsoft support or other technical support personal to troubleshoot query performance issues. The generated XML Showplans are schema validated, and the new XML Showplan format is easily portable and can be e-mailed to a remote site for review. It can be imported and graphed by a remote user without requiring access to the source database. Using the XML format for the Showplan output provides some nice advantages over the text and graphical formats. It can be processed using any XML technology, such as XQuery, XPath, DOM, or SAX. If you support mobile databases, one additional nice touch is that SQL Server CE uses the same format. One important point to note is that while the new export to XML format is available, you don't necessarily need to use it. The older text and graphical Showplan formats are still supported.

Database Tuning Advisor

The Database Tuning Advisor is another new feature that's bundled in SQL Server 2005 to enable you to fine-tune the performance of your database applications. The Database Tuning Advisor is essentially an updated version of the Index Tuning Wizard that was provided in the earlier releases of SQL Server. However, the new Database Tuning Advisor goes far beyond just suggesting new indexes, and that's one of the reasons for its new name. The Database Tuning Advisor is able to work with partitions; it supports scheduled execution, as well as improved evaluation what-if analysis. The other reason is the fact that the new Database Tuning Advisor is now a full-fledged application rather than just a series of wizard dialogs. You can see an example of the Database Tuning Advisor in Figure 2-8.

Partitioning Recommendations

In addition to recommending indexes, the new Database Tuning Advisor provides full support for SQL Server 2005 data partitioning. The Database Tuning Advisor

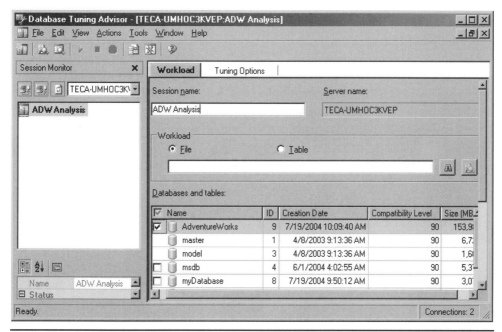

Figure 2-8   *Database Tuning Advisor*

can recommend the use of both aligned and nonaligned partitions. (An aligned partition uses a clustered index that's in the same order as the table, while a nonaligned partition uses a non-clustered index that's in a different order than the base table.) In addition to being able to recommend adding partitions, the Database Tuning Advisor can also recommend dropping existing partitions. You can refer to Chapter 2 for more information on data partitioning in SQL Server 2005.

Pause and Resume

The old Index Tuning Wizard, like a typical wizard application, operated in a one-time run mode where you stepped through the wizard screens from start to finish. The new Database Tuning Advisor, by contrast, can be stopped and restarted with the saved state. You can even resume the state on different client workstations.

Scheduled Tuning

The Database Tuning Advisor supports a couple of different scenarios for scheduled tuning. First, unlike the old Index Tuning Wizard, which could run for long periods of time while it came up with the optimum index recommendations, the new Database Tuning Advisor can be set up to run for a specified amount of time and then deliver a "best effort" tuning recommendation based on the given run time. If the old Index Tuning Wizard wasn't allowed to finish, it was unable to generate any recommendations. In contrast, you can set up the Database Tuning Advisor to run for four hours and give the best recommendation that it can given what it was able to accomplish in the allotted time. In addition, the Database Tuning Advisor has the ability to schedule its runs without the need to run the tool interactively or to perform the scheduling using difficult scripting.

What-If Tuning

Another cool new feature of the Database Tuning Advisor is the ability to perform evaluative or what-if tuning. This feature allows you to test a given run scenario in terms of selective testing of its recommendations. For instance, if the Database Tuning Advisor recommended that you add four different indexes but you felt that you didn't really need all four, you can rerun the work load using your chosen indexes and then see how your choice compares with the Database Tuning Advisor's original recommendations.

Profiler Enhancements

While certainly not a new feature, Profiler has been given a number of enhancements in the new release. One of the most fundamental changes in Profiler is found at the architectural level. Profiler is closely tied to the SQL Server engine, and in previous releases when updates were applied to the SQL Server engine that affected the information used by Profiler, a corresponding update needed to be applied to the client systems that were used to run Profiler. With the SQL Server 2005 release, Microsoft has extracted the definition of valid events and columns from the SQL Server engine and stored them in XML files. When Profiler first starts, it checks the version of SQL Server that it's connecting to. If Profiler connects to a known version of SQL Server, then it uses its cached definitions. If it connects to an updated version of SQL Server, then it downloads the new XML profiling information. This enables Profiler to seamlessly work with updated versions of SQL Server without requiring updates to the Profiler client each time an update is applied to the SQL Server engine.

Profiling Analysis Services

One of the biggest changes in Profiler for SQL Server 2005 is its ability to profile MDX statements that are run against Analysis Services. The new Profiler can work against a SQL Server 2005 Analysis Services instance in exactly the same way that it has worked with the relational SQL Server engine in previous releases.

Aggregated Views

The aggregated views feature of the new SQL Server 2005 Profile enables you to group events together and show the total number for the entire grouping. For instance, you could choose to view the profiler events according to system process ID (SPID) and the Login Event and see the total number of failed logins by a particular SPID. This feature can enable you to more easily see important trends and events without requiring you to take the Profiler's output, store it in a table, and then perform queries against it.

New Trace Permission

Another important enhancement in SQL Server 2005 that directly affects Profiler is the new Trace permission. With earlier releases of SQL Server, you needed to be a System Administrator in order to run Profiler. While that wasn't a problem for most normal performance troubleshooting activities, it did prove to be a hurdle for running audits where you didn't necessarily want to give the auditor full system administrative privileges. SQL Server 2005 includes a new Trace role that you can assign to a login, giving that login the ability to run Profiler without being a member of the system administrator's group. Obviously, because Profiler potentially allows access to all of the data, you need to be very careful about granting the Trace permission.

Data Extraction by Event Type

The new SQL Server 2005 Profiler is also able to extract information from the Profiler output according to event type. For instance, this feature enables you to extract all of the T-SQL statements from a given Profiler session and then write those events as a .sql file that can be executed using SQL Server Management Studio. Profiler provides this same capability for MDX and DMX statements as well. Another really cool use for this feature is the ability to extract deadlock information. This deadlock information can then be presented in the graphical view using Profiler.

Create Trace Wizard

Another new feature that's found in SQL Server 2005 is the reintroduction of the Trace Wizard. The Trace Wizard was originally introduced in SQL Server 7 but was subsequently dropped from the SQL Server 2000 release. Microsoft has added the Create Trace Wizard back into SQL Server 2005. Essentially, the Create Trace Wizard makes it easier to run Traces by walking the administrator through common trace scenarios.

New Management Frameworks

In addition to the new management tools found in the SQL Server 2005, the SQL Server management framework has also been completely revamped. A new .NET-based management framework called System Management Objects (SMO) can be used to write custom server management applications for SQL Server 2005. New .NET-based management APIs have also been added for Analysis Services and replication management. Another significant new change for the SQL Server 2005 administrative tool set is support for WMI configuration and WMI events. In the following section of this chapter, you'll find out more about each of these new management frameworks in SQL Server 2005.

SQL Server Management Objects (SMO)

Like its predecessor, Distributed Management Objects (DMO), the SMO object framework is designed to be able to programmatically manage every aspect of SQL Server. However, unlike the older DMO object framework, which was based on COM, the new SMO object framework has been implemented as a .NET class library. This means that SMO requires the .NET Framework to be installed on the systems that are used to run SMO management applications. SMO can be used to manage SQL Server 7 and SQL Server 2000 systems as well as SQL Server 2005.

For backward compatibility, DMO will continue to be supported by SQL Server 2005, but it has not been enhanced to support the new features found in the new release. For instance, DMO cannot be used to manage the SQL Service Broker, the new HTTP Endpoints feature, the new XML and varbinary(max) data types, or any of the other numerous new features that Microsoft has added to the SQL Server 2005 release. In other words, DMO is limited to supporting only those features that were found in the previous releases of SQL Server. The new SMO object framework provides over 150 new classes to represent the new features found in SQL Server 2005. To make it easy to migrate older DMO applications to SMO, the object framework used by SMO is closely based on the same object framework that was used by DMO. While the object frameworks are not identical, they are quite similar. For instance, both SMO and DMO possess objects that represent servers, databases, tables, columns, and the other major database objects.

In addition to being able to access all of the new features found in SQL Server 2005, the new SMO object framework provides a couple of other important new features. First, SMO uses optimized instantiation of objects, which means that it can create an instance that represents a high-level object like a server object without needing to retrieve all of the properties that compose that object. In the case of an object like a server, this means that the SMO doesn't need to retrieve all of the database information plus all of the database object information for all of the databases on the server when the server object is created. Full instantiation is delayed until the object is explicitly referenced. Optimized instantiation results in much better performance—especially for VLDB implementations. SMO also has the ability to capture and batch together groups of SQL statements for better performance. There's also an enhanced scripting capability that's enabled by a new Scripter class. The Scripter class is able to discover and create creation scripts for database objects and their dependencies.

SMO is implemented in the Microsoft.SqlServer.Management.Smo, Microsoft .SqlServer.Management.Smo.Common, and Microsoft.SqlServer.Management .Smo.Agent namespaces.

Analysis Management Objects (AMO)

Just as SMO is used to manage SQL Server servers, Analysis Management Objects (AMO) is used to manage Analysis Services. Among other items, AMO can be used to manage Analysis Services servers, data sources, cubes, dimensions, measures, and data mining models. Like SMO, AMO is a .NET-based object framework that requires the CLR in order to run. AMO is conceptually based on the older COM-based Decision Support Objects (DSO) library. As is the case with DMO, SQL Server 2005 still supports DSO for backward compatibility of existing applications. AMO generates XML-based messages that can be used to create or change Analysis Server objects. These XML messages can be saved as XML documents. AMO is implemented in the Microsoft.SqlServer.Management .AnalysisServices namespace.

Replication Management Objects (RMO)

Exactly as SMO has been designed to control all aspects of SQL Server configuration and management, the new .NET-based Replication Management Objects (RMO) is designed to configure and manage the database replication process in SQL Server 2005. As with SMO and AMO, RMO applications require the presence of the CLR. The new RMO object framework contains classes that enable the management of SQL Server replications, administration, synchronization, and monitoring. RMO is implemented in the Microsoft.SqlServer.Replication namespace.

Windows Management Instrumentation (WMI)

SQL Server 2005 can also be managed using the Windows Management Instrumentation (WMI) API. WMI is Microsoft's cross-product management standard, but prior to the SQL Server 2005 release, WMI wasn't as effective at managing SQL Server as DMO or SQL Server Enterprise Manager. For shops attempting to standardize on the WMI management framework, this made enterprise deployments of SQL Server difficult, as manual intervention was often required. To address enterprise manageability, SQL Server 2005's WMI management capabilities have been extended with a new WMI Configuration Provider and new WMI events.

WMI Configuration Provider

SQL Server 2005's new WMI Configuration Provider enables a remote management application to connect to SQL Server and perform management functions. The WMI configuration API is designed to function in a disconnected fashion. The WMI provider is implemented in the Microsoft.SqlServer.Smo.Wmi namespace.

WMI Events

SQL Server 2005's new WMI events enable SQL Server to be monitored by Microsoft Operations Manager (MOM) and other third-party WMI-compliant management applications. SQL Server 2005 can raise WMI events for virtually all of the operations that can be traced using Profiler. For example, events can be generated for create database, drop database, alter database, and all of the other operations that can be traced. Just as when using Trace, there's some overhead generated when you use WMI events, but they provide very rich management information. WMI events can be raised by SQL Server, Analysis Services, DTS, and Reporting Services.

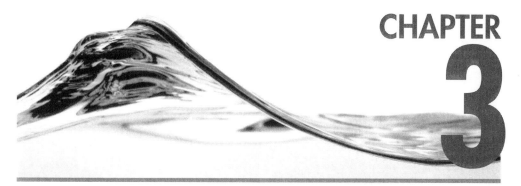

Availability and Recovery Features

IN THIS CHAPTER:

Protection Against Database or Server Failure

Database Availability Enhancements

Backup and Restore

N ew improvements in the SQL Server 2005 release have continued to improve SQL Server's availability by increasing its failover clustering capabilities and providing new database options that offer both continuous availability and improved database recovery capabilities. Achieving high availability is relatively easy on a small scale but gets exponentially more difficult as the size of the system increases. SQL Server 2005 provides a number of new features that enhance database availability and recoverability by addressing the primary obstacles that hinder enterprise-level database availability. Some of the factors that have hindered database availability in previous versions of SQL Server include things like delayed failover times, the need to have exclusive database access for selected maintenance operations, and occasional difficulty in getting the server to respond during high CPU usage time, such as when some user's code has gone into an infinite loop. Another factor that can adversely affect database availability is hardware upgrades. Even though hardware upgrades are planned events, they typically require system downtime in order to perform the upgrade. SQL Server 2005 provides a new capability designed to decrease the downtime required by one of the most common hardware upgrades. In this chapter, we'll take a look at these new availability and recovery options found in SQL Server 2005 so that you can understand how these features can be used to implement SQL Server 2005 in a highly available and recoverable production database environment.

Protection Against Database or Server Failure

A database server failure is a breakdown that's caused by either a hardware failure or a software issue that renders the server inoperable for a period of time. Database server failure can also be caused by environmental factors such as a disaster. In this section, you'll learn about some of the most important new features that SQL Server 2005 provides to address database server failures.

Improved Failover Clustering

One key high-availability benefit that SQL Server 2005 derives in part from its support for Windows Server 2003 is significantly improved support for failover clustering. Taking advantage of the enhanced clustering support found in Windows Server 2003, SQL Server 2005 can now be implemented on clusters of up to eight nodes on Windows Server 2003 Datacenter Edition. In addition, SQL Server 2005 supports four-node clustering on Windows Server 2003 Enterprise Edition and

Windows 2000 Datacenter Server. A maximum of two-node clustering is supported in Windows 2000 Advanced Server.

With Windows clustering services, each server in the cluster is called a *node*. All of the nodes in a cluster are in a state of constant communication. If one of the nodes in a cluster becomes unavailable, another node will assume its duties and begin providing the same services as the failed node. This process is called *failover*. Users who are accessing the cluster are switched automatically to the new node.

Clustering can be set up in a couple of basic ways: Active-Active clustering, where all of the nodes are performing work, or Active-Passive, where one of the nodes is dormant until the active node fails. Windows Server 2003 also supports N+I configurations (N active with I spare), which provide a very flexible and cost-effective clustering scenario to enable highly available applications. For example, with an eight-node cluster in an N+I configuration, you can have seven of the eight nodes set up to be available and providing different services while the eighth node is a passive node that can assume the services of any of the seven active nodes. Figure 3-1 illustrates an example eight-node cluster, where seven nodes are active and one node is in standby waiting to step in if any of the seven active nodes fail.

Some of the clustering-specific improvements in SQL Server 2005 include support for an unattended cluster setup. In addition, all of the different services within SQL Server 2005 are fully cluster-aware, including:

▶ Database Engine

▶ Analysis services

▶ Reporting services

▶ Notification services

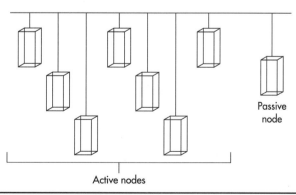

Figure 3-1   *Eight-node cluster support*

- ▶ SQL Server Agent
- ▶ Full-Text Search
- ▶ Service Broker
- ▶ SQLiMail

In addition, all of the major management tools in SQL Server 2005 are also cluster-aware, including:

- ▶ SQL Server Management Studio
- ▶ Service Control Manager
- ▶ SQL Profiler
- ▶ SQL Query Analyzer

You can find more information about the SQL Server 2005 management tools in Chapter 1.

Database Mirroring

Probably the biggest new feature in the area of availability is SQL Server 2005's support for Database Mirroring. The new Database Mirroring feature protects against database or server failure by giving SQL Server 2005 an instant standby capability. Database Mirroring essentially provides database-level failover. In the event that the primary database fails, the database mirror enables a second, standby database to be available in about 2–3 seconds. Database Mirroring provides zero data loss, and the mirrored database will always be up-to-date with the current transaction that's being processed on the primary database server. The impact of running Database Mirroring to transaction throughput is zero to minimal. The database failover support can be set up to be performed either automatically or manually. The manual failover mode is good for testing, but you'll want your production databases to be able to fail over automatically. Database Mirroring works with all of the standard hardware items that support SQL Server—there's no need for special systems, and the primary server and the mirrored server do not need to be identical. In addition, unlike in high-availability clustering solutions, there's no need for any shared storage between the primary server and the mirrored server. You can see an overview of how the new Database Mirroring feature works in Figure 3-2.

Database Mirroring is implemented using three systems: the primary server, the mirroring server, and the witness. Don't be confused by the names. The primary server is just the name of the system currently providing the database services. All

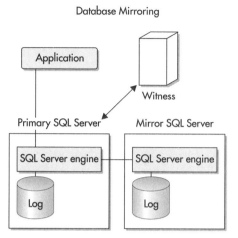

Figure 3-2   *Database Mirroring*

incoming client connections are made to the primary server. The mirror server's job is to maintain a copy of the primary server's mirrored database. Depending on the configuration of the mirrored server, the primary server and the mirror can seamlessly switch roles. The witness essentially acts as an independent third party, helping to determine which system will assume the role of the primary server. Each system gets a vote as to who will be the primary server. It takes two votes to decide on the primary server. This is important because it's possible that the communications between the primary server and the mirror server could be cut off, in which case each system would elect itself to function as the primary server. The witness would cast the deciding vote.

Database Mirroring works by sending transaction logs between the primary server and the mirroring server. So in essence, the new Database Mirroring feature is a real-time log shipping application. Database Mirroring can be set up with a single database, or it can be set up for multiple databases. When a client system writes a request to the primary server, that request actually gets written to the primary server's log file before being written into the data file, because SQL Server uses a write-ahead log. Next, that transaction record gets sent to the mirroring server, where it gets written to mirroring server's transaction log. After the mirroring server has written the record to its log, it sends an acknowledgment to the primary server that the record has been received, giving both systems the same data in each of their log files. In the case of Commit operations, the primary server waits to receive an acknowledgment from the mirroring server before sending its response back to the client, telling it the operation is completed. In order to keep the data files up-to-date on the mirroring server, it is essentially in a state of continuous recovery, taking the data from the log and updating the data file.

Database Mirroring is initialized by taking a backup of the database that you want to mirror on your primary server and then restoring that backup to your mirroring server. In other words, the mirrored database must exist on the mirror server before the mirroring process can begin. This puts the underlying database data and schema in place. The backup and restore process can use any of SQL Server's standard media types, including tape or disk. Next, you use the ALTER DATABASE command as shown here to start the mirroring process:

```
ALTER DATABASE <database name> SET PARTNER = '<partner server name>'
```

The ALTER DATABASE command must first be run on the mirroring server, pointing it to the name of the primary SQL Server in the SET PARTNER clause. Then the ALTER DATABASE command is run a second time, this time on the primary server. When the ALTER DATABASE command is run on the primary server, the name of the mirroring server is supplied in the SET PARTNER clause. Once the ALTER DATABASE command has completed on the primary server, database mirroring is set into motion and the primary server will begin shipping logs to the mirroring server. The next step in setting up Database Mirroring is to set up the witness. Much as you set up the primary and mirroring server, you set up the witness by again running the ALTER DATABASE command on the primary server, as shown in the following listing:

```
ALTER DATABASE <database name> SET WITNESS = '<witness server name>'
```

In this case, the database name would be the same database name that was used in the earlier commands. However, this time the SET WITNESS clause is used to specify the witness server. Once the witness server has been set up, Database Mirroring has all of the information that it needs to perform database failover.

Database mirroring essentially gives you a fault-tolerant virtual database. However, that isn't the entire Database Mirroring story. Implementing an instant standby database enables the database to be quickly available after a failure, but what about the user connections to that failed database? That's where the new Transparent Client Redirect feature comes into play.

Transparent Client Redirect

The Transparent Client Redirect feature works very closely with the new Database Mirroring feature to allow client systems to be automatically redirected to the mirroring server when the primary server becomes unavailable. This new feature is implemented in the new SQL Server 2005 Microsoft Data Access Components (MDAC), and no changes are required to the client- or data-layer applications. The MDAC middleware is aware of both the primary and mirroring servers. MDAC acquires the mirroring server's name upon its initial connection to the primary server. When the connection to the primary server is lost, MDAC will first try to reconnect to the primary server. If that first connection attempt fails, then MDAC will automatically redirect its second connection attempt to the mirroring server. Just as with clustering, if the connection is lost in the middle of a transaction, then that transaction will be rolled back and must be redone after the client connects to the mirroring server.

When to Use Clustering or Database Mirroring

Both clustering and database mirroring are enterprise-ready solutions that are capable of providing a backup system in case of database or server failure. They have many similarities. Both are capable of enabling zero data loss, both have automatic failure detection, both provide automatic failover, and both enable client reconnection. However, there are some important differences. As its name implies, Database Mirroring works at the database level, while clustering works at the server level. Database Mirroring provides nearly instant 2–3 second failover time, while clustering typically has about a 30-second failover time—sometimes longer, depending on the level of database activity and the size of the databases on the failed server. Database Mirroring also protects against disk failures slightly better because there is no shared disk storage, as there is in a clustering solution. There is virtually no distance limitation for Database Mirroring, while clustering has a limit of about 100 miles, because there is a time limit for transmitting the heartbeat between cluster nodes. In addition, Database Mirroring is a simpler technology that's easier to implement than clustering. On the other hand, Database Mirroring can't be used for the system databases, while clustering does protect the system databases as well as the user databases. Basically, clustering is the better solution for protecting an entire server, while Database Mirroring is the better solution for protecting a single critical database or application.

Database Availability Enhancements

Although the previous scenarios all address important factors that reduce database availability, there's probably no single factor that affects database availability and recoverability more than database maintenance. While it's certainly possible to go for years without a database failure, database maintenance is a daily issue that you can't avoid. SQL Server 2005 tackles the challenges of this vital area head-on with the addition of two new features: Database Snapshots and early restore access. In the next part of this chapter, we'll look at each of these new availability and recoverability features in more detail.

Database Snapshot

The new Database Snapshot feature provides a read-only snapshot of a database at a specific point in time. A Database Snapshot is best suited either for creating copies of a database for reporting or for creating a backup copy of the database that you can use to revert a production database back to a prior state. When a Database Snapshot is created, the system makes a metadata copy of the specified database at that particular point in time. Any subsequent changes that are made to the original database are not reflected in the Database Snapshot. Applications connect to a Database Snapshot exactly as if it were another database. A Database Snapshot can be created for any database. Database Snapshots are created as part of the CREATE DATABASE DDL statement. You can see how to create a view on the example AdventureWorks database in the following listing:

```
CREATE DATABASE AdWSnapShot_080104_0700 ON
( NAME = AdventureWorks_Data,
    FILENAME = 'C:\Program Files\Microsoft SQL Server
      \MSSQL.1\MSSQL\DATA\AdventureWorks_data_040422_1800.ss')
AS SNAPSHOT OF AdventureWorks;
```

In this example, you can see that a Database Snapshot named AdWSnapShot_080104_0700 is created on the AdventureWorks database. Database Snapshots are created using the AS SNAPSHOT OF clause that you can see in the listing. When you create a Database Snapshot, you must specify all of the data files that are used in the source database. Since the AdventureWorks database consists of a single data file, only the AdventureWorks_Data file must be specified in the CREATE DATABASE statement. You do not specify the log files.

Creating a Database Snapshot is an inexpensive operation server-wise, as the server basically uses metadata in conjunction with recovery to create the viewpoint. It's important to understand that Database Snapshots are not a complete copy of a database. Instead, creating a Snapshot is a metadata-only operation. A Database Snapshot uses the same data pages as the original database, so it doesn't require a great deal of additional disk space. Database Snapshots are built using copy-on-write technology where anytime a change is made to one of the source database's data pages, a copy of that page is saved for the Database Snapshot and then the updated page is written the same way it normally would be. When the Database Snapshot is accessed, it uses the shared data pages until it gets to the changed page, and then it

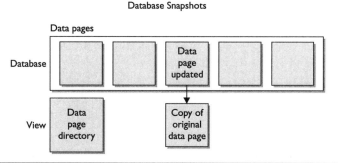

Figure 3-3   *Database Snapshots*

will look at the pages that have been copied rather than the data pages that contain the updated data. In this way, the Database Snapshot needs storage for only those pages that have been changed since the time the Database Snapshot was created. Figure 3-3 illustrates how Database Snapshots work.

Database Snapshots can be combined with Database Mirroring to create a reporting server based on the data that's on the mirrored server (Figure 3-4). Normally, the data on the mirrored server is always in recovery mode, so it can't be accessed by an application. However, you can create a Database Snapshot that's based on the mirrored database and that Database Snapshot can be accessed in read-only mode for reporting.

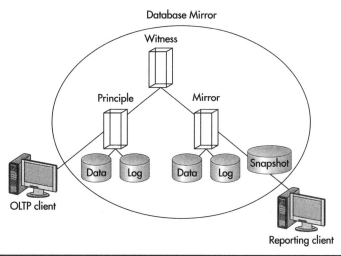

Figure 3-4   *Database Mirroring and Database Snapshot create a reporting server*

Although the database on the mirroring server can't be directly accessed because it's in an ongoing state of recovery, that doesn't affect the Database Snapshot, which accesses a snapshot of the data pages in the mirroring server's database. Creating a Database Snapshot on the mirroring server enables you to better utilize the processing power of the mirroring server by enabling you to shift your static reporting to that server. One thing to consider when using Database Snapshots on a Database Mirror is that in the event of a failover, the existing Database Snapshots that were created on the mirroring server will remain intact.

It's important to realize that Database Snapshots are an availability feature, not a failover feature. They provide more ways to access your data, increasing your data's availability. They are not a failover feature—if the original database is unavailable, the Database Snapshot will also be unavailable.

Early Restore Access

Every time the SQL Server database is started or a database is restored, that database must go through a period of recovery where any transactions that are in the log are applied to the data files. The phase of recovery is often referred to as redo. As soon as the redo portion of the recovery process is complete, then all of the undo operations are performed as any incomplete transactions in the log are rolled back. With SQL Server 2000, the database was not available until all of the redo and undo operations were completed. If a database was brought down while it was active and that database was quite busy, then there could be a somewhat lengthy delay before that database was available again, as you needed to wait until all of the entries in the log were processed.

SQL Server 2005's new Early Restore Access enables the databases to become available immediately after the redo portion of the recovery process is completed. With SQL Server 2005, when the database is restarted, all of the open transactions that are in the log are redone and then the database is immediately available. The net result is that the database is available much sooner. For the transactions that weren't committed, SQL Server still holds the locks on the data pages used by those transactions so that the transactions will remain consistent even though the database is in use. SQL Server 2005 then begins the process of undoing these transactions while the database is active. Users can initiate read/write operations to the database during the undo phase of recovery. However, any attempts to access the data that SQL Server has locked during the undo process will experience blocking until the undo process releases the locks on that data. Figure 3-5 illustrates the difference in availability between SQL Server 2000 and SQL Server 2005.

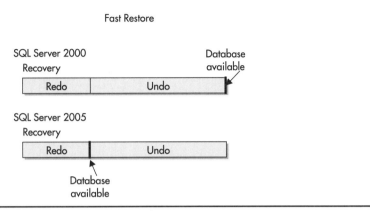

Figure 3-5 *Early restore access*

The RESTORE action is now very granular and defines the scope of the redo option. You can restore full, partial, or filegroup backups. If you indicate that you want to restore a filegroup, then only that filegroup's data is added to the roll-forward operation. If you indicate that you want to restore a full backup, then all of the data in the backup set will be used for the redo operation.

Online Index Operations

With prior versions of SQL Server, when an index was being rebuilt you couldn't perform any update operations on the table until the index rebuild had finished. SQL Server 2005's new online index operations feature extends SQL Server's availability by enabling applications to update, insert, and delete rows from the table while the index is being rebuilt. The new online index feature performs this magic by keeping two copies of the index: one that the applications can continue to use and a second temporary index that's used while the index is being rebuilt. The SQL Server engine maintains both indexes with any changes as the rebuild is being performed. When the rebuild is finished, the old index is dropped and replaced with the new index. Online index rebuild is supported for CREATE INDEX, ALTER INDEX REBUILD, ALTER INDEX DISABLE, DROP INDEX, ALTER TABLE ADD CONSTRAINT, and ALTER TABLE DROP CONSTRAINT statements. Although SQL Server 2005 now supports online index rebuild, it does come at the cost of additional overhead, so you can still choose to rebuild your indexes offline.

The following listing illustrates how the new online indexing feature is used:

```
CREATE INDEX MyIndex ON Person.Contact(LastName) WITH (ONLINE=ON)
```

Here, you can see that the standard CREATE INDEX statement is used to create an index named MyIndex on the LastName column of the table named PersonContact that's in the AdventureWorks database. The ONLINE=ON clause enables the index to be created online.

Fine Grained Online Repairs

Another new feature that enhances the availability of SQL Server 2005 is the ability to perform fine-grained restores. While not the table-level restores that some people have looked for since that feature was removed after SQL Server 6.5, the new fine-grained restore feature in SQL Server 2005 enables you to restore select filegroups in a database while the remainder of the database continues to be available. For SQL Server 2000, that basic unit of availability is the database. All of the components of the database must be intact before that database is available. With SQL Server 2005, the unit of availability is now the filegroup. SQL Server 2005 enables you to restore a filegroup at a time or even a page or group of pages at a time, and the rest of database can continue to be available as long as the primary filegroup is up.

Damaged Page Tracking

A closely related new feature that ties in with SQL Server 2005's ability to perform page-level restores is the ability to track damaged pages. Any bad pages that are encountered on a read operation are tracked in a table, and by using the fine-grained restore capability, you can restore on a page-by-page basis while the database remains online. Any transaction that uses data from a damaged page is rolled back. If the bad page happens to turn up during a transaction rollback, then the database will be forced to restart.

Dedicated Administrator Connection

Another new feature found in SQL Server 2005 that helps to provide better availability is the new dedicated administrator's connection. The dedicated administrator's connection provides the DBA with access to the server regardless of the server's current workload. This enables the DBA to access to the server and kill any runaway processes. To start the new SQLCMD tool in dedicated administrative mode, you would enter the following command:

```
C:\Sqlcmd -A
```

More information about using the dedicated administrator's connection appears in Chapter 1.

Hot-Plug Memory

Another new availability feature that's derived from Windows Server 2003 is Hot-Plug memory. Hot-Plug memory allows you to add RAM while the system is running. As you might expect, this feature requires support from the underlying OS and the hardware platform. In the case of SQL Server 2005, this means that SQL Server must be running on Windows Server 2003 to be able to take advantage of this availability feature. If the platform supports this feature, you can add memory on the fly and SQL Server 2005 will be able to dynamically recognize the additional RAM without requiring a server reboot or any downtime. While Hot-Plug memory allows you to dynamically add RAM on the fly, it doesn't allow you to remove it.

Improved Dynamic Configuration

All configuration within SQL Server 2005 is now dynamic, including CPU and I/O affinity. With SQL Server 2005, you can now change these values and the effects will take place immediately. There's no longer any need to restart the server. In addition, changes to Address Windowing Extensions (AWE) are also all dynamic. SQL Server 2005 can automatically adjust to changes to the physical AWE size dynamically. This feature is designed to work in conjunction with the ability to use Hot-Plug memory on the fly. This feature requires Windows Server 2003.

SQL Server Transaction Isolation Levels

Another area that affects database recoverability is the transaction isolation level that is used by the application. SQL Server 2005 provides a new level of transaction called Snapshot Isolation, giving it added flexibility for data access. The standard four ANSI isolation levels that were supported on earlier version of SQL Server (Serializable, Repeatable Read, Read Committed, Read Uncommitted) all protect transactions from one another by taking locks on the underlying data rows so that other applications can't change the data. These transaction levels all continue to be supported. The new Snapshot Isolation provides increased data availability for read applications. With Snapshot Isolation, SQL Server 2005 performs a type of optimistic locking where SQL Server doesn't take any locks on the rows involved in a transaction. Instead, it keeps track of the row's state when the transaction is opened. When a Snapshot transaction is opened, the system essentially copies the row data for the transaction, enabling your application to continue to see the row data as it was at the time the transaction was started. No locks are placed on the rows. This enables non-blocking consistent reads in an OLTP application. Because Snapshot Isolation doesn't hold any locks, data writers don't block readers and readers don't block writers. The new Snapshot Isolation level is really meant for applications that have an emphasis on read operations. When your application reads the rows in a transaction, it may be reading old data because other applications are able to change the data. While this new isolation level does allow writes, there is additional overhead in all updates. Snapshot Isolation is useful when you need a time-consistent view of all of the data in your database. For update applications, Snapshot Isolation is best used in scenarios where the cost of locking the data outweighs the cost of occasionally rolling back a transaction.

Backup and Restore

SQL Server 2005 also sports several new features in the area of backup and restore technology. While many of the previous availability features were related to some of these new backup and restore features—particularly fine-grain online operations— this section focuses primarily on those changes that Microsoft has made to make the backup and restore process more robust and easier to implement.

Partial Restore

With SQL Server 2000, the database was not available during a restore operation. With SQL Server 2005, the database is online as soon as the primary filegroup is restored. Only the data being restored is unavailable. If a user accesses data that's found in the primary filegroup, the operation will succeed with no indication to the user that the rest of the database is still being restored. If the user does attempt to access data from a filegroup that is currently being restored or that is still offline, then the database will return a message that the data is offline.

Media Reliability Enhancements

SQL Server 2005 also provides a number of enhancements in the way that it deals with media. In particular, it now allows backups to be performed to mirrored devices, it provides enhanced checksum integrity, and it enables a restore operation to continue even if errors are encountered.

Backup Media Mirroring

One of the new media reliability features found in SQL Server 2005 is the ability to support media mirroring. Media mirroring enables you to simultaneously perform a backup to multiple backup devices. For instance, you can back up your database to both tape1 and tape2 at the same time, obtaining two identical copies of the backup set. Redundant backup media provide an important safeguard that can help protect your organization from media errors and help to ensure the ability to perform a successful restore. The following example illustrates using the new media mirroring feature:

```
BACKUP DATABASE AdventureWorks TO
 TAPE='\\.\tape1'
MIRROR TO
 TAPE='\\.\tape2'
WITH FORMAT, MEDIANAME = 'ADWBackup'
```

This example shows the AdventureWorks database being backed up to tape1 and mirrored to tape2. Performance of the backup is not affected by adding a backup mirror. Up to four mirrors can be applied to a single backup.

Improved Verification of Backups

With SQL Server 2000, using the RESTORE VERIFYONLY command just caused SQL Server to read the tape without going any farther into the restore process. Using the RESTORE VERIFYONLY command in SQL Server 2005 does everything short of actually restoring the data in the restore media, giving you a much better idea of the viability of the data in the backup set.

Continue Past Restore Errors

Another new media reliability enhancement is the ability of the restore operation to continue past media errors. Prior versions of SQL Server would abort a restore operation if any error was encountered during the restore process. However, in cases where this was the only media version available, this could be a serious impediment to recovering whatever data was available. With this new feature, SQL Server 2005 will allow the restore process to continue as far as possible, ignoring the media errors it encounters. After the restore process has finished, the database can be manually repaired.

Database Page Checksums

The new Database Page Checksum feature enables the database to detect disk and I/O errors that are not reported by the disk subsystem. When the Database Page Checksum feature is enabled, SQL Server will calculate a checksum value as the page is written to disk and write that checksum along with the data. When the page is read, another checksum is calculated and compared to the original checksum written with the data. If they are different, an error is reported. The following command shows how Database Page Checksums can be added to an existing database:

```
ALTER DATABASE AdventureWorks
 SET PAGE_VERIFY CHECKSUM
```

Concurrent Database and Log Backups

Another new feature in the SQL Server 2005 backup area is the ability to perform database backups and log backups concurrently. Using SQL Server 2000, you had to wait to back up the log until after the database backup had completed. With SQL Server 2005, database backups no longer block log backups. Likewise, you can also back up files and filegroups at the same time that you back up the transaction log. However, you are limited to performing one data file backup at a time per each database.

Backup of Full-Text Catalogs

One other backup enhancement that's part of SQL Server 2005 is the ability to back up Full Text Catalogs. With SQL Server 2000, Full Text Catalog data was maintained outside of SQL Server by the Microsoft Search Service. Backing up the SQL Server database that contained full-text data didn't automatically result in the full-text catalog being backed up as well. This opened up the possibility of the catalog being out-of-sync with the full-text data being restored. SQL Server 2005 fixes this problem by including the ability to automatically back up all of the external full-text catalogs at the same time that the database is backed up. This ensures that the full-text catalog and the data remain consistent between the backup and restore operations. The DATABASE ATTACH and DEATTACH commands also have an option to include any full-text catalogs. Links in the database point to the external files used. When the database is backed up, these external files are also backed up, ensuring database consistency.

Database
Development Features

CHAPTER

4

Programmability Features

IN THIS CHAPTER:

Common Language Run-time (CLR) Integration

T-SQL Enhancements

ADO.NET Enhancements

T he new development features found in SQL Server 2005 are the accumulation of many man-years worth of effort by both the SQL Server development team and the .NET Framework development team. The most significant of these new development features is the integration of the .NET Common Language Run-time (CLR). The integration of the CLR brings with it a whole host of new capabilities, including the capability to create database objects using any of the .NET compatible languages, including C#, VB.NET, and Managed C++. In this chapter, you'll get an introduction to those new .NET CLR integration features as well as see some examples showing how they are used. Next, the chapter will address a topic that's more familiar to SQL Server DBAs and developers: the new features found in T-SQL. Then, the chapter will take a walk on the client side and present some of the new development features found in the updated .NET Framework Data Provider for SQL Server that ships with SQL Server 2005.

Common Language Run-time (CLR) Integration

Undoubtedly the most significant new feature in the SQL Server 2005 release is the integration of the Microsoft .NET Framework. The integration of the CLR with SQL Server extends the capability of SQL Server in several important ways. While T-SQL, the existing data access and manipulation language, is well suited for set-oriented data access operations, it also has limitations. Designed more than a decade ago, T-SQL is a procedural language, not an object-oriented language. The integration of the CLR with SQL Server 2005 brings with it the ability to create database objects using modern object-oriented languages like VB.NET and C#. While these languages do not have the same strong set-oriented nature as T-SQL, they do support complex logic, have better computation capabilities, provide easier access to external resources, facilitate code reuse, and have a first-class development environment that provides much more power than the old Query Analyzer.

The integration of the .NET CLR with SQL Server 2005 enables the development of stored procedures, user-defined functions, triggers, aggregates, and user-defined types using any of the .NET languages. The integration of the .NET CLR with SQL Server 2005 is more than just skin deep. In fact, the SQL Server 2005 database engine hosts the CLR in-process. Using a set of APIs, the SQL Server engine performs all of the memory management for hosted CLR programs.

The managed code accesses the database using ADO.NET in conjunction with the new SQL Server .NET Data Provider. A new SQL Server object called an *assembly* is the unit of deployment for .NET objects with the database. To create CLR database objects, you must first create a DLL using Visual Studio 2005. Then, you import that DLL into SQL Server as an assembly. Finally, you link that assembly to a database object such as a stored procedure or a trigger. In the next section, you'll get a more detailed look at how you actually use the new CLR features found in SQL Server 2005.

Assemblies

To create .NET database objects, you must write managed code and compile it into a .NET assembly. The most common way to do this would be to use Visual Studio 2005 and then create a new SQL Server project and compile it into a DLL. More details about how you actually go about creating a new managed code project with Visual Studio 2005 are presented in the section ".NET Stored Procedures" later in this chapter.

After the assembly is created, you can then load the assembly into SQL Server using the T-SQL CREATE ASSEMBLY command, as you can see here:

```
CREATE ASSEMBLY MyCLRDLL
FROM '\\SERVERNAME\CodeLibrary\MyCLRDLL.dll'
```

The CREATE ASSEMBLY command takes a parameter that contains the path to the DLL that will be loaded into SQL Server. This can be a local path, but more often it will be a path to a networked file share. When the CREATE ASSEMBLY is executed, the DLL is copied into the master database.

If an assembly is updated or becomes deprecated, then you can remove the assembly using the DROP ASSEMBLY command as follows:

```
DROP ASSEMBLY MyCLRDLL
```

Because assemblies are persisted in the database, when the source code for that assembly is modified and the assembly is recompiled, the assembly must first be dropped from the database using the DROP ASSEMBLY command and then reloaded using the CREATE ASSEMBLY command before the updates will be reflected in the SQL Server database objects.

You can use the sys.assemblies view to view the assemblies that have been added to SQL Server 2005, as shown here:

```
SELECT * FROM sys.assemblies
```

Since assemblies are created using external files, you may also want to view the files that were used to create those assemblies. You can do that using the sys.assembly_files view, as shown here:

```
SELECT * FROM sys.assembly_files
```

SQL Server .NET Data Provider

If you're familiar with ADO.NET, you may wonder exactly how these new CLR database procedures will connect with the database. After all, ADO.NET makes its database connection using client-based .NET data providers like the .NET Framework Data Provider for SQL Server, which connects to SQL Server database, or the .NET Framework Data Provider for Oracle, which connects ADO.NET applications to Oracle databases. While that's great for a networked application, going through the network libraries isn't the most efficient connection mode for code that's running directly on the server. To address this issue, Microsoft created the new SQL Server .NET Data Provider. The SQL Server .NET Data Provider establishes an in-memory connection to the SQL Server database.

A reference to the new SQL Server .NET Data Provider is automatically added to your Visual Studio 2005 applications when you create a new SQL Server project. To create a new SQL Server project type, you first open up Visual Studio 2005 and then select the File | New Project option from the menu. Then, from the New Projects dialog, select the project type (e.g., Visual Basic Projects, Visual C# Projects), and then scroll through the list of templates until you see the SQL Server project template shown in Figure 4-1.

NOTE

The creation of SQL Server projects is supported in Visual Studio 2005 (code named Whidbey), which is scheduled to be released at the same time as SQL Server 2005.

After you select the SQL Server Project template, give your project a name and click OK to create the project. All of the required references will automatically be added to your SQL Server project. The new SQL Server .NET Data Provider is added as the sqlaccess reference that you can see highlighted in Figure 4-2. Plus, you can see the System.Data reference, which provides support for ADO.NET and its data-oriented objects such as the DataSet and the SQL Server data types.

In addition to adding the proper references, one of the important things that Visual Studio 2005's SQL Server templates automatically do for you is add the correct import directives. When you're creating SQL Server CLR database objects, you should be

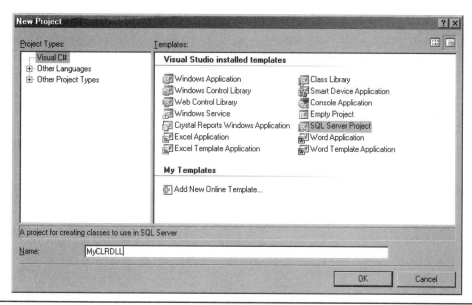

Figure 4-1   *Creating a New SQL Server Project with Visual Studio 2005*

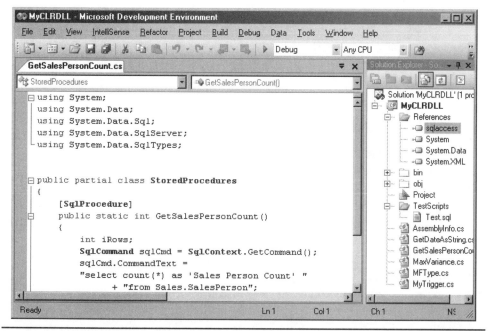

Figure 4-2   *The SQL Server .NET Data Provider Reference*

sure to include an import statement for the System.Data.SqlServer namespace in your project. The System.Data.SqlServer namespace contains the .NET classes that compose the SQL Server .NET Data Provider. The import directive enables you to refer to the classes in the System.Data.SqlServer namespace using just their short class names rather than their much longer fully qualified names, which are always prefixed with the namespace name (e.g., System.Data.SqlServer). For a C# project, the import directive is as follows:

```
using System.Data.SqlServer;
```

For a VB.NET project, you import the System.Data.SqlServer namespace as follows:

```
Imports System.Data.SqlServer
```

Unlike typical ADO.NET projects where you must explicitly open a connection to a named SQL Server instance using the connection object's Open method, the SQL Server .NET Data Provider implicitly makes a connection to the local SQL Server system, and as you'll see in the following examples, there's no need to create an ADO.NET Connection object and invoke its Open method.

NOTE

Strictly speaking, Visual Studio 2005 is not needed in order to create .NET database objects for SQL Server 2005. You can develop CLR database objects using the .NET Framework 2.0 and the .NET Framework SDK. However, Visual Studio 20005 provides project templates and project deployment options that give it significant advantages over manually creating these objects using just the .NET SDK.

.NET Stored Procedures

Stored procedures are one of the most likely database objects that you'll want to create using one of the managed .NET languages, because stored procedures often contain complex logic and embody business rules that are difficult to express in T-SQL. To create a CLR stored procedure in Visual Studio 2005, you can use the Project | Add Stored Procedure option to display the Visual Studio installed templates dialog that's shown in Figure 4-3.

From the Add New Item dialog, select the Stored Procedure option from the list of templates displayed in the Templates list and then provide the name of the stored procedure in the Name field that you can see at the bottom of the screen. Here, you can see that the stored procedure will be named GetSalesPersonCount. Visual Studio 2005 will add a new class to your project for the stored procedure. The generated

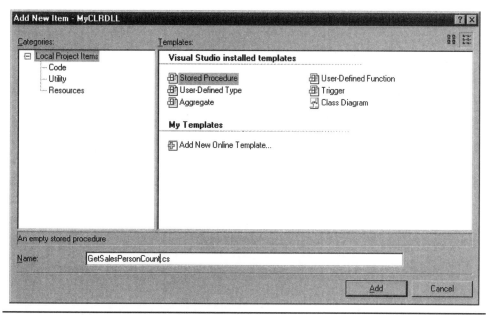

Figure 4-3   *Adding a CLR stored procedure*

class file is named after your stored procedure name and will include all of the required import directives as well as stub code that names the stored procedure. It's up to you to fill in the rest of the code that makes the stored procedure work. The following example illustrates the source code required to create a simple CLR stored procedure:

```
using System;
using System.Data;
using System.Data.Sql;
using System.Data.SqlServer;
using System.Data.SqlTypes;


public partial class StoredProcedures
{
    [SqlProcedure]
    public static int GetSalesPersonCount()
    {
        int iRows;
        SqlCommand sqlCmd = SqlContext.GetCommand();
        sqlCmd.CommandText =
```

```
            "SELECT COUNT(*) AS 'Sales Person Count' "
                + "FROM Sales.SalesPerson";
            iRows = (int)sqlCmd.ExecuteScalar();
            return iRows;
        }
};
```

The first important point to note in this code is the directive that imports the System.Data.SqlServer namespace. This enables the MyCLRDLL project to use the SQL Server .NET Data Provider without always needing to reference the fully qualified name. The second thing to notice is the [SqlProcedure] attribute that precedes the method name; it tells the compiler this method will be exposed as a SQL Server stored procedure. Next, you can see that the default class name for this stored procedure is set to StoredProcedures. This class contains a static method named GetSalesPersonCount that returns an int data type. For C#, the method must be defined as static. For VB.NET code, the method would need to be defined as Shared. The code here essentially retrieves the number of rows from the table Sales.SalesPerson in the sample AdventureWorks database. Notice that within the class, the Open method was not used. This is a radical departure for the client-based ADO.NET code. Instead, the SQL Server .NET Data Provider automatically opens a connection to the local server on your behalf.

After the CLR stored procedure source code has been compiled into an assembly, you can then add that assembly to the database and create the CLR stored procedure. You can do this in two ways: If you're developing in Visual Studio 2005, then you can simply use the Build | Deploy Solution option to install the new CLR stored procedure in the SQL Server database. Or, you can perform the deployment steps manually. To help you understand how CLR objects are used in the database, I'll explain the manual deployment steps in the next section.

After generating the DLL, the next step is to use that DLL to create a new SQL Server object called an *assembly*. The following code illustrates creating an assembly for the MyCLRDLL.DLL:

```
CREATE ASSEMBLY MyCLRDLL
FROM '\\MyFileShare\Code Library\MyCLRDLL.dll'
```

The CREATE ASSEMBLY command uses the first argument to name the assembly. Here, I've named it MyCLRDLL, which happens to be the same name as the actual .NET DLL, but using the same names isn't a requirement. The argument after the FROM clause tells the CREATE ASSEMBLY statement where to find the physical DLL on the disk. This could be on the local drive, or it could be on a UNC path.

NOTE

*At the time of this writing, the first time you manually run the **CREATE ASSEMBLY** command the Microsoft.VisualStudio.DataTools.SqlAttributes.dll also needs to be present in the directory that contains the .NET DLL that you want to add as an assembly.*

When the assembly is created, the DLL is copied into the target SQL Server database and the assembly is registered. The following code illustrates creating the GetSalesPersonCount stored procedure that uses the MyCLRDLL assembly:

```
CREATE PROCEDURE GetSalesPersonCount
AS EXTERNAL NAME
MyCLRDLL.StoredProcedures.GetSalesPersonCount
```

The EXTERNAL NAME clause is new to SQL Server 2005. Here, the EXTERNAL NAME clause specifies that the stored procedure GetSalesPersonCount will be created using a .NET assembly. An assembly can contain multiple classes and methods; the EXTERNAL NAME statement uses the following syntax to identify the correct class and method to use from the assembly:

Assembly Name.ClassName.MethodName

In the case of the previous example, the registered assembly is named MyCLRDLL. The class within the assembly is StoredProcedures, and the method within the class that will be executed is GetSalesPersonCount.

After the CLR stored procedure has been created, it can be called exactly like any T-SQL stored procedure, as the following example illustrates:

```
DECLARE @mycount INT
EXEC @mycount = GetSalesPersonCount
PRINT @mycount
```

.NET User-Defined Functions

Creating .NET-based *user-defined functions (UDFs)* is another new feature that's enabled by the integration of the .NET CLR. User-defined functions that return scalar types must return a .NET data type that can be implicitly converted to a SQL Server data type. Scalar functions written with the .NET Framework can significantly outperform T-SQL in certain scenarios because unlike T-SQL functions, .NET functions are created using compiled code. User-defined functions can also return table types, in which case the function must return a result set.

To add a UDF using Visual Studio 2005, you can use the Project | Add User-Defined Function menu option shown in Figure 4-4.

You can either add this to an existing project as I did (adding it to the sample MyCLRDLL that I created in the earlier example), or create a new SQL Server project. The following example shows a simple UDF named GetDateAsString that performs a basic date-to-string conversion:

```csharp
using System;
using System.Data.Sql;
using System.Data.SqlTypes;

public partial class UserDefinedFunctions
{
    [SqlFunction]
    public static SqlString GetDateAsString()
    {
        DateTime CurrentDate = new DateTime();
        return CurrentDate.ToString();
    }
};
```

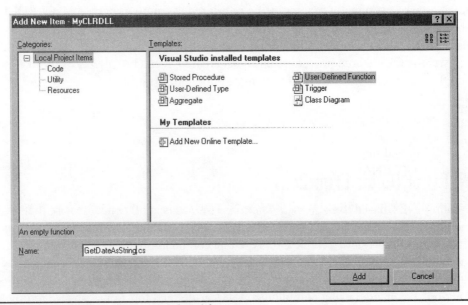

Figure 4-4   *Adding a CLR user-defined function*

Here, notice that the System.Data.SqlServer namespace was not needed, as this particular function does not perform any data access. Next, you can see that by default, Visual Studio 2005 generated the UserDefinedFunctions class to contain all of the methods that this assembly will expose as UDFs. You can also see that the [SqlFunction] attribute is used to identify the GetDateAsString method as a UDF. The code here simply converts the system date to a string data type.

To create the function, the assembly must first be created as you saw in the stored procedure example. If you're using Visual Studio 2005, you can simply select the Build | Deploy Solution option. If you're doing this manually and this is included in an assembly with other CLR objects, you'll first need to drop those objects, then drop the assembly, and finally re-create the assembly and objects. Since this method was added to the MyCLRDLL that was already used in an assembly and a stored procedure, the DROP PROCEDURE statement and the DROP ASSEMBLY statement must first be run to delete the dependent database objects before the updated .NET DLL can be reloaded into an assembly. After the existing objects are deleted, the following CREATE ASSEMBLY statement can be run to reload the new DLL:

```
CREATE ASSEMBLY MyCLRDLL
FROM '\\MyFileShare\Code Library\MyCLRDLL.dll'
```

Then the CREATE FUNCTION statement is used to create a new SQL Server function that executes the appropriate method in the assembly. The following listing illustrates how the CREATE FUNCTION statement can create a .NET user-defined function:

```
CREATE FUNCTION GetDateAsString()
RETURNS nvarchar(256)
EXTERNAL NAME
MyCLRDLL.UserDefinedFunctions.GetDateAsString
```

For user-defined functions, the CREATE FUNCTION statement has been extended with the EXTERNAL NAME clause, which essentially links the user-defined function name to the appropriate method in the .NET assembly. In this example, the GetDateAsString function is using the assembly named MyCLRDLL. Within that assembly, it's using the UserDefinedFunctions class and the GetDateAsString method within that class.

After the function has been created, it can be called like a regular SQL Server function. You can see how to execute the GetDateAsString function in the following example:

```
SELECT dbo.GetDateAsString()
```

.NET Triggers

In addition to stored procedures and user-defined functions, the new .NET integration capabilities found in SQL Server 2005 also provide the ability to create .NET *user-defined triggers (UDTs)*. To add a UDT using Visual Studio 2005, you can use the Project | Add Trigger menu option, as shown in Figure 4-5.

As with the other CLR database objects, you select the Trigger option from the list of templates and then provide the name of the trigger in the name prompt. Visual Studio 2005 will generate a stub file that you can add your code to. The following example code listing illustrates a simple CLR trigger named MyTrigger:

```
using System;
using System.Data;
using System.Data.Sql;
using System.Data.SqlServer;
using System.Data.SqlTypes;

public partial class Triggers
{
    // Enter existing table or view for the target
    //  and uncomment the attribute line
    [SqlTrigger (Name="MyTrigger",
     Target="Person.ContactType", Event="FOR INSERT")]
    public static void MyTrigger()
    {
        SqlTriggerContext oTriggerContext =
            SqlContext.GetTriggerContext();
        SqlPipe sPipe = SqlContext.GetPipe();
        SqlCommand sqlCmd = SqlContext.GetCommand();
        if (oTriggerContext.TriggerAction == TriggerAction.Insert)
        {
            sqlCmd.CommandText = "SELECT * FROM inserted";
            sPipe.Execute(sqlCmd);
        }
    }
}
```

Like the other examples, the stub file includes the appropriate import directives as well as generating a class, in this case appropriately named Triggers, and a method with its appropriate method attribute. This code example makes use of a couple of

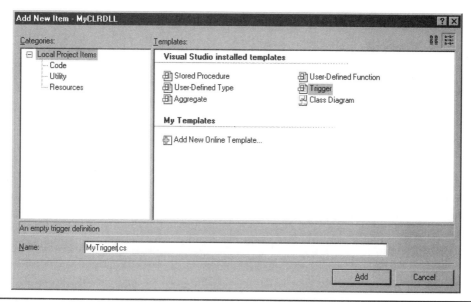

Figure 4-5   *Adding a CLR trigger*

new ADO.NET objects: the SqlTriggerContext object and the SqlPipe object. The SqlTriggerContext object provides information about the trigger action that's fired and the columns that are affected. The SqlTriggerContext object is always instantiated by the SqlContext object. Generally, the SqlContext object provides information about the caller's context. Specifically, in this case, the SqlContext object enables the code to access the virtual table that's created during the execution of the trigger. This virtual table stores the data that caused the trigger to fire.

Next, a SqlPipe object is created. The SqlPipe object represents a conduit that passes information between the CLR and the calling code. Here, the SqlPipe object enables the extended trigger to communicate with the external caller. Then the SqlContext object is used to determine if the trigger action was an insert operation. If so, then the contents of the virtual trigger table are retrieved and sent to the caller using the SqlPipe object's Execute method.

Once the code has been created, you can either deploy it to the database using the Visual Studio 2005 Build | Deploy solution option or manually drop and re-create the assembly and any dependent objects as you saw in the stored procedure and UDF examples earlier in this chapter. To manually create a CLR trigger, you can use the

CREATE TRIGGER state that you can see in the next example. The following code shows how to create the extended trigger on the Person.ContactType table in the AdventureWorks database:

```
CREATE TRIGGER MyTrigger
ON Person.ContactType
FOR INSERT
AS EXTERNAL NAME
MyCLRDLL.Triggers.MyTrigger
```

Much as in the other .NET examples, the extended trigger is created using the CREATE TRIGGER statement. The CREATE TRIGGER statement has been extended with the AS EXTERNAL NAME clause, which associates the trigger to a method in an assembly. Here, the EXTERNAL NAME clause points to the assembly named MyCLRDLL. Within the Triggers class of that namespace, the MyTrigger method contains the code that will be executed when this extended trigger is fired.

The .NET trigger will be fired for every insert operation that's performed on the Job table. For example, the following INSERT statement will add a row to the Person.ContactType table, which will cause the .NET trigger to fire:

```
INSERT INTO Person.ContactType VALUES(102, 'The Big Boss',
  '2004-07-20 00:00:00.000')
```

The example trigger, MyTrigger, performs a select statement on the inserted row value. Then it uses the SqlPipe object to send the results back to the caller. In this example, the trigger will send the contents of the inserted row values back to the caller.

CLR User-Defined Data Types

Another important new feature in SQL Server 2005 that is enabled by the integration of the .NET CLR is the ability to create true *user-defined types (UDTs)*. Using UDTs, you can extend the raw types provided by SQL Server and add data types that are specialized to your application or environment.

In the following example, you'll see how to create a UDT that represents a gender code: either M for male or F for female. While you could store this data in a standard one-byte character field, using a UDT ensures that the field will accept only these two values with no additional need for triggers, constraints, or other data validation techniques.

If you're using Visual Studio 2005, the best way to create a UDT is to use the SQL Server templates. To create a new UDT, you right-click your project in Visual

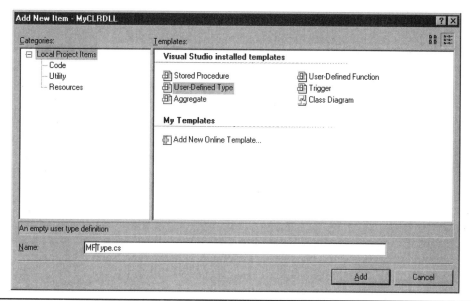

Figure 4-6   *Creating a .NET SQL Server UDT*

Studio 2005 and select Add | Add Class from the context menu. This will display the Add New Item dialog that you can see in Figure 4-6.

Select User-Defined Type from the list of SQL Server templates. Enter the name that you want to assign to the class and then click Open to have Visual Studio generate a stub file for the UDT. The stub file implements the four methods that SQL Server 2005 requires for all UDTs. These methods are generic to fulfill the SQL Server UDT contract requirements—it's up to you to add the code to make the UDT perform meaningful actions. The four required UDT methods are listed in Table 4-1.

Method	Description
IsNullable	This required method is used to indicate if the object is nullable. SQL Server 2005 requires all UDTs to implement the nullability, so this method must always return true.
Parse	This required method accepts a string parameter and stores it as a UDT.
ToString	This required method converts the contents of the UDT to a string.
Default constructor	This required method creates a new instance of the UDT.

Table 4-1   *Required UDT Methods*

You can see the completed MFType class that is used to implement a UDT for M (male) and F (female) codes in this listing:

```csharp
using System;
using System.Data.Sql;
using System.Data.SqlTypes;


[Serializable]
[SqlUserDefinedType(Format.SerializedDataWithMetadata,
MaxByteSize=512)]
public class MFType: INullable
{
    string m_value;
    public override string ToString()
    {
        string s = "null";
        if (m_value != null)
        {
            s = m_value.ToString();
            return s;
        }
        else return m_value.ToString();
    }
    public bool IsNull
    {
        get
        {
            if (m_value == null)
                return true;
            else return false;
        }
    }

    public static MFType Null
    {
        get
        {
            MFType h = new MFType();
            return h;
        }
    }

    public static MFType Parse(SqlString s)
    {
```

```
        if (s.IsNull || s.Value.ToLower() == "null")
            return Null;
        MFType u = new MFType();
        u.Value = s.ToString();
        return u;
    }


    // Create a Value Property
    public SqlString Value
    {
        get
        {
            return (m_value);
        }
        set
        {
            if (value == "M" || value == "F")
            {
                m_value = value.ToString();
            }
            else
            {
                throw new ArgumentException
                    ("MFType data type must be M or F");
            }
        }
    }
}
```

The first section of this code is essentially a template that's required by all user-defined types. The class's attributes must be serializable, the class must implement the INullable interface, and the class name is set to the name of the UDT. You can optionally add the IComparable interface. In this example, MFType is the class name. A string variable named m_value is declared to hold the contents of the code. Next, you can see the required ToString method. The ToString method checks to see if the contents of the m_value variable are null. If so, then the string "null" is returned. Otherwise, the m_value's ToString method returns the string value of the contents.

The next section of code defines the IsNull property. This property's get method checks the contents of the m_value variable and returns the value of true if m_value is null. Otherwise, the get method returns the value of false. Next, you can see the Null method, which was generated by the template to fulfill the UDT's requirement for nullability.

The Parse method accepts a string argument, which it stores in the object's Value property. You can see the definition for the Value property a bit lower down in the code. The Parse method must be declared as static, or if you're using VB.NET, it must be a Shared property.

The Value property is specific to this implementation. In this example, the Value property is used to store and retrieve the value of the UDT. It's also responsible for editing the allowable values. In the set method, you can see that only the values of M or F are permitted. Attempting to use any other values causes an exception to be thrown that informs the caller that the "MFType data type must be M or F."

Very much like a CLR stored procedure or function, after the code is completed, it is compiled into a DLL. That DLL is then imported as a SQL Server assembly using the CREATE ASSEMBLY statement or the Visual Studio 2005 Deploy Solution option. (The Visual Studio 2005 Deploy Solution option creates both the assembly and the UDT.)

To manually add the UDT to a database, you can use a CREATE TYPE statement similar to this one:

```
CREATE TYPE MFType EXTERNAL NAME MyCLRDLL.MFType
```

As when creating the other .NET database objects, the EXTERNAL NAME keyword is used to specify the assembly and the namespace for the UDT. In this case, since the UDT itself is implemented as a class, no method name is required. The value of MyCLRDLL identifies the assembly, and the value of MFType specifies the UDT's class. To see the UDTs that have been created for a database, you can query the sys.Types view, as shown here:

```
SELECT * FROM sys.Types
```

Once the UDT is created, you can use it in T_SQL much like SQL Server's native data types. However, since UDTs contain methods and properties, there are differences. The following example shows how the MFType UDT can be used as a variable and how its Value property can be accessed:

```
DECLARE @mf MFType
SET @mf.Value='N'
PRINT @mf.Value
```

In this listing, the UDT variable is declared using the standard T-SQL DECLARE statement. You can access the UDT's members by prefixing them with the (.) symbol. In this listing, the SET statement is used to attempt to assign the value of N to the UDT's Value property. Because N isn't a valid value, the following error is generated:

```
.Net SqlClient Data Provider: Msg 6522, Level 16, State 1, Line 2
A CLR error occurred during execution of 'MFType':
System.ArgumentException: MFType data type must be M or F
at MFType.set_Value(SqlString value)
```

Just as UDTs can be used as variables, they can also be used to create columns. The following listing illustrates creating a table that uses the MFType UDT:

```
CREATE TABLE MyContacts
(ContactID int,
FirstName varchar(25),
LastName varchar(25),
Gender MFType)
```

While creating columns with the UDT type is the same as when using a native data type, assigning values to the UDT is a bit different than the standard column assignment. Complex UDTs can contain multiple values. In this case, since the UDT uses a simple value, you can assign values to it exactly as you can any of the built-in data types. This example shows how to insert a row in the example MyContacts table that contains the MFType UDT:

```
INSERT INTO MyContacts VALUES(1, 'Michael', 'Otey', 'M')
```

To retrieve the contents of the UDT using the SELECT statement, you need to use the UDT.Member notation, as shown here, when referencing a UDT column:

```
SELECT ContactID, LastName, Gender.Value FROM MyContacts
```

CLR User-Defined Aggregates

A *user-defined aggregate (UDAGG)* is another new type of .NET database object that was introduced in SQL Server 2005. Essentially, a user-defined aggregate is an extensibility function that enables you to aggregate values over a group during the processing of a query. SQL Server has always provided a basic set of aggregation functions like MIN, MAX, and SUM that you can use over a query. User-defined aggregates enable you to extend this group of aggregate functions with your own custom aggregations. Like native aggregation functions, user-defined aggregates allow you to execute calculations on a set of values and return a single value. When you create a UDAGG, you supply the logic that will perform the aggregation. In this section, you'll see how to create a simple UDAGG that calculates the median value for a set of numbers.

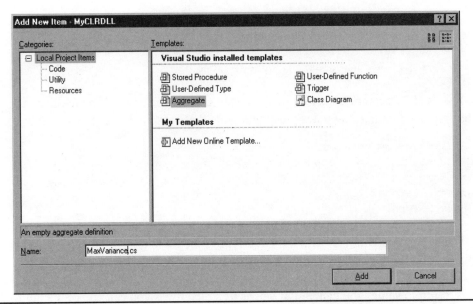

Figure 4-7   *Adding a user-defined aggregate*

To create a new UDAGG using Visual Studio 2005, select the Project | Add Aggregate option from the menu to display the Add New Item dialog that you can see in Figure 4-7.

Select Aggregate from the list of SQL Server templates and then enter the name for the class and click Open. Visual Studio will generate a stub file for the Aggregate class. Much like a UDT, the Aggregate class's stub file implements four methods that SQL Server 2005 requires for all user-defined aggregates. The four required methods for all UDAGGs are listed in Table 4-2.

Method	Description
Init	This required method initializes the object. It is invoked once for each aggregation.
Accumulate	This required method is invoked once for each item in the set being aggregated.
Merge	This required method is invoked when the server executes a query using parallelism. This method is used to merge the data from the different parallel instances together.
Terminate	This required method returns the results of the aggregation. It is invoked once after all of the items have been processed.

Table 4-2   *Required Aggregate Methods*

You can see the example MaxVariance class that is used to implement a user-defined MaxVar aggregate in the following listing:

```
[Serializable]
[SqlUserDefinedAggregate(Format.SerializedDataWithMetadata, MaxByteSize = 512)]
public class MaxVariance
{
    int m_LowValue;
    int m_HighValue;

    public void Init()
    {
        m_LowValue = 999999999;
        m_HighValue = -999999999;
    }
    public void Accumulate(SqlInt32 Value)
    {
        if (Value > m_HighValue) m_HighValue = (int)Value;
        if (Value < m_LowValue) m_LowValue = (int)Value;
    }
    public void Merge (MaxVariance Group)
    {
        if (Group.GetHighValue() > m_HighValue)
            m_HighValue = Group.GetHighValue();
        if (Group.GetLowValue() < m_LowValue)
            m_LowValue = Group.GetLowValue();
    }
    public SqlInt32 Terminate ()
    {
        return m_HighValue - m_LowValue;
    }
    // Helper methods
    public int GetLowValue()
    {
        return m_LowValue;
    }
    public int GetHighValue()
    {
        return m_HighValue;
    }
}
```

At the top of this class, you can see the serialization attribute that's required by UDAGG classes. Next, two variables are declared to hold the minimum and maximum values that are encountered by the aggregate. After that, in the Init method the two variables are assigned high and low values, ensuring that they will be assigned values from the list. While the Init method is called just once, the Accumulate method is called once for each row in the result set. In this example, the Accumulate method compares the incoming value with the values stored in the m_HighValue and m_LowValue variables. If the incoming value is higher than the current high value, it is stored in the m_HighValue variable. If the value is lower than the value of m_LowValue, it is stored in the m_LowValue. Otherwise, no action is performed by the Accumulate method for this UDAGG.

NOTE

Because UDAGGs are serialized, you need to be aware of the total storage requirement of the UDAGG. The UDAGG is serialized following each invocation of the Accumulate method, and it cannot exceed the maximum column size of 8000 bytes.

The Merge method is used when the UDAGG is processed in parallel, which typically won't be the case for most queries. If the Merge is called, its job is to import the current aggregation values from the parallel instance. You can see here that it does that using two helper methods that essentially export the values in the m_HighValue and m_LowValue variables. These values are compared to the exiting values, and if they are higher or lower, they will replace the current values in m_HighValue and m_LowValue.

The Terminate method is called once after all of the results have been processed. For this example, the Terminate method simply subtracts the lowest value found from the highest value found and returns the difference to the caller.

After compiling the .NET class into a DLL, you can import the DLL as a SQL Server assembly using either the Visual Studio 2005 Deploy Solution option or manually using the CREATE ASSEMBLY statement and CREATE AGGGRATE statements. The manual CREATE AGGREGATE statement is shown here:

```
CREATE AGGREGATE MaxVariance(@MyInt int)
RETURNS int
EXTERNAL NAME MyCLRDLL.MaxVariance
```

This example shows the creation of an aggregate named MaxVariance. This aggregate can be used with integer data types, and it returns an integer value. In the EXTERNAL NAME clause, you can see that the code for this UDAGG is found in the MaxVariance class of the MyCLRDLL assembly.

You can use the UDAGG just like SQL Server's built-in aggregate functions. One small difference is that the UDAGG needs to be prefixed with the schema name to allow the system to locate it. The following line illustrates using the MaxVariance UDAGG:

```
SELECT dbo.MaxVariance(MinQty) FROM Sales.SpecialOffer
```

The result of this UDAGG will be the difference between the high and low values found in the Sales.SpecialOffer column.

.NET Database Object Security

No discussion of the new CLR features would be complete without the security issues associated with using .NET assemblies and the SQL Server CLR. Unlike T-SQL, which doesn't have any native facilities for referencing resources outside the database, .NET assemblies are fully capable of assessing both system and network resources. Therefore, securing them is an important aspect of their development. With SQL Server 2005, Microsoft has integrated the user-based SQL Server security model with the permissions-based CLR security model. Following the SQL Server security model, users are able to access only database objects—including those created from .NET assemblies—to which they have user rights. The CLR security extends this by providing control over the type of system resources that can be accessed by .NET code running on the server. CLR security permissions are specified at the time the assembly is created by using the WITH PERMISSION_SET clause of the CREATE ASSEMBLY statement. Table 4-3 summarizes the options for CLR database security permissions that can be applied to SQL Server database objects.

Using the SAFE permission restricts all external access. The EXTERNAL_ACCESS permission enables some external access of resources using managed APIs. SQL Server impersonates the caller in order to access external resources. You must have the new EXTERNAL_ACCESS permission in order to create objects with this permission set. The UNSAFE permission is basically an anything-goes type of permission. All system resources can be accessed, and calls to both managed and unmanaged code are allowed. Only system administrators can create objects with UNSAFE permissions.

When to Use CLR Database Objects

Database objects created using the CLR are best suited for replacing extended stored procedures that require access to external system resources, for creating database objects that require complex logic, or for creating database objects that are potentially transportable between the database and the data tier layer of an application. They are not as well suited to raw data access and update functions as T-SQL.

CRL Security	External Access Allowed	Calls to Unmanaged Code
SAFE	No external access	No calls to unmanaged code
EXTERNAL_ACCESS	External access permitted via management APIs	No calls to unmanaged code
UNSAFE	External access allowed	Calls to unmanaged code allowed

Table 4-3   *CLR Database Object Security Options*

T-SQL Enhancements

With all the new .NET-related features, you may wonder if Microsoft is planning to drop support for T-SQL, but that's definitely not the case. T-SQL is still the best language to use for raw data access, and as you might have noticed, the T-SQL syntax was used in the previous examples, so rest assured that T-SQL will be around for the foreseeable future. In fact, Microsoft has made a number of important enhancements to T-SQL that you'll learn about in this section of the chapter.

Top Enhancements

In SQL Server 2000, you were forced to use a constant value in conjunction with the TOP clause. In other words, you could select the TOP 5 or the TOP 10 rows, where the value of 5 or 10 was a constant. With SQL Server 2005, the TOP function now enables the use of an expression in conjunction with the TOP clause. An expression can be any allowed T-SQL expression, including a variable or a scalar subquery. The TOP clause is also supported in the INSERT, UPDATE, and DELETE statements. This gives the TOP clause a great deal more flexibility than ever before. An example of using the new TOP clause is shown here:

```
USE AdventureWorks
DECLARE @MyTop INT
SET @MyTop = 15
SELECT TOP (@MyTop) CustomerID, SalesPerson FROM Sales.Customer
```

Common Table Expressions (CTE)

Another new T-SQL feature is support for *common table expressions (CTEs)*. CTEs are a lot like views; however, they are embedded in a query. The main reason Microsoft introduced CTEs to SQL Server 2005 is to provide a mechanism for handling recursive queries. Recursion is achieved by the fact that a CTE is allowed to refer to itself. To avoid the possibility of overwhelming the system with a poorly constructed recursive query, SQL Server implements a server-wide limit on the maximum level of recursion allowed, with a default maximum of 100 levels. A CTE is implemented as part of the WITH keyword and can be used with SELECT, INSERT, UPDATE, and DELETE statements. To implement recursive queries using the new CTE, you must use a special syntax, as shown in the simple code example that follows. This example performs a simple recursive query using the HumanResources.Employee table in the example AdventureWorks database:

```
USE AdventureWorks
WITH EmployeeChart(EmployeeID, ManagerID, Title)
AS
(SELECT EmployeeID, ManagerID, Title
 FROM HumanResources.Employee
 WHERE EmployeeID = 3
 UNION ALL
SELECT L2.EmployeeID, L2. ManagerID, L2.Title
 FROM HumanResources.Employee AS L2
 JOIN EmployeeChart
  ON L2.ManagerID = EmployeeChart.EmployeeID)
SELECT * from EmployeeChart
```

To use a CTE, you first write a WITH clause, which you use to name the CTE and specify the columns to bind to a SELECT statement. There must be a semicolon in front of the WITH keyword if it is not the first statement in a batch. The first SELECT statement is called the *anchor member,* and it must not refer to itself. In this case, it retrieves the EmployeeID, ManagerID, and Title columns from the AdventureWorks Employee table. The second SELECT statement references the CTE and is called the *recursive member.* In this case, it retrieves the same columns and is joined to the anchor member on the ManagerID column. You can see the results of this CTE in the following listing:

```
EmployeeID  ManagerID   Title
----------- ----------- ---------------------------------------------------
3           12          Engineering Manager
4           3           Senior Tool Designer
9           3           Design Engineer
11          3           Design Engineer
158         3           Research and Development Manager
263         3           Senior Tool Designer
267         3           Senior Design Engineer
270         3           Design Engineer
5           263         Tool Designer
265         263         Tool Designer
79          158         Research and Development Engineer
114         158         Research and Development Engineer
217         158         Research and Development Manager

(13 row(s) affected)
```

PIVOT and UNPIVOT

The addition of the PIVOT and UNPIVOT relational operators is another new feature found in SQL Server 2005's T-SQL. The new PIVOT and UNPIVOT operators are most useful for OLAP scenarios where you're dealing with tabular data rather than relational data. The PIVOT operator transforms a set of rows into columns. As you might expect, the UNPIVOT operator reverses the PIVOT operator, transforming the pivoted columns back into rows. However, depending on the situation, the UNPIVOT operation may not exactly reverse the PIVOT operation. This situation occurs because the PIVOT operation is often set up such that it will omit certain values. If a value is omitted during the PIVOT operation, it obviously cannot be unpivoted. Therefore, the UNPIVOT operator doesn't always result in an exact mirror image of the original pivot condition.

You can see how the PIVOT operator works in the following listings. Given a simple select on a file named OrderSum, you can see a set of orders for a CustomerID of 1, where each order has an associated year.

```
OrderId       CustomerID  OrderYear
-----------   ----------- -----------
100           1           2000
101           1           2000
102           1           2000
103           1           2001
104           1           2001
105           1           2002
106           1           2003
107           1           2004

(8 row(s) affected)
```

Using SQL Server 2005's new PIVOT operator, you can transform this result set, which lists each year vertically, into a result set that lists the years horizontally for each customer and sums up the number of orders for each year. The sample PIVOT operation is shown in the following listing:

```
SELECT * FROM OrderSum
 PIVOT (COUNT(OrderID)
   FOR OrderYear IN([2000], [2001], [2002], [2003], [2004]))
   AS P
 WHERE CustomerID = 1
```

Here, the PIVOT operation is used with the SELECT statement to create a new result set. The first value of the pivot operator identifies the value that will be placed in the pivot column. In this example, the COUNT(OrderID) aggregation sums up the number of orders for each pivot value. The FOR keyword identifies the column whose values will be pivoted. This example shows the pivot operation being performed on the OrderYear column. The values identified by the IN keyword list are the values from the pivoted column that will be used as column headings. You can see the pivoted result set in the following listing:

```
CustomerID  2000         2001         2002         2003         2004
----------- ----------- ----------- ----------- ----------- -----------
1           3            2            1            1            1
Warning: Null value is eliminated by an aggregate or other SET operation.

(1 row(s) affected)
```

DDL Triggers

Earlier versions of SQL Server only allowed triggers to be used with data manipulation events such as inserting or updating a row. SQL Server 2005 extends this by allowing triggers to be placed on DDL events such as creating and dropping database objects such as tables, views, procedures, and logins. DDL triggers can be associated with CREATE, ALTER, and DROP statements. This enables the DBA to place restrictions on the type of DDL operations that can be performed in a given database, or you can use these triggers to send notification messages regarding important schema changes that take place in the database. The following example shows how to add a DDL trigger named NoTableUpdate to the DROP Table and ALTER Table DDL statements:

```
CREATE TRIGGER NoTableUpdate
ON DATABASE FOR DROP_TABLE, ALTER_TABLE
AS
PRINT 'DROP TABLE and ALTER TABLE statement are not allowed'
ROLLBACK
```

Here, you can see how the new DDL trigger can be used to restrict the use of the DROP TABLE and ALTER TABLE statements. If an ALTER TABLE or DROP TABLE statement is issued, the NoTableUpdate trigger will print an error message and roll back the attempted DDL operation. An attempt to issue an ALTER TABLE statement in the database containing the NoTableUpdate trigger is shown here:

```
DROP TABLE and ALTER TABLE statement are not allowed
.Net SqlClient Data Provider: Msg 3609, Level 16, State 2, Line 1
Transaction ended in trigger. Batch has been aborted.
```

To make alterations to the tables in a database after this trigger is in place, you will first need to drop the DDL trigger.

DML Output

Another new T-SQL feature found in SQL Server 2005 is the ability to produce output from T-SQL INSERT, UPDATE, and DELETE DML statements. The new Output clause returns the modified data. For instance, the following DELETE Statement removes all of the rows from the OrderSum table:

```
DECLARE @MyOrderSumTVar TABLE(
    OrderID int,
    CustomerID int,
    OrderYear int);
DELETE FROM OrderSum

OUTPUT DELETED.* INTO @MyOrderSumTVar
```

SELECT * FROM @MyOrderSumTVar

 NOTE

The OrderSum example table was created in an earlier example in this chapter.

Here the OUTPUT DELETED.* clause specifies that all deleted rows will be output. With earlier versions of SQL Server, you would just see the number of rows that were affected by the statement. You can see the results of the new T-SQL DML Output clause here:

```
(8 row(s) affected)
OrderID      CustomerID   OrderYear
-----------  -----------  -----------
100          1            2000
101          1            2000
102          1            2000
103          1            2001
104          1            2001
105          1            2002
106          1            2003
107          1            2004

(8 row(s) affected)
```

WAITFOR

Another new T-SQL feature in SQL Server 2005 is enhanced support for the WAITFOR command. In previous versions of SQL Server, the WAITFOR command was able to wait for only a predefined time. With SQL Server 2005, the WAITFOR command is able to wait for the results of a RECEIVE statement. The primary reason behind this feature is to facilitate T-SQL programming support for the new queuing capabilities provided by the SQL Service Broker subsystem. (You can learn more about the new SQL Service Broker in Chapter 6.) The following listing shows how the new WAITFOR command can be used in conjunction with a RECEIVE statement:

```
WAITFOR (RECEIVE TOP (1) * FROM dbo.ServiceBrokerQueue)
```

New varchar(max) Data Type

The new varchar(max) data type provides an alternative to text/image data type. The new varchar(max) data type is an extension to the varchar, nvarchar and varbinary data types. Like the text, ntext, and image data types, the varchar(max) data type supports up to 2GB of data. However, unlike the existing text, ntext, and image data types, the varchar(max) data type can contain both character and binary data. Likewise, it provides no support for text pointers.

Microsoft introduced the new varchar(max) data type to make working with these large data types more like working with standard string data. This allows you to use the same programming model for varchar(max) data that you use to work with standard varchar data. All string functions work on varchar(max) data types, and the SUBSTRING functions can be used to read chunks of data. In addition, the T-SQL UPDATE statement has been enhanced to support updating chunks within a varchar(max) data type. You can create a column using the new varchar(max) data type, as shown here:

```
CREATE TABLE NewBLOB
(
    DataID INT IDENTITY NOT NULL,
    BLOBData VARCHAR(MAX) NOT NULL
)
```

Transaction Abort Handling

Another important advance embodied by T-SQL in SQL Server 2005 is improved transaction abort handling. With SQL Server 2005, a new Try/Catch model has been added to the transaction. The new Try/Catch structure enables transaction abort errors to be captured with no loss of the transaction context. With SQL Server 2000, although you can abort a transaction there's no way to maintain the context of the transaction so that you can completely recover the aborted transaction. SQL Server 2005's new Try/Catch transaction abort handling enables you to maintain the complete context of the aborted transaction, giving you the option of re-creating the transaction. The following code listing shows the basic T-SQL Try/Catch structure:

```
BEGIN TRY
    <SQL Statements>
END TRY
BEGIN CATCH TRAN_ABORT
    <SQL Statements>
END CATCH
```

The transaction is attempted in the Try block. If the RAISERROR with TRAN_ABORT statement is issued in the Try block, control is transferred to the Catch block. Within the Catch block, the @@error variable can be evaluated to determine the error condition.

When to Use T-SQL Database Objects

T-SQL database objects are not being phased out in SQL Server 2005. In fact, T-SQL is still the best choice for objects that need to perform raw data access operations. For instance, if you have stored procedures whose main function is inserting, updating, or deleting rows of data, then these objects should be developed using T-SQL rather than one of the .NET languages.

ADO.NET Enhancements

In addition to the new CLR and T-SQL features, the SQL Server 2005 release also provides some extensive improvements on the client side by bundling an update to ADO.NET. As ADO.NET continues to mature, it's finally getting those missing features that were present in its predecessor, the COM-based ADO, along with a couple of brand-new features. As you'll see as I describe the new features that Microsoft has added to ADO.NET, many of them expose some of the new capabilities that have been added to the SQL Server database engine. In addition to the major new features listed in the sections that follow, as you might expect, the new ADO.NET also supports new T-SQL varchar(max) and XML data types.

Server Cursor Support Using the SqlResultSet

One of the most important new features provided in the new ADO.NET is support for *server-side cursors*. This is one of the areas where ADO.NET was missing features found in COM-based ADO. Prior versions of ADO.NET supported only client-side cursors, such that the client platform had to do the work of maintaining the result set. With server-side cursors, you can shift that work to the server. Microsoft added this new feature chiefly to support the new in-process SQL Server .NET Data Provider, which runs on the server. Microsoft added this feature for in-process server-side requirements because on the server, there's a need to dynamically scroll through the results of short-lived result sets and there's little user interaction. Server-side cursors do hold state, which decreases scalability and increases the need for round-trips to the server. However, because of scalability issues Microsoft added this to only the server-side System.Data.SqlServer namespace. Server-side cursor support is not part of the client-side System.Data.SqlClient namespace.

With ADO.NET 2.0, the new SqlResultSet object exposes server-side cursors to your application. Theses cursors are both updatable and dynamically scrollable. The new server-side cursors are instantiated by the new ExecuteResultSet method in the System.Data.SqlServer SqlCommand object. The following example demonstrates the use of the ADO.NET SqlResultSet object:

```
using System;
using System.Data;
using System.Data.Sql;
using System.Data.SqlServer;
using System.Data.SqlTypes;

public partial class StoredProcedures
{
    [SqlProcedure]
    public static void GetProductName()
    {
        SqlPipe myPipe = SqlContext.GetPipe();
        myPipe.Send("GetProductName: Opening server cursor");
        SqlCommand cmd = SqlContext.GetCommand();
        cmd.CommandType = CommandType.Text;
        cmd.CommandText = "SELECT Name FROM Production.Product WHERE MakeFlag = 1";

        SqlResultSet resultset = cmd.ExecuteResultSet
            (ResultSetOptions.Scrollable |
            ResultSetOptions.Updatable);

        if (resultset.HasRows == true)
```

```
    {
        while (resultset.Read())
        {
            myPipe.Send(resultset.GetString(0));
            // You could optionally update with
            //resultset.Update();
            // or scroll back using
            //resultset.ReadLast();
        }
        resultset.Close();
    }
    myPipe.Send("GetProductName: Server cursor closed");
  }
};
```

Here, you can see the new CLR stored procedure called GetProductName. First, the SqlPipe object is used to send a progress message to the client. Then, the new SqlCommand object is instantiated that will retrieve the contents of the Name column on the Production.Product table of the sample AdventureWorks database. Next, an instance of the SqlResultSet object is created. Much like SqlDataReader, the SqlResultSet object is instantiated using the SqlCommand object. In this case, a scrollable, updatable cursor is opened using the ExecuteResultSet method. After the cursor is opened, your application can scroll forward, scroll backward, and make updates. Since server-side cursors hold state and consume server resources for as long as they're open, it's very important to be sure to close them when they're no longer needed.

Asynchronous Support

Another feature that was present in ADO that was missing in the earlier releases of ADO.NET is support for asynchronous queries. *Asynchronous queries* provide client applications the ability to submit queries without blocking the user interference. In the middle tier of applications, the new ADO.NET asynchronous support provides the ability for server applications to issue multiple database requests on different threads without blocking the threads. This new asynchronous support will also work with prior versions of SQL Server, including SQL Server 7 and 2000. With SQL Server 2005, ADO.NET provides asynchronous support for both opening a connection and executing commands. The implementation is the same as other asynchronous operations found in the .NET Framework. The asynchronous operation is started using the object's BEGIN*xxx* method and is ended using the END*xxx* method. The IAsyncResult object is used to check the completion status of the command.

```
SqlConnection cn = new SqlConnection
  ("SERVER=TECA-YUKON;INTEGRATED SECURITY=True;"
    + "DATABASE=AdventureWorks;async=True");
SqlCommand cmd = new SqlCommand("SELECT * FROM Production.Product", cn);
cmd.CommandType = CommandType.Text;
try
{
    cn.Open();
    IAsyncResult myResult = cmd.BeginExecuteReader();
    while (!myResult.IsCompleted)
    {
        // Perform other code actions
    }
    // Process the contents of the reader
    SqlDataReader rdr = cmd.EndExecuteReader(myResult);

    // Close the reader
    rdr.Close();
}
catch (Exception ex)
{
    MessageBox.Show(ex.Message);
}
finally
{
    cn.Close();
}
```

ADO.NET 2.0's asynchronous support is implemented in the client namespaces such as the System.Data.SqlClient namespace. The first important point to notice in this example is the connection string. In order to implement asynchronous support, the connection string must contain the ASYNC=true keywords. Next, note the IAsynchResult object within the Try block. The SqlCommand object's BeginExecuteReader method is used to start an asynchronous query that returns all of the rows in the Production.Product table. Control is returned to the application immediately after the statement is executed. The application doesn't need to wait for the query to finish. Next, a While loop is used to check the status of the IAsyncResult object. When the asynchronous command completes, the IsCompleted property is set to true. At this point, the While loop completes and the EndExecuteReader command is used to assign the asynchronous query to a SqlDataReader for processing.

Multiple Active Result Sets (MARS)

The ability to take advantage of SQL Server 2005's new multiple active result sets (MARS) feature is another enhancement found in the new ADO.NET version. In prior versions of ADO.NET and SQL Server, you were limited to one active result set per connection. And while COM-based ADO and OLE DB had a feature that allowed the application to process multiple result sets, under the covers that feature was actually spawning new connections on your behalf in order to process the additional commands. The new MARS feature in ADO.NET takes advantage of SQL Server 2005's capability to have multiple active commands on a single connection. In this model, you can open a connection to the database, then open the first command and process some results, then open the second command and process results, and then go back to the first command and process more results. You can freely switch back and forth between the different active commands. There's no blocking between the commands, and both commands share a single connection to the database. The feature provides a big performance and scalability gain for ADO.NET 2.0 applications. Since this feature relies on a SQL Server 2005 database, it can be used only with SQL Server 2005 databases and doesn't work with prior versions of SQL Server. The following example illustrates using MARS:

```
SqlConnection cn = new SqlConnection
  ("SERVER=TECA-YUKON;INTEGRATED SECURITY=True;"
    + "DATABASE=AdventureWorks");
SqlCommand cmd1 =
  new SqlCommand("SELECT * FROM HumanResources.Department", cn);
cmd1.CommandType = CommandType.Text;
try
{
    cn.Open();
    SqlDataReader rdr = cmd1.ExecuteReader();
    while (rdr.Read())
    {
        if (rdr["Name"].ToString() == "Production")
        {
            SqlCommand cmd2 = new SqlCommand
              ("SELECT * FROM HumanResources.Employee "
                + "WHERE DepartmentID = 7", cn);
            cmd2.CommandType = CommandType.Text;
            SqlDataReader rdr2 = cmd2.ExecuteReader();
            while (rdr2.Read())
            {
                // Process results
```

```
            }
            rdr2.Close();
        }
    }
    rdr.Close();
}
catch (Exception ex)
{
    MessageBox.Show(ex.Message);
}
finally
{
    cn.Close();
}
```

In this example, you can see that both cmd1 and cmd2 share the same SqlConnection object, named cn. The cmd1 object is used to open a SqlDataReader that reads all of the rows from the HumanResources.Department table. When the Department named Production is found, the second SqlCommand object, named cmd2, is used to read the contents of the HumanResources.Employee table. The important point to note is that the SqlCommand named cmd2 is able to execute using the active SqlConnection object that is also servicing the cmd1 object.

Paging

Integrated support for paging is another welcome new feature found in the SQL Server 2005 version of ADO.NET. Paging is always a difficult area to work with in client applications, and the new ADO.NET provides the basic support for paging by enabling the application to select and bind to a range of rows from a result set. For scalability, the new paging implementation doesn't hold any state on the server. However, this also means that it's possible for the membership of the paging set to change between executions. This means that the new paging feature is best suited to data that's fairly stable and doesn't change frequently. The paging support in the new ADO.NET is ordinal based, and to use it, you must specify a starting row in the result set and the number of rows to include in the page. The rows of the page set are read using the standard DataReader. The following example PageProductsTable subroutine illustrates using the new ADO.NET paging function:

```
private SqlDataReader PageProductsTable(int nStartRow, int nPageSize)
{
    SqlConnection cn = new SqlConnection
```

```
    ("SERVER=TECA-YUKON;INTEGRATED SECURITY=True;"
      + "DATABASE=AdventureWorks");
  SqlCommand cmd =
    new SqlCommand("SELECT * FROM Production.Product", cn);
  cmd.CommandType = CommandType.Text;
  cn.Open();
  return cmd.ExecutePageReader
    (CommandBehavior.Default, nStartRow, nPageSize);
}
```

In this example, the PageProductsTable method takes as arguments two integers that define the starting position and the paging size of the rows to be read. It returns an ADO.NET SqlDataReader object. Inside the routine, the SqlConnection and SqlCommand objects are created as normal. After the SqlConnection object is opened, the SqlCommand object's ExecutePageReader method is called to retrieve a page of results. The first argument of the ExecutePageReader method is the CommandBehaviorDefault enumerator that tells the SqlCommand object how to handle the connection when the operation is finished. The second argument is an ordinal that identifies the starting row. The third argument specifies the number of rows to be returned. You can use ADO.NET 2.0's paging capabilities, as you can see in the following example:

```
DataTable dt = new DataTable("Products");
dt.Load(PageProductsTable(10, 10));
dataGridView1.DataSource = dt;
```

Here, a new DataTable object is created, and then the Load method is used to pipe the results of the paged SqlDataReader into the DataTable. The DataTable is then bound to a dataGridView object.

Bulk Insert

Another significant enhancement in ADO.NET 2.0 is the new SqlBulkCopy object. The SqlBulkCopy object provides a high-performance method for transferring objects between different databases or different SQL Server systems. The following example illustrates how the new SqlBulkCopy object is used:

```
// Create source & destination connections
SqlConnection cnSource = new SqlConnection
  ("SERVER=TECA-YUKON;INTEGRATED SECURITY=True;"
    + "DATABASE=AdventureWorks");
```

```
SqlConnection cnDest = new SqlConnection
  ("SERVER=TECA-YUKON;INTEGRATED SECURITY=True;"
    + "DATABASE=AdventureWorks2");

cnSource.Open();
cnDest.Open();

// Read the source data
SqlCommand cmd = new SqlCommand
  ("SELECT * FROM Sales.SpecialOffer", cnSource);
SqlDataReader rdr = cmd.ExecuteReader();

// Create SqlBulkCopy object and write the destination data
SqlBulkCopy bulkData = new SqlBulkCopy(cnDest);
bulkData.DestinationTableName = "SpecialOffers";
bulkData.WriteToServer(rdr);

bulkData.Close();
cnSource.Close();
cnDest.Close();
```

In this example, two connection objects are created that point to different databases in the same system. The first connection object uses the AdventureWorks database, and the second object uses a copy called AdventureWorks2. Both connection objects are opened, and then a SqlDataReader is used to read the data from the source connection. Next, a SqlBulkCopy object is created and attached to the destination connection object. Then, the SqlBulkCopy object's WriteToServer method is called using the SqlDataReader that's attached to the source connection. The WriteToServer method copies the data from the source to the destination. It's important to note that the target object must exist on the destination connection. There are additional methods in the SqlBulkCopy object that you can use to perform custom schema mapping between the source and the destination tables.

Common Connection Model

One of the problems that ADO.NET 1.0 also had was the fact that it was not provider agnostic. In other words, you needed to use a specific provider to connect to a specific target database platform. For example, the SqlClient could connect only to SQL Server systems, not to Oracle systems. Likewise, the OracleClient could connect only to Oracle systems, not to SQL Server systems. While you could build your code to load the correct provider on the fly, the result wasn't elegant, and it was certainly not convenient. ADO.NET 2.0 solves this problem by adding a new Provider Factory capability that is capable of instantiating the appropriate provider at run time. The following example illustrates how the new Provider Factory is used:

```
DbDataReader rdr;
DbProviderFactory provider =
    DbProviderFactories.GetFactory("System.Data.SqlClient");

using (DbConnection cn = provider.CreateConnection())
{
    using (DbCommand cmd = provider.CreateCommand())
    {
        cmd.CommandText = "SELECT * FROM Production.Location";
        cmd.Connection = cn;
        cn.ConnectionString =
            ("SERVER=TECA-YUKON;INTEGRATED SECURITY=True;"
                + "DATABASE=AdventureWorks");
        cn.Open();
        rdr = cmd.ExecuteReader(CommandBehavior.CloseConnection);
        DataTable dt = new DataTable("Product Locations");
        dt.Load(rdr);
        dataGridView1.DataSource = dt;
    }
}
```

Here, you can see that the GetFactory method is used to create an instance of the System.Data.SqlClient data provided at run time. Then, a DbCommand object is used to execute a command to retrieve the contents of the Production.Location table, which are passed to the DbDataReader. Finally, the results of the DbDataReader are loaded to a DataTable that's bound to a dataGridView object.

NOTE

You need to include the System.Data.Common namespace to use the DbProvider objects.

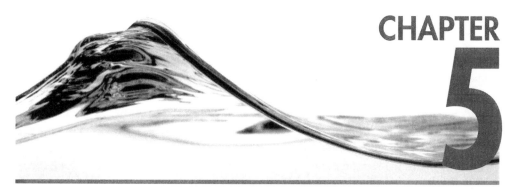

Notification Services

IN THIS CHAPTER:

Notification Services was first introduced in 2002 as a web download for SQL Server 2000. With SQL Server 2005, Notification Services has been added as a new subsystem to the base product. Notification Services is a framework that enables you to develop custom messaging applications that are able to push customized information to multiple subscribers and devices. Notification Services is used by a variety of well-known companies to deliver personalized information to their customers. For instance, MSN mobile uses Notification Services to send personalized news and other information to a variety of mobile devices. Another well-known Notification Services implementation can be found at ESPN.com, which provides a service that subscribers can use to find sports scores. SQL Server 2005's Notification Services allows you to build these same types of notification-style applications. While you can build notification applications from scratch, SQL Server 2005's Notification Services gives you a big head start on this type of project by providing a robust, scalable, and tested framework that you can use as the basis for your own notification applications.

In this chapter, you'll learn about the new Notification Services subsystem. In the first part of this chapter, you'll get an overview of this new subsystem. Next, you'll learn about how you go about building Notification Services applications. To begin with, you'll get an overview of the development process and then see some sample code that illustrates how the Notification Services framework is used to build notification-style applications.

Notification Services Overview

A Notification Services *application* is a software layer that sits between an information source and the intended recipient of that information. The Notification Services application monitors certain predefined events and can intelligently filter and route the information about those events to a variety of different target devices using a personalized delivery schedule. Notification Services applications consist of three basic components: events, subscriptions, and notifications. Figure 5-1 provides a very high-level overview of a Notification Services application.

Events

In a Notification Services application, *events* are just what they sound like—things happening that you want to be informed about. In the case of the ESPN.com example, an event might be something like the final scores of some sporting event.

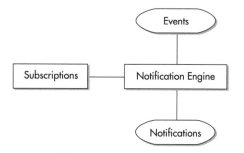

Figure 5-1   *Notification Services overview*

For NASDAQ, an event might be a given stock price rising to a certain level. With SQL Server 2005's Notification Services, events are stored as rows in a table in the Notification Services database.

Subscriptions

Subscriptions are how the users of a Notification Services application tell the system about the type of events that they are interested in. For example, with the sports-based Notification Services example, a user might create a subscription to get the final scores of the Los Angeles Lakers games. In the stock prices Notification Services example, a user might create a subscription to be notified when the price of Microsoft stock climbs over a $50 per share. SQL Server 2005's Notification Services stores subscriptions, like events, as rows in a table.

Notifications

A *notification* is essentially a message that will be sent to the end user that contains the information regarding the event that the user subscribed to. For the ESPN notification services example, this might be an e-mail message that your favorite team defeated their rivals and what the final score was. Notifications can be delivered in various formats to a variety of different target devices.

Notification Engine

The job of the Notification Services application is to monitor the external events and to look for matches between events and the registered subscriptions. When an event matches a subscription, the Notification Services engine sends a notification to the end user. The scalability of a Notification Services application depends in large part on how well the Notification Services engine matches events to subscriptions. Microsoft has designed the underlying Notification Services framework to be scalable at an Internet level, meaning that with the appropriate platform, SQL Server 2005's Notification Services can scale upward to handle millions of events, subscriptions, and notifications. To do that, Notification Services takes advantage of SQL Server 2005's extremely efficient relational database engine to join the rows from the events table with the rows in the subscriptions table in order to match events to subscriptions.

Notification Services Architecture

SQL Server 2005's Notification Services is a platform that's designed to enable you to develop and deploy highly scalable notification applications. SQL Server 2005 Notification Services applications are created using T-SQL and XML, and they are executed using the integrated .NET Framework that is built into SQL Server 2005. There are both 32-bit and 64-bit versions of the Notification Services platform. You can see an overview of the SQL Server 2005 Notification Services architecture in Figure 5-2.

At the top of Figure 5-2, you can see the Notification Services application. This application is written by the developer; its main task is to add subscription information into the Notification Services subscriptions table. This application can be an ASP.NET web application, a standard Win32 Windows application, or any type of application that's capable of calling .NET managed APIs either directly or via the .NET COM Interop classes.

On the left side of Figure 5-2, you can see the events portion of the SQL Server 2005 Notification Services architecture. Events are added to the system by *event providers*. These event providers monitor external data sources looking for changes. SQL Server 2005 ships with two built-in event providers: a *file system watcher,* which is able to detect changes in operating system files, and the *SQL Server event provider,* which monitors a SQL Server or Analysis Services database for changes. Notification Services can also be extended to look at other external data sources through the use of custom event providers. When an event provider encounters a data change, it records that event in the events table of the Notification Services database.

The *Notification Services generator* (or engine), shown in the center of Figure 5-2, uses the logic provided by the Notification Services developer to match the events stored by the event providers to the subscriptions entered by the application's end users. When an event matches a subscription, the Generator adds a row

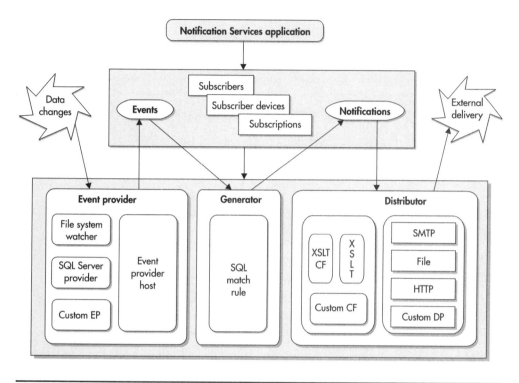

Figure 5-2   *Notification Services architecture overview*

containing the event and subscriber information into the notifications table of the
Notification Services database.

The *distributor,* shown in the lower right of Figure 5-2, monitors the notifications
table for new entries. When the generator adds a new entry to the notifications
table, the distributor retrieves that entry and formats it for delivery. By default,
the distributor will format the notification using an XML style sheet (XSLT) that
renders the output in a way that's compatible with the specified output device.
Once the notification has been formatted, the Distributor then passes it on to the
distribution provider for delivery to the target user. Out of the box, SQL Server 2005
comes with three built-in distribution providers: an SMTP provider; a File provider;
and an HTTP provider that can be used for SOAP, .NET Alerts, and SMS notifications.
As you can probably surmise, the SMTP provider delivers notifications via an e-mail
server such as Exchange. The File provider delivers the notification in the form of an
operating system file. The HTTP provider delivers the notification as an HTML web

page or using one of the other HTTP-related protocols. In addition to these, you can also extend the delivery capabilities of the distributor by adding a custom distribution provider.

Developing Notification Services Applications

In the first part of this chapter, you got an overview of the new SQL Server 2005 Notification Services. In this next section, we'll dig in a little deeper so that you learn about the actual steps involved in developing SQL Server 2005 Notification Services applications. First, you'll get an overview of the development process, and next we'll dive in and build a very simple Notification Services application.

Development Stages

The process for developing Notification Services applications begins with defining the schema and rules that govern how the application works. Next, you must compile the application. Then, you need to construct an interface that allows the user to add subscriptions to the application. Finally, you'll need to add any custom components that may be needed by the application. Let's look at each of these steps in more detail.

Define the Schema and Rules

The Notification Services developer uses a combination of XML and T-SQL to define the application's schema and rules. When you define the schema and the rules for a Notification Services application, you are essentially describing the events that the application will monitor as well as the application's subscriptions, its notifications, and the logic that will be used to match the events to the subscriptions. The Notification Services application's schema and rules are primarily defined in two files: adf.xml and config.xml. You can create these files using a standard text editor or an XML-aware editor such as Visual Studio 2005 or XMLSpy. More detailed information about the specific contents of the adf.xml and config.xml files is presented a little later in this chapter.

Compile the Application

After the schema and the rules have been created, the next step in building a Notification Services application is to compile all of the code and register a service that will run the Notification Services applications. To compile the application, SQL Server 2005 provides the nscontrol command line utility, which is used to create, register, and also update the Notification Services application. In addition, the SQL Server Management Studio provides a dialog that enables you to interactively create Notification Services applications.

Build the Notification Subscription Management Application

The first two steps build the core engine of the Notification Services application. However, users still need a way of adding their own subscription information to the Notification Services application. To enable users to enter their subscription information, the Notification Services application needs a subscription management interface, which is typically a Web or GUI application built using ASP.NET, VB.NET, or C# technologies in conjunction with a development platform like Visual Studio 2005.

Add Custom Components

Finally, the last step in building your Notification Services application is to optionally add any custom components that might be needed by the application. Custom components would include any required event providers, content formats, or notification delivery protocols that are not included in the base SQL Server 2005 Notification Services product.

Example Notification Services Application

The example Notification Services application that is presented in the next part of this chapter monitors the value of a column in a SQL Server table. When that column value exceeds a certain threshold, the sample Notification Services application will send an e-mail notification to the end user. This sample is a simplified version of the Stock example that was included with the SQL Server 2000 Notification Services sample programs. To make all of this work, the application starts by using the SQL Server 2005 provider to inspect a table in the database. An event will need to be created that checks the value of a column in that table, the user must enter a subscription for that event, and a rule must be added to allow SQL Server to match the events to the subscriptions. When an event matches the event rule, the e-mail distribution provider will send an XML-formatted notification to the end user. Now that you've got an overview of the sample Notification Services application, let's see how it's built.

Creating the Application Definition and Application Configuration Files

Notification Services applications consist of two primary files: an *application definition file (ADF)* and an *application configuration file (ACF)*—both XML files that must be built in accordance with their xsd schemas. The XSD schemas serve to make sure that both documents possess the required elements and attributes. The ACF file defines the name of the Notification Services application as well as its instance name and the application's directory path. The instance name is essentially the name of a Windows service that runs the Notification Services application.

The ADF file is the core file for the Notification Services; the different sections of the ADF describe the event, subscription, rules, and notification structure that will be employed by the Notification Services application. For the SQL Server 2000 release, you needed to do all of the XML coding by hand to create these two files. This was also true for the early betas of SQL Server 2005. However, the final SQL Server 2005 release will have graphical tools that enable you to create the ACF and ADF files without manually coding XML in a text editor.

In addition to these two primary files that define the Notification Services application and structure, a Notification Services application also needs a subscription management application that is responsible for adding subscription information to the Notification Services application's database. While the ADF and the ACF are built primarily using XML and T-SQL, the subscription management application is typically built using a high-level language with a graphical user interface.

TIP

Visual Studio.NET's multiple project solution structure enables you to easily group both the XML application definition files and the subscription management code as two projects that are part of a common solution.

The following listing shows the ACF file, config.xml, that's used in this chapter's example Notification Services application:

```xml
<?xml version="1.0" encoding="utf-8"?>
<NotificationServicesInstance xmlns:xsd="http://www.w3.org/2001/XMLSchema"
  xmlns:xsi="http://www.w3.org/2001/XMLSchema-instance"
  xmlns="http://www.microsoft.com/MicrosoftNotificationServices
    /ConfigurationFileSchema">
    <InstanceName>NSSampleInstance</InstanceName>
      <SqlServerSystem>tecayukon</SqlServerSystem>
    <Applications>
        <Application>
            <ApplicationName>NSSample</ApplicationName>
            <BaseDirectoryPath>C:\NSSample</BaseDirectoryPath>
                <ApplicationDefinitionFilePath>ADF.xml
                </ApplicationDefinitionFilePath>
        </Application>
    </Applications>
    <DeliveryChannels>
```

```
    <DeliveryChannel>
        <DeliveryChannelName>EmailChannel
            </DeliveryChannelName>
            <ProtocolName>SMTP</ProtocolName>
    </DeliveryChannel>
  </DeliveryChannels>
</NotificationServicesInstance>
```

You can see that the ACF is a relatively simple document. This file can be created using any text or XML-aware editor. The most important points to notice are the SqlServerSystem, InstanceName, ApplicationName, BaseDirectoryPath, and ApplicationDefinitionFilePath tags. As you might guess, the SqlServerSystem name tag contains the name of the SQL Server system that will host the Notification Services databases, the InstanceName tag defines the instance name for the application, and the ApplicationName tag defines the name of the Notification Services application. The BaseDirectoryPath tells the compiler where to find the ADF file, and the ApplicationDefinitionFilePath tag supplies the name of the XML document that contains the ADF code. In addition to these basic items, the ACF also uses the DeliveryChannel tag to define how notifications will be delivered. In this example, the DeliveryChannel tag uses the SMTP protocol to deliver e-mail notifications.

Defining the ADF Event Schema

The core definitions that control how a Notification Services application works are found in the ADF. The first thing that needs to be done to build the example application is to build the schema for the events. In the ADF file the EventClasses element contains the XML code that's used to define the Notification Services events. The EventClasses element can contain multiple event definitions. Each event definition is described in a separate EventClass subelement. The following code snippet from the example adf.xml file illustrates the XML code used to create the sample:

```
<?xml version="1.0" encoding="utf-8" ?>
<Application xmlns:xsd="http://www.w3.org/2001/XMLSchema"
  xmlns:xsi="http://www.w3.org/2001/XMLSchema-instance"
  xmlns="http://www.microsoft.com/MicrosoftNotificationServices/
  ApplicationDefinitionFileSchema">
    <!-- Describe the Events  -->
    <EventClasses>
        <EventClass>
            <EventClassName>DataEvents</EventClassName>
            <Schema>
                <Field>
                    <FieldName>DataID</FieldName>
                    <FieldType>int</FieldType>
```

```
                <FieldTypeMods>not null</FieldTypeMods>
            </Field>
            <Field>
                <FieldName>DataValue</FieldName>
                <FieldType>int</FieldType>
                <FieldTypeMods>null</FieldTypeMods>
            </Field>
        </Schema>
        <IndexSqlSchema>
            <SqlStatement>CREATE INDEX DataEventsIndex
                ON DataEvents ( DataID )</SqlStatement>
        </IndexSqlSchema>
        <Chronicles>
            <Chronicle>
                <ChronicleName>DataEventsTable</ChronicleName>
                <SqlSchema>
                    <SqlStatement>
                    IF EXISTS(SELECT name FROM dbo.sysobjects
                    WHERE name = 'DataEventsTable')
                    DROP TABLE dbo.DataEventsTable
                    CREATE TABLE DataEventsTable
                    (
                        [DataID]     int,
                        [DataValue]     int
                    )
                    </SqlStatement>
                </SqlSchema>
            </Chronicle>
        </Chronicles>
    </EventClass>
</EventClasses>
```

All ADF files must begin with the application elements, which as you might guess, represent the Notification Services application. The primary elements within the application element that define the application are the EventClasses, SubscriptionClasses, and NotificationClasses elements. The preceding code listing contains the EventClasses section of the ADF. Because this sample application uses only a single event, the EventClasses element contains only one EventClass element, named DataEvents. The Schema section within the EventClass element defines the event schema that the Notification Services application will monitor. In this case, two columns are defined:

the DataID column, which is a simple identifier, and the DataValue column, which contains an associated value. The resemblance of these two definitions to SQL Server columns is no coincidence. Notification Services uses these definitions to create columns in the Notification Services database. To ensure good performance, the IndexSqlSchema tag is use to create an index over the DataID column.

The Chronicles section defines tables that store event data for use by scheduled subscriptions. The Chronicles section has two required tags: the ChronicleName tag and the SqlSchema tag. The ChronicleName tag supplies the name of the Chronicle table, and the SqlSchema tag contains the T-SQL statements that create the table. Because this code is used during both the Notification Services creation and update processes, it must first check for the existence of the table and drop it if it's found. The next line of T-SQL code then creates the table.

Defining the ADF Providers

After defining the events that the application will monitor, the next step in creating the Notification Services application is defining the provider that will deliver those events to the application. In the following code snippet from the next section of the adf.xml file, you can see the definition for the SQL Server event provider that is used to connect the Notification Services application to a SQL Server:

```
<!-- Specify the SQL Server Event Provider -->
<Providers>
    <HostedProvider>
        <ProviderName>SQLData</ProviderName>
        <ClassName>SQLProvider</ClassName>
        <SystemName>tecayukon</SystemName>
        <Schedule>
            <Interval>P0DT00H00M60S</Interval>
        </Schedule>
        <Arguments>
            <Argument>
                <Name>EventsQuery</Name>
                <Value>SELECT DataID, DataValue FROM DataEventsTable</Value>
            </Argument>
            <Argument>
                <Name>EventClassName</Name>
                <Value>DataEvents</Value>
            </Argument>
        </Arguments>
    </HostedProvider>
</Providers>
```

The Providers section of the ADF describes the event providers used by the Notification Services application. In this example, the HostedProvider element defines the SQL Server event provider. The ProviderName element is used to assign a name to the provider, and the SystemName element supplies the name of the SQL Server system that the provider will connect to.

The Schedule element defines how often the provider will connect to the system; this interval is governed by the value defined in the Interval element. The value in the Interval element uses the XML duration data type. The 0DT portion of this value represents a date interval with a value of 0. The 00HR portion represents an hourly interval with a value of 0. The 00M segment represents a minute interval with a value of 0. The 60S portion represents a seconds interval with a value of 60. In other words, this interval is set at 60 seconds.

The Arguments element supplies the query that will be used to extract data from the event source. In this example, the contents of the DataID and DataValue column in the DataEventsTable will be retrieved every 60 seconds for the event class named DataEvents that was defined in the preceding EventClass element.

Defining the ADF Subscription Schema

Once the events have been described, the next step in creating the ADF file is defining the subscriptions. The following code listing shows the next portion of the adf.xml file that describes the subscriptions used by the sample Notification Services application:

```
<!-- Describe the Subscription -->
<SubscriptionClasses>
    <SubscriptionClass>
        <SubscriptionClassName>DataSubs</SubscriptionClassName>
        <Schema>
            <Field>
                <FieldName>DeviceName</FieldName>
                <FieldType>nvarchar(255)</FieldType>
                <FieldTypeMods>not null</FieldTypeMods>
            </Field>
            <Field>
                <FieldName>SubLocale</FieldName>
                <FieldType>nvarchar(10)</FieldType>
                <FieldTypeMods>not null</FieldTypeMods>
            </Field>
            <Field>
                <FieldName>DataID</FieldName>
                <FieldType>int</FieldType>
```

```
                        <FieldTypeMods>not null</FieldTypeMods>
                    </Field>
                    <Field>
                        <FieldName>DataTriggerValue</FieldName>
                        <FieldType>int</FieldType>
                        <FieldTypeMods>not null</FieldTypeMods>
                    </Field>
                </Schema>
                <IndexSqlSchema>
                    <SqlStatement>CREATE INDEX DataSubIndex ON DataSubs
                        ( DataID )</SqlStatement>
                </IndexSqlSchema>
                <EventRules>
                    <EventRule>
                        <RuleName>DataSubEventRule</RuleName>
                        <Action>
                            SELECT dbo.DataNotificationsNotify
                                (s.DeviceName, s.SubLocale, e.DataID, e.DataValue)
                                FROM DataSubs s JOIN DataEvents e
                                ON s.DataID = e.DataID
                                LEFT OUTER JOIN DataEventsTable t
                                ON s.DataID = t.DataID
                                WHERE s.DataTriggerValue &lt;= e.DataValue
                                AND (s.DataTriggerValue &gt; t.DataValue
                                OR .DataValue IS NULL)

                            INSERT INTO DataEventsTable (DataID, DataValue)
                            SELECT e.DataID, e.DataValue
                                FROM DataEvents e
                                WHERE e.DataID NOT IN
                                    (SELECT DataID from DataEventsTable)

                            UPDATE DataEventsTable
                                SET DataValue = e.DataValue
                                FROM DataEvents e, DataEventsTable t
                                WHERE e.DataID = t.DataID
                                AND e.DataValue &gt; t.DataValue
                        </Action>
                        <EventClassName>DataEvents</EventClassName>
                    </EventRule>
                </EventRules>
            </SubscriptionClass>
        </SubscriptionClasses>
```

Like the EventClasses, the SubscriptionClasses section of the ADF document can describe multiple subscriptions, where each subscription is described in a separate SubscriptionClass element. This example uses a single SubscriptionClass named DataSubs. The Schema section describes the subscription. The DeviceName field identifies that target device type. The SubLocale is used to optionally change the language that the subscriber will use to receive the notification. The DataID and DataTriggerValue fields identify the event that will be subscribed to and the data value that will trigger a notification. Again, as with the EventClass, the IndexSqlSchema element is used to create an index on the DataID column for better performance. Notification Services uses these descriptions to create database columns on SQL Server.

After the subscriptions have been set up, the next section of code in the EventRules element defines the logic that the Notification Services application will use to match events to subscriptions. While the Event and Subscription information is defined using XML, the event rules are created using T-SQL code that's stored in the EventRules Action element. In this example, the most important thing to notice is that the DataSubs table is joined to the DataEvents table where the DataValue from the DataEvents table is greater than the DataTriggerValue but less than a new value. When the join condition is met, a row for the subscriber will be created. The following INSERT and UPDATE statements are used to update the Chronicle table when a value isn't found or when the value is greater than the existing chronicle value.

The ADF Notification Schema

The next part of defining the ADF file is setting up the NotificationClasses schema. The NotificationClasses describe how the notification information will be delivered. The following code listing from the final section of the adf.xml file contains the NotificationClass definition. The NotificationClasses element could describe multiple notification types where each type is described in its own NotificationClass element. Because this sample application uses only one type of notification, the NotificationClasses section contains a single NotificationClass element.

```
<!-- Describes the Notifications -->
<NotificationClasses>
    <NotificationClass>

<NotificationClassName>DataNotifications</NotificationClassName>
        <Schema>
            <Fields>
                <Field>
```

```
                    <FieldName>DataID</FieldName>
                    <FieldType>int</FieldType>
                </Field>
                <Field>
                    <FieldName>DataValue</FieldName>
                    <FieldType>int</FieldType>
                </Field>
            </Fields>
        </Schema>
        <!-- Specify the Content Format XSLT -->
        <ContentFormatter>
            <ClassName>XsltFormatter</ClassName>
            <Arguments>
                <Argument>
                    <Name>XsltBaseDirectoryPath</Name>
                    <Value>C:\NSSample</Value>
                </Argument>
                <Argument>
                    <Name>XsltFileName</Name>
                    <Value>NSSample.xslt</Value>
                </Argument>
            </Arguments>
        </ContentFormatter>
    </NotificationClass>
</NotificationClasses>
<Generator>
    <SystemName>tecayukon</SystemName>
</Generator>
<Distributors>
    <Distributor>
        <SystemName>tecayukon</SystemName>
    </Distributor>
</Distributors>
<ApplicationExecutionSettings>
    <PerformanceQueryInterval>PT5S</PerformanceQueryInterval>
</ApplicationExecutionSettings>

</Application>
```

In this listing, you can see that the notification class is named DataNotifications. The DataNotification classes' Schema element defines information that will be sent to the subscriber. Here you can see that the value of the DataID and DataValue fields will be sent as part of the notification.

The ContentFormatter element defines how the notification will be formatted when it is sent to the subscriber. This example illustrates using the built-in XSLTFormatter. The Arguments element describes the directory where the XSLT file is found as well as the name of the file. In this listing, you can see that the XSLT file is found in the C:\NSSample directory and is named NSSample.xslt.

The Generator, Distributor, and ApplicationExecutionSettings elements specify the SQL Server system that will be used to generate notifications, the system that will be used to distribute notifications, and the interval at which system performance counters will be updated, respectively.

Formatting the Notification Output

In the previous listing, you saw that the notification was formatted using the NSSample.xslt style sheet. You can see what that example style sheet looks like in the following listing:

```
<?xml version="1.0" encoding="UTF-8" ?>
<xsl:stylesheet version="1.0"
  xmlns:xsl="http://www.w3.org/1999/XSL/Transform">
  <xsl:template match="notifications">
    <HTML>
    <BODY>
      <xsl:apply-templates />
      <I>This message was generated using
      <BR/>Microsoft SQL Server Notification Services</I><BR/><BR/>
    </BODY>
    </HTML>
  </xsl:template>
  <xsl:template match="notification">
    <P>The data value of <B><xsl:value-of select="DataID"/></B>
    <BR/>reached the value <B><xsl:value-of select="DataValue"/></B>
    </P>
  </xsl:template>
</xsl:stylesheet>
```

The style sheet used to format the Notification Services application's output is a standard HTML style sheet. In the template section, you can see where the DataID and DataValue fields from the NotificationClass are displayed in the notification.

Creating the Notification Services Application

After the required XML and T-SQL application code has been created, you're ready to build the Notification Services application. Notification Services applications can be created interactively using the SQL Server Management Studio, or they can be created using the nscontrol utility.

Creating Notification Services Applications Using SQL Server Management Studio   After the config.xml and adf.xml files that define the Notification Services have been created, you can use them to build your Notification Service application from the SQL Server Management Studio by first opening the Object Browser and right-clicking the Notification Services node. Then, you can select the New Notification Services Instance option from the context menu to display a screen like the one in Figure 5-3.

To create a new Notification Services application using the New Notification Services Instance dialog, you click Browse and navigate to the directory that contains your application's config.xml file. Next, you select the config.xml file and click OK. If you want the application to be immediately enabled after it is created, you need to check the Enable Instance After It Is Created check box.

Creating Notification Services Applications Using Nscontrol   Nscontrol is a command-line tool that's used to create and administer Notification Services applications. Nscontrol understands a number of different action commands that you can use to

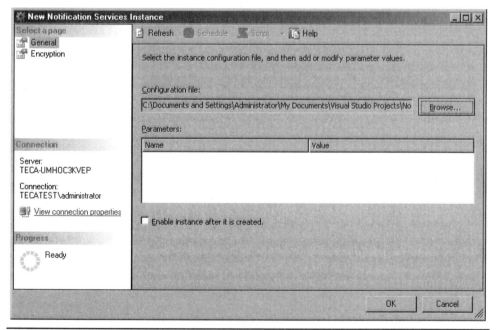

Figure 5-3   *The New Notification Services Instance dialog*

Nscontrol Command	Description
nscontrol create	Creates a Notification Services application and its databases.
nscontrol delete	Deletes a Notification Services application and its databases.
nscontrol disable	Disables a Notification Services application.
nscontrol displayargumentkey	Displays the key used to encrypt event data.
nscontrol enable	Enables a Notification Services application.
nscontrol listversions	Displays the version of Notification Services and any registered applications.
nscontrol register	Registers a Notification Services application.
nscontrol status	Displays the status of a Notification Services application.
nscontrol unregister	Unregisters a Notification Services application.
nscontrol update	Updates a Notification Services application.

Table 5-1   *Nscontrol Commands*

work with Notification Services applications. Table 5-1 lists the available nscontrol action commands.

Creating a Notification Services application is a multistep process. First, the application needs to be created using the nscontrol create command. This creates the database used by the Notification Services application. Next, the application needs to be registered using the nscontrol register command. This creates the service that is used to run the application. Then, the application needs to be enabled using the nscontrol enable command. The following batch file illustrates the command sequence needed to create the example NSSample Notification Services application:

```
echo off
cls
set NSdir="C:\Program Files\Microsoft SQL Server\90\NotificationServices\9.0.242\bin"
echo =======================================
echo Beginning NSSampleInstance Creation
echo =======================================
echo .
echo Create the application databases
%NSdir%\nscontrol create -in config.xml

echo Register the application
%NSdir%\nscontrol register -name NSSampleInstance -service

echo Enable the application
%NSdir%\nscontrol enable -name NSSampleInstance
```

```
echo start the NS app as a service
net start NS$NSSampleInstance

echo Display the status of the app
%NSdir%\nscontrol status -name NSSampleInstance
```

The nscontrol create command –in argument specifies the name of the Notification Services ACF. In this example, the ACF is named config.xml. Running the nscontrol create command creates two databases on the server, NSSampleInstanceMain and NSSampleInstanceNSSample, which store the Notification Services application definition and data events.

The nscontrol register command uses the –name argument to identify the instance name of the Notification Services application to register. The –service switch directs it to register a service named NS$NSSampleInstance.

The nscontrol enable command uses the –name parameter to identify the instance name of the application that will be enabled.

Once the application is enabled, its service can be started using the net start command. For testing, you can also execute the NS$NSSampleInstance application from the command prompt or the Run dialog.

Adding Subscribers to the Application

Subscribers are added to Notification Services applications using the managed code APIs that Microsoft provides with SQL Server 2005 Notification Services. Microsoft's .NET Framework APIs enable you to add, update, and delete subscribers, as well as subscriber devices and subscriptions. While the Notification Services API is provided via managed code classes, you can also access the API from unmanaged code by using Win32-based COM applications.

The Notification Services API is located in Microsoft.SqlServer.NotificationServices .dll, which must be added to your .NET project as a reference. Then, you can use the Notification Services classes to manage subscriptions to your notification services applications. The following code sample shows how you can add a subscription using the managed code API:

```
using Microsoft.SqlServer.NotificationServices;
using System.Text;

public class NSSubscriptions
{
    private string AddSubscription(string instanceName, string
      applicationName, string subscriptionClassName, string subscriberId)
    {
```

```
        // Create the Instance object
        NSInstance myNSInstance = new NSInstance(instanceName);

        // Create the Application object
        NSApplication myNSApplication = new NSApplication
         (myNSInstance, applicationName);

        // Create the Subscription object
        Subscription myNSSubscription = new Subscription
          (myNSApplication, subscriptionClassName);
        myNSSubscription.Enabled = true;
        myNSSubscription.SubscriberId = subscriberId;

        // Set the subscription data fields
        myNSSubscription["DeviceName"] = "MyDevice";
        myNSSubscription["SubscriberLocale"] = "USA";
        myNSSubscription["DataID"] = 1;
        myNSSubscription["DataTriggerValue"] = 100;

        // Add the subscription
        string subscriptionId = myNSSubscription.Add();
        return subscriptionId;
    }
}
```

At the top of this listing, you can see an import directive for the Microsoft.SqlServer
.NotificationServices namespace. Using the import directive enables you to use the
classes in the NotificationServces namespace without requiring you to fully qualify
the names. Next, inside the AddSubscriptions method you can see the code that adds
the subscription. First, a Notification Services instance object is created, followed by
an Application object. Then, the Application object is used to create a subscription object
named myNSSubscriptions. The Subscription object's properties are assigned values,
and then its Add method is called to actually add the subscription to the database.

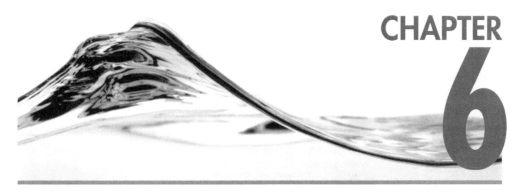

SQL Server
Service Broker

IN THIS CHAPTER:

SQL Server Service Broker Overview

Developing with the SQL Server Service Broker

Administering the Service Broker

The SQL Server Service Broker is a new subsystem that adds guaranteed asynchronous queuing support to SQL Server 2005. Asynchronous queuing adds a dimension of scalability to SQL Server 2005. Asynchronous queuing is found in many other highly scalable applications, including the operating system's I/O subsystems, web servers, and even the internal operations of the SQL Server database engine itself. The addition of asynchronous queuing to SQL Server 2005 brings the capability of handling asynchronous queuing to end-user database applications as well. Asynchronous queuing is an important factor for scalability because it allows a program to respond to more requests than the platform may be able to physically handle. For instance, in the case of a web server if ten thousand users simultaneously requested resources from the server, without asynchronous queuing the web server would be overwhelmed as it attempted to launch threads to handle all of the incoming requests. Asynchronous queuing enables all of the requests to be captured in a queue so that instead of being overwhelmed, the web server can process entries from the queue at its maximum levels of efficiency. In the case of the web server, asynchronous queuing enables the server to effectively handle a far greater number of user connections than would otherwise be possible. The SQL Server Service Broker enables you to build this same type of scalability into your database applications.

In this chapter, you'll learn about the new features provided by the SQL Server Service Broker. You'll get an overview of the new subsystem and learn about its core components. Then you'll see the basics of how you create SQL Server Service Broker applications. Here you learn about the SQL Server Service Broker's metadata and its programming model. First, you'll see how to create message types and queues. Then, you'll see how to use the new T-SQL commands that enable messaging applications to add entries to a queue as well as receive the entries that have been added to a queue. Finally, you'll learn about some of the administrative features found in the SQL Server Service Broker subsystem.

SQL Server Service Broker Overview

The SQL Server Service Broker adds the ability to perform asynchronous queuing to SQL Server 2005. The new queuing capability is built into the SQL Server engine and is fully transactional. Transactions can incorporate queued events and can be both committed and rolled back. You can access the SQL Server Service Broker using new SQL statements. Examples of these commands will be presented in the next section of this chapter. In addition, the new SQL Server Service Broker also supports reliable delivery of messages to remote queues. This means that queuing applications built using the SQL Server Service Broker can span multiple

SQL Server systems and still provide guaranteed message delivery—even to remote queues. The messages that are sent across the queues can be very large, up to 2GB. The SQL Server Service Broker will take care of the mechanics required to break apart the large messages into smaller chunks that are sent across the network and then reassemble at the other end. There are both 32-bit and 64-bit versions of the SQL Server Service Broker.

Queue Application Design

While the idea of queuing in applications may be a bit foreign to most database designers, queues are common in highly scalable applications. One of the most well-known of these types of applications is the airline reservation systems used by all major airlines such as United, Delta, and American, as well as by travel brokers such as Expedia and CheapTickets.com. To get an idea of how queuing is used in one of these applications, you can refer to Figure 6-1, where you can see the design of a sample queued application.

Figure 6-1 presents a high-level overview of an example airline reservation system. Here you can see that the application's presentation layer is delivered to the end user's browser by an application running on a web farm. That application could be written using ASP.NET or some other web development language. The front-end

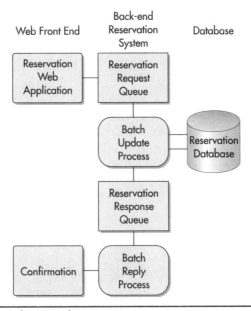

Figure 6-1   *Queued application design*

application will then interact with the actual reservation system that's normally running on another system.

Because applications like these must support thousands of simultaneous users, they can't afford to lock rows while a given user waits to decide on the final details of a flight or even starts a reservation and then goes to lunch, planning to finish later. Row locking in this type of scenario would seriously inhibit the application's scalability and even the application's usability. Queuing solves this problem by enabling the application to make an asynchronous request for a reservation; it sends the request to the back-end reservation system and is immediately freed for other work. At no point in the process of placing the reservation have any locks been placed on the database tables. The back-end reservation system, which is essentially operating in batch mode, will take the reservation request off the queue and then perform the update to the database. Since the update is being done in batch mode, it happens very quickly with no user interaction and minimal time is needed to lock rows while the update is performed. If the request is successful, the end user's reservation is confirmed. Otherwise, if the request is denied because all of the seats were booked or for some other reason, then the reservation will not be accepted and the user will be contacted with the status.

Dialogs

Dialogs are an essential component of Microsoft's new SQL Server Service Broker. Essentially, *dialogs* provide two-way messaging between two endpoints. The endpoints for these messages can be two applications running on different servers or instances, or they can be two applications running on the same server. Figure 6-2 illustrates the SQL Server Services Broker's dialog.

The main purpose of a SQL Server Service Broker dialog is to provide an ordered sequence of events. The SQL Server Service Broker dialogs maintain reliable event ordering across servers or threads even if there are network, application, or server failures that temporarily disrupt the processing of the queued events. When the queue processing is restored, the events will continue to be processed in order from the point of the last processed queued event. Dialogs enable queued messages to

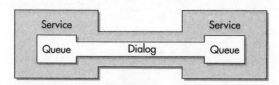

Figure 6-2   *SQL Server Service Broker dialog*

always be read in the same order that they are put into the queue. Dialogs can be set up to process events in either full-duplex mode or half-duplex mode.

Conversation Group

Another core component of the SQL Server Service broker subsystem is the conversation group. A *conversation group* is a set of related SQL Server Service Broker dialogs. An application might require multiple dialogs to complete a task, and a conversation group enables you to logically group together all of those related dialogs. For instance, an order entry application might have one dialog to process orders, another to process inventory, another to handle shipping, and yet another to handle billing requests. All of these related dialogs can be grouped together to form a conversation group. In this case, the conversation group basically represents all of the dialogs for an application. Figure 6-3 shows the relationship of the conversation group and the SQL Server Service Broker dialog.

The main purpose behind the conversation group is to provide a locking mechanism for related queues. In this sense, it's important to understand that the locking is not applied to any underlying database tables. Instead, the locking that's enabled by the conversation group is applied to entities in the queues. In the case of an order, this might mean that no process can read the orders for any of the queues in your conversation group while your application holds a lock on those entries.

In addition to locking, the conversation group also enables the application to maintain state. Maintaining state is always one of the most difficult aspects of an asynchronous application because there can be lengthy time delays between the arrival of messages. Keeping active threads open during that time period isn't an option

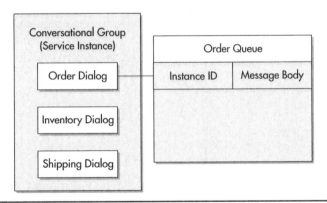

Figure 6-3   *SQL Server Service Broker conversation group*

because all the unused threads would consume excessive system resources and limit scalability. Instead, the conversation group maintains the state of an entity using a state table. The conversation group uses an instance ID (a GUID) as the primary key for identifying the entries in the group of queues.

SQL Server Service Broker Activation

SQL Server Service Broker activation is another unique feature of the SQL Server Service Broker subsystem. Activation enables you to create a stored procedure that is associated with a given input queue. The purpose of the stored procedure is to automatically process messages from that queue. As each new message comes in, the associated stored procedure is automatically executed to handle the incoming messages. If the stored procedure encounters an error, it can throw an exception and be automatically recycled.

Periodically, the SQL Server Service Broker checks the status of the input queue to find out if the stored procedure is keeping up with the incoming messages on the input queue. If the SQL Server Service Broker determines that there are waiting messages on the queue, then it will automatically start up another instance of the queue reader to process the additional messages. This process of automatically starting additional queue readers can continue until the preset MAX_QUEUE_READERS value is reached. Likewise, when the SQL Server Service Broker determines that there are no remaining messages on the queue, it will begin to automatically reduce the number of active queue readers.

SQL Server Service Broker queues don't necessarily need to be associated with stored procedures. Messages that require more complex processing can also be associated with external middle-tier procedures. Since these middle-tier processes are external to the database, they need to be activated differently. To enable the automatic activation of external processes, the SQL Server Service Broker also supports firing a SQL Server event. These events can be subscribed to using WMI (Windows Management Instrumentation). In this case, when an event comes into the queue the SQL Server event is fired and read by the WMI subscriber, which in turns starts up the external queue reader.

Message Transport

The SQL Server Service Broker message transport protocol enables messages to be sent across the network. The SQL Server Service Broker message transport is based on TCP/IP, and the overall architecture of the SQL Server Service Broker message transport is a bit like the architecture used by TCP/IP and FTP. The SQL Server Service Broker Message transport is composed of two protocols: the Binary Adjacent

Broker protocol, which is a lower-level protocol like TCP, and the Dialog protocol, which is a higher-level protocol like FTP and rides on top of the lower-level Binary Adjacent Broker protocol.

Binary Adjacent Broker Protocol

The Binary Adjacent Broker protocol is a highly efficient low-level TCP/IP protocol that provides the basic message transport. It is a bidirectional and multiplexed protocol and so can handle the message transport for multiple SQL Server Service Broker dialogs. The Binary Adjacent Broker protocol doesn't worry about message order or confirming message delivery. That's all handled by the Dialog protocol. Instead, the Binary Adjacent Broker protocol simply sends messages across the network as quickly as it can.

Dialog Protocol

The Dialog protocol handles end-to-end communications for a SQL Server Service Broker dialog. Designed to provide one-time-only in-order delivery of messages, it handles sending messages and acknowledging them. It also provides symmetric failure handling, where both end nodes are notified of any message delivery failures. In addition, the Dialog protocol is responsible for authentication and encryption of messages.

Developing with the SQL Server Service Broker

As you saw in the first part of this chapter, the SQL Server Service Broker is a subsystem that enables the development of database-oriented messaging applications. While the first part of this chapter provided you with an overview of the primary components of the SQL Server Service Broker subsystem and gave you an idea of the functions and interactions of those components, this section of the chapter will dive in a little deeper and will provide you with a rundown showing how you develop applications using the SQL Server Service Broker.

Programming Model

The SQL Server Service Broker utilizes a set of metadata to describe the kinds of messages that an application can receive, which directions the messages are sent, and how the messages are related. Essentially, the SQL Server Service Broker's metadata describes the messaging infrastructure used by an application. Additionally, the metadata has associated permissions that can be used to secure the messaging application. Figure 6-4 illustrates the SQL Server Service Broker's metadata model.

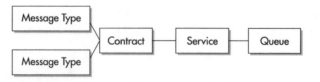

Figure 6-4 *SQL Server Service Broker metadata*

The *message type* is the most basic object in the SQL Server Service Broker's metadata. The message type is used to describe the messages that will be used. For XML messages, the message types can have an optional schema associated with the message. If there is an associated schema, the SQL Server Service Broker will ensure that the message complies with the schema definition. If there is no schema, the messages are treated as binary data.

The next primary object in the SQL Server Service Broker's metadata is the *contract*. Message types are grouped into contracts. The contract describes all of the messages that can be received using a particular dialog. For example, if a reservation request and response dialog comprises a simple reservation system, the contract will specify that those two message types are both grouped together and related to the reservation system. The contact essentially specifies which message types are allowed by a given dialog.

Contracts are grouped together to form a *service,* which essentially represents all of the dialogs that are required to process the messages for that service. A service is associated with one or more queues and is the primary object that's addressed by the SQL Server Service Broker application. The application opens a dialog to a service. The application isn't concerned with the physical details of how the service is implemented, as the physical implementation details are defined by the metadata. The queue contains the messages that are received by a SQL Server Service Broker application.

T-SQL DDL and DML

T-SQL has been enhanced with several new statements that enable the native integration of SQL Server Service Broker messaging with traditional database procedures. Table 6-1 summarizes the new T-SQL DDL statements that are used to create SQL Server Service Broker objects.

In addition to the new T-SQL DDL statements that are used to create the new SQL Server Service Broker objects, there are also a group of new T-SQL statements that work with the messages in a SQL Server Service Broker application. Table 6-2 lists the new SQL Server Service Broker–related T-SQL DML statements.

T-SQL DDL	Description
CREATE MESSAGE TYPE	Creates a new message type
CREATE CONTRACT	Creates a new contract in a database
CREATE QUEUE	Creates a new queue in a database
CREATE ROUTE	Creates a new route in a database
CREATE SERVICE	Creates a new service in a database
ALTER MESSAGE TYPE	Changes a message type
ALTER CONTRACT	Changes a contract
ALTER QUEUE	Changes a queue
ALTER ROUTE	Changes a route
ALTER SERVICE	Changes a service
DROP MESSAGE TYPE	Deletes a message type from a database
DROP CONTRACT	Deletes a contract from a database
DROP QUEUE	Deletes an queue from a database
DROP ROUTE	Deletes a route from a database
DROP SERVICE	Deletes a service from a database

Table 6-1   *T-SQL Statements for SQL Server Service Broker Objects*

SQL Server Service Broker Example Application

In the first part of this section, you got a high-level overview of how you use the
SQL Server Service Broker to develop asynchronous messaging applications. This
section will now dive in deeper and demonstrate how you use T-SQL to create the
required SQL Server Service Broker objects and go on to show how you use them in

T-SQL DML	Description
BEGIN DIALOG	Opens a new dialog
END CONVERSATION	Ends a conversation used by a dialog
MOVE CONVERSATION	Moves a conversation to a new dialog
GET SERVICE INSTANCE	Retrieves a service instance ID from a queue
RECEIVE	Receives a message from a queue
SEND	Sends a message to a queue

Table 6-2   *T-SQL Statements for SQL Server Service Broker Messages*

a simple application. The sample application is a simple reservation system that accepts a simple reservation request on an input queue and then responds with a message on a response queue.

Creating the SQL Server Service Broker Objects

The code that's used to create the required SQL Server Service Broker objects is shown in the following listing:

```
CREATE MESSAGE TYPE ResRequest
       ENCODING varbinary
CREATE MESSAGE TYPE ResResponse
       ENCODING varbinary

CREATE CONTRACT ResContract
  (ResRequest SENT BY any,
   ResResponse SENT BY any)

CREATE QUEUE ResRequestQueue WITH ACTIVATION
  (STATUS = ON,
   PROCEDURE_NAME = ResRequestProc,
   MAX_QUEUE_READERS = 5,
   EXECUTE AS SELF)

CREATE QUEUE ResResponseQueue

CREATE SERVICE ResRequestService ON QUEUE
   ResRequestQueue(ResContract)

CREATE SERVICE ResResponseService ON QUEUE
   ResResponseQueue(ResContract)
```

The first step to creating a SQL Server Service Broker application is the creation of message types, which describe the messages that will be sent. The first two statements create two simple message types. The first parameter is used to name the message type, and the ENCODING keyword indicates whether the message will be binary or XML. In this example both message types, ResRequest and ResResponse, are created as binary messages, meaning they will accept any type of data.

Next, a contract is created. The contract describes all of messages that can be received using a particular dialog. The first argument is used to name the contract. The SENT BY clause is used to designate which messages are associated with the contract and where those messages come from.

Then queues must be created. This example shows the creation of two queues: the ResRequestQueue and the ResResponseQueue. The ResRequestQueue uses the ACTIVATION keyword to automatically fire off a stored procedure that will read the contents of the queue. This stored procedure must exist at the time the queue is created; otherwise, an error will be generated. The ResRequest stored procedure is shown a bit later in this section. The MAX_QUEUE_READERS keyword specifies the maximum number of readers that the SQL Server Service Broker will automatically activate. The EXECUTE AS option allows you to execute the activated procedure under a different user context.

After the queues are created, you can display the contents of the queues by using the SELECT statement exactly as if the queue were a standard database table. The following line of code shows how you can display the contents of the Request queue:

```
SELECT * FROM ResRequestQueue.
```

Just after the queues are created, they are empty. However, running SELECT statements on the queue is a great way to check out functionality of the SQL Server Service Broker applications you are developing.

After the queues have been created, the next step is to create a service. You create a service using the CREATE SERVICE statement. The first parameter names the service. The ON QUEUE clause identifies the queue associated with the service, and then the contracts that are associated with the service are listed.

If one of the services were located on a remote system, you would also need to create a route. The CREATE ROUTE statement basically supplies the SQL Server Service Broker with the system address where the remote service is found, which tells SQL server how to deliver the message to the remote system.

Sending Messages to a Queue

After the necessary SQL Server Service Broker objects have been created, you're ready to use them in your queuing applications. The following code listing shows how you can add a message to the ResRequestQueue queue:

```
DECLARE @ResRequestDialog UNIQUEIDENTIFIER

BEGIN TRANSACTION

BEGIN DIALOG @ResRequestDialog
  FROM SERVICE ResResponseService
  TO SERVICE 'ResRequestService'
  ON CONTRACT ResContract
```

```
  WITH LIFETIME = 1000;

SEND ON CONVERSATION @ResRequestDialog
  MESSAGE TYPE ResRequest (N'My Request Message');

SEND ON CONVERSATION @ResRequestDialog
 MESSAGE TYPE ResResquest (N'My Request Message2');

COMMIT TRANSACTION
```

At the start of this listing, you can see that a variable named ResRequestDialog is created; it contains a unique identifier that will be assigned by a SQL Server Service Broker dialog. Next, a transaction is started. It's a good idea to wrap all of the actions that are performed by the SQL Server Service Broker in a transaction. This enables you to commit and optionally roll back any changes to the queues. Then, the BEGIN DIALOG statement is used to open up a new SQL Server Service Broker dialog. When you declare a dialog, you always need to specify two endpoints. The FROM SERVICE identifies the initiator of the messages, while the TO SERVICE keyword identifies the target endpoint. Here, the sender is named ResResponseService and the target is named ResResquestService. While this example uses simple names, Microsoft recommends that you use a URL name to uniquely identify the SQL Server Service Broker objects. For example, to ensure uniqueness in the network Microsoft recommends using names like [http://MyCompany.com/MyApp/ResResponseService]. The ON CONTRACT keyword specifies the contract that's used for the dialog. The contract specifies which messages this dialog is able to send or receive.

Then, two SEND operations are executed. These statements send two messages to the target service, which will receive those messages and add them to the queue that is associated with that service. Finally, the transaction is committed.

Retrieving Messages from a Queue

Now that you've seen how to add a message to a queue, the next example will illustrate how to create a stored procedure that will read the messages off the queue. As you may recall from the earlier SQL Server Service Broker object creation examples, the target queue, ResRequestQueue, was created with activation. This means that an associated stored procedure named ResRequestProc will be automatically started when a message arrives on the queue. You can see the code for that stored procedure in the following listing:

```
CREATE PROC ResRequestProc
AS
DECLARE @ResRequestDialog UNIQUEIDENTIFIER
DECLARE @message_type_id int
DECLARE @message_body NVARCHAR(1000)
DECLARE @message NVARCHAR(1000)

while(1=1)
BEGIN

    BEGIN TRANSACTION

        WAITFOR   (RECEIVE top(1)
        @message_type_id = message_type_id,
        @message_body = message_body,
        @ResRequestDialog = conversation_handle
         FROM ResRequestQueue), TIMEOUT 200;

        if (@@ROWCOUNT = 0)
        BEGIN
           COMMIT TRANSACTION
           BREAK
        END

        IF (@message_type_id = 2) -- End dialog message
           BEGIN
               PRINT ' Dialog ended '
             + cast(@ResRequestDialog as nvarchar(40))
           END
        ELSE
           BEGIN
               BEGIN TRANSACTION
                   BEGIN DIALOG @ResRequestDialog
                   FROM SERVICE ResRequestService
                       TO SERVICE 'ResResponseService
                       ON CONTRACT ResContract
                       WITH LIFETIME = 1000;

                   SELECT @message = 'Received:' + @message_body;
```

```
            SEND ON CONVERSATION @ResRequestDialog
            MESSAGE TYPE ResResponse (@message);

            PRINT CONVERT(varchar(30), @message)
        COMMIT TRANSACTION
      END CONVERSATION @ResRequestDialog
  END
  COMMIT TRANSACTION
END
```

A variable that will contain the response dialog identification is declared at the top of this stored procedure, followed by three variables that will be used to pull back information from the queue that's being read. Then a loop is initiated to read all of the entries from the queue. Within the loop, a transaction is started and the RECEIVE statement is used to receive a message. In this example, the TOP(1) clause is used to limit the procedure to receiving only a single message at a time. If the TOP clause were omitted, you could receive all of the messages that were present on the queue. The RECEIVE statement populates the three variables. The message_type_id identifies the type of message, which is typically either a user-defined message or an End Dialog message. The @message_body variable contains the contents of the actual message, while the @ResRequestDialog variable contains a handle that identifies the sending dialog.

Then, the result set is checked to ensure that a message was actually received. If no rows were received, then the last transaction is committed and the procedure is ended. Otherwise, if rows were received, the message *type*id is checked to see if the message is a user message or an End Dialog message. If it's a user message, the contents will be processed. First, a dialog is opened to the ResResponseService. This dialog will be used to send the modified message to the ResResponse Queue. Again, the ResContract is specified, which restricts the message types that will be allowed.

After the dialog is opened, the received message is modified by concatenating the string "Received:" with the contents of the message that was received, and then the SEND statement is used to send the modified message to the ResResponseQueue. Finally, the dialog conversation is ended and the transaction is committed.

Administering the Service Broker

The SQL Server Service Broker provides a number of configuration options that govern how the SQL Server Service Broker subsystem operates. In this section, you'll get a brief look at some of the most important configuration options. You'll learn about SQL Server Service Broker security, as well as look at some of the system views that SQL Server 2005 provides to enable you to get information about the SQL Server Service Broker objects and applications.

System Configuration Options

There are several system configuration options that can be set using the sp_configure system stored procedure to influence the behavior of the SQL Server Service Broker subsystem. Table 6-3 lists the available sp_configure options for the SQL Server Service Broker.

Dialog Security

When dialogs are created, they can optionally be secured using the WITH ENCRYPTION clause. When a dialog is created using the WITH ENCRYPTION clause, a session key is created that's used to encrypt the messages sent using the dialog. One important point about dialog security is the fact that it is an end-to-end form of security. In other words, the message is encrypted when it is first sent from a dialog, and it is not decrypted until the message reaches its endpoint. The message contents remain encrypted as the message is forwarded across any intermediate hops. To implement dialog security, the SQL Server Service Broker uses certificate-based authentication, where the certificate of the sending user is sent along with the message.

sp_configure Parameter	Description
broker tcp listen port	Sets the port that the SQL Server Service Broker uses for network connections. The default value is 4022.
broker authentication mode	Sets type of remote authentication that will be used for connections. A value of 1 means no authentication will be used. A value of 2 means that authentication is supported. A value of 3 means authentication is required. The default value is 3.
broker forwarding size limit	Sets the maximum disk space in MB to store messages to be forwarded. The default value is 10.
broker message forwarding	Sets the type of message forwarding that is allowed. A value of 1 means no forwarding is allowed. A value of 2 allows forwarding with the domain. A value of 3 allows external forwarding. The default value is 1.

Table 6-3   *Options for sp_configure*

Because of the asynchronous nature of SQL Server Service Broker, the security information is stored in the message headers and retrieved by the receiving service when the message is retrieved. This design enables SQL Server Service Broker applications to avoid the need to establish a connection to authenticate messages.

System Views

SQL Server 2005 supplies several new system views that enable you to retrieve information about SQL Server Service Broker objects and their current statuses. Table 6-4 lists the new Service Broker catalog views.

System View	Description
sys.service_message_types	Lists all the message types that have been created. System message types are listed at the top, while user-defined messages types are listed at the end of the display.
sys.service_contracts	Lists all of the contracts that have been created.
sys.service_contract_message_usages	Lists the relationships between contracts and message types. Relationships can be one-to-one or one-to-many.
sys.services	Lists the created services.
sys.service_contract_usages	Lists the relationships between contracts and services. Relationships can be one-to-one or one-to-many.
sys.service_instances	Lists the services that are active at the current time.
sys.conversation_endpoints	Lists the conversation endpoints that are currently active.
sys.routes	Lists the created routes.
sys.remote_service_bindings	Lists the relationships of the services and the users that will execute the service.
sys.transmission_queue	Lists all of the messages that are queued to be sent.
sys.service_queues	Lists the queues that have been created.

Table 6-4 *New Service Broker Catalog Views*

XML Integration

XML (eXtensible Markup Language) has emerged as one of the most important Internet technologies. XML's flexible text-based structure enables it to be used for an incredibly wide array of network tasks, including data/document transfer, web page rendering, and even as a transport for interapplication remote Procedure Calls (RPC) via SOAP (Simple Object Access Protocol). XML has truly become the lingua franca of computer languages.

Microsoft first added support for XML to SQL Server 2000, starting with support for the FOR XML clause as part of the SELECT statement and the OpenXML function. As XML continued to grow rapidly in enterprise acceptance and usage, Microsoft quickly provided additional functionality by producing a series of web releases. SQL for XML 1.0 added support for UpdateGrams, Templates, and BulkLoad to the base SQL Server 2000 release. The next two web releases, SQLXML 2.0 and SQLXML 3.0, further enhanced the SQL Server 2000 product by adding support for XML Views and SOAP in addition to several other new capabilities. While SQL Server 2000's support for XML provided a great starting point for integrating hierarchical XML documents with SQL Server's relational data, it had some limitations. Once the XML data was stored in a SQL Server database using either the Text or Image data type, there was little that you could do with it. SQL Server 2000 was unable to natively query the hierarchical data that made up the XML document without using complex T-SQL or client-side code.

SQL Server 2005 builds on this starting point by adding support for many new XML features. At a high level, SQL Server 2005 provides a new level of unified storage for XML and relational data. SQL Server 2005 adds a new XML data type that provides support for both native XML queries as well as strong data typing by associating the XML data type to an XSD (Extensible Schema Definition). In addition, it provides bidirectional mapping between relational data and XML data. The XML support is well integrated into the SQL Server 2005 relational database engine, as it provides support for triggers on XML, replication of XML data, and bulk load of XML data, as well as enhanced support for data access via SOAP and many other enhancements. In this chapter you'll get an introduction to the most important new XML features provided by SQL Server 2005.

The Native XML Data Type

Without a doubt the most important XML related enhancement that Microsoft has added to SQL Server 2005 is support for a new native XML data type. The XML data type, literally named XML can be used as a column in a table or a variable or parameter in a stored procedure. It can be used to store both typed and untyped data. If the data stored in an XML column has no XSD schema, then it is considered untyped. If there is an associated XSD schema, then SQL Server 2005 will check the schema to make sure that the data store complies with the schema definition. In all cases, SQL Server 2005 checks data that is stored in the XML data type to ensure that the XML document is well formed. If the data is not well formed, SQL Server 2005 will raise an error and the data will not be stored. The XML data type can accept a maximum of 2GB of data and is stored like the varbinary(max) data type. The following listing illustrates creating a simple table that uses the new XML data type for one of its columns.

```
CREATE TABLE MyXMLDocs
  (DocID INT PRIMARY KEY IDENTITY,
  MyXmlDoc XML)
```

The most important thing to note in this example is the definition of the MyXmlDoc column, which uses the data type of XML to specify that the column will store XML data. You can store XML data into an XML column using the standard T-SQL INSERT statement. The following example shows how you can populate an XML column using a simple INSERT statement:

```
INSERT INTO MyXmlDocs Values
('<MyXMLDoc>
    <DocumentID>1</DocumentID>
    <DocumentText>Text</DocumentText>
</MyXMLDoc>')
```

NOTE

One important point to notice here is that because the XML data is untyped, any valid XML document can be inserted into the XML data type.

Strongly Typed XML Data Types

The native XML data type checks to ensure that any data that's stored in an XML variable or column is a valid XML document. On its own, it doesn't check any more than that. However, Microsoft designed the XML data type to be able to support more sophisticated document validation using an XSD schema. When an XSD schema is defined for an XML data type column, the SQL Server engine will check to make sure that all of the data that is stored in the XML column complies with the definition that's contained in the XSD schema.

The following listing shows a sample XSD schema for the simple XML document that was used in the preceding example:

```
<xs:schema xmlns:xs="http://www.w3.org/2001/XMLSchema"
elementFormDefault="qualified" targetNamespace="MyXMLDocSchema"
xmlns="MyXMLDocSchema">
  <xs:element name="MyXMLDoc">
    <xs:complexType>
      <xs:sequence>
        <xs:element name="DocumentID" type="xs:string" />
        <xs:element name="DocumentBody" type="xs:string" />
      </xs:sequence>
    </xs:complexType>
  </xs:element>
</xs:schema>
```

This XSD schema uses the namespace of MyXMLDocSchema and defines an XML document that has a complex element named MyXMLDoc. The MyXMLDoc complex element contains two simple elements. The first simple element must be named DocumentID, and a second simple element is named DocumentBody. Both elements contain XML string-type data.

To create a strongly typed XML column or variable, you first need to register the XSD schema with SQL Server using the CREATE XMLSCHEMA T-SQL DDL statement. The following listing shows how you combine the CREATE XML SCHEMA COLLECTION statement with the sample MyXMLDocSchema to register the schema with the SQL Server 2005 database:

```
CREATE XML SCHEMA COLLECTION MyXMLDocSchema AS
N'<?xml version="1.0"?>
<xs:schema xmlns:xs="http://www.w3.org/2001/XMLSchema"
  elementFormDefault="qualified" targetNamespace="http://MyXMLDocSchema">
  <xs:element name="MyXMLDoc">
    <xs:complexType>
      <xs:sequence>
        <xs:element name="DocumentID" type="xs:string" />
        <xs:element name="DocumentBody" type="xs:string" />
      </xs:sequence>
    </xs:complexType>
  </xs:element>
</xs:schema>'
```

The CREATE XML SCHEMA COLLECTION DDL statement takes a single argument that names the collection. Next, after the AS clause it expects a valid XSD schema enclosed in single quotes. If the schema is not valid, an error will be issued when the statement is executed. The CREATE XML SCHEMA COLLECTION statement is database specific, and the schema that is registered can be accessed only in the database for which the schema is registered.

Once you've registered the XML schema with SQL Server 2005, you can go ahead and associate XML variables and columns with that schema. Doing so ensures that any XML documents that are contained in those variables or columns will adhere to the definition provided by the associated schema. The following example illustrates how you can create a table that uses a strongly typed XML column:

```
CREATE TABLE MyXMLDocs
  (DocID INT PRIMARY KEY IDENTITY,
   MyXmlDoc XML(MyXMLDocSchema))
```

Here you can see that the MyXMLDocs table is created using the CREATE TABLE statement much as in the preceding example. In this case, however, the MyXMLDoc column is created using an argument that specifies that name of the registered XSD schema definition. If you refer to the earlier listing, you can see that the schema was registered using the name MyXMLDocSchema. After the MyXMLDoc column has been associated with the schema that was registered, any data that's inserted into this column will be strongly typed according to the schema definition and any attempt to insert data that doesn't match the schema definition will be rejected. The following listing illustrates an INSERT statement that can add data to the strongly typed MyXMLDoc column:

```
INSERT INTO MyXMLDocs Values
  ('<MyXMLDoc xmlns="http://MyXMLDocSchema">
       <DocumentID>1</DocumentID>
       <DocumentBody>"My text"</DocumentBody>
       </MyXMLDoc>')
```

NOTE

Because this example uses a typed XML data type, the data must conform to the definition provided by the associated XSD schema.

In this case, the XML document must reference the associated XML namespace http://MyXMLDocSchema. And the XML document must contain a complex element named MyXMLDoc, which in turn contains the DocumentID and DocumentBody elements. The SQL Server engine will reject any attempt to insert any other XML documents into the MyXMLDocs column. If the data does not conform to the supplied XSD schema, SQL Server will return an error message like the one shown in the following listing:

```
Msg 6965, Level 16, State 1, Line 1
XML Validation: Invalid content,expected
element(s):MyXMLDocSchema:DocumentID where element 'MyXMLDocSchema:Do' was
specified
```

> **NOTE**
>
> *As you might expect from their dependent relationship, if you assign a schema to a column in a table, that table must be altered or dropped before that schema definition can be updated.*

Retrieving a Registered XML Schema

Once you import a schema using CREATE XML SCHEMA COLLECTION, the schema components are stored in SQL Server's metadata. The stored schema can be listed by querying the sys.xml_namespaces system view, as you can see in the following example:

```
SELECT * FROM sys.xml_namespaces
```

This statement will return a result set showing all of the registered schemas in a database like the one that follows:

```
xml_collection_id name                                       xml_namespace_id
----------------- ---------------------------------- ----------------
1                 http://www.w3.org/2001/XMLSchema    1
65540             http://MyXMLDocSchema               1
(2 row(s) affected)
```

You can also use the new XML_SCHEMA_NAMESPACE function to retrieve the XML schema. The following query retrieves a schema from the database for a given namespace.

```
SELECT XML_SCHEMA_NAMESPACE(N'dbo',N'MyXMLDocSchema')
```

This statement will return a result set showing all of the columns that use the registered schema, as you can see in the following listing:

```
------------------------------------------------------------------
<xsd:schema xmlns:xsd=http://www.w3.org/2001/XMLSchema
targetNamespace="http://MyXMLDocSchema" xmlns:t=http://MyXMLDocSchema
```

```
elementFormDefault="qualified"><xsd:elementname="MyXMLDoc">
<xsd:complexType><xsd:complexContent><xsd:restriction base="xsd:any
```

```
(1 row(s) affected)
```

The elementname attribute lists the columns that use the typed XML data type.

XML Data Type Methods

SQL Server 2005 provides several new built-in methods that work much like user-defined types for working with the XML data type. These methods enable you to drill down into the content of XML documents that are stored using the XML data type. On its own, just being able to store XML data in SQL Server has limited value. To really facilitate deep XML integration, you also need a way to query and manipulated the data that's stored using the new XML data type, and that's just what the following XML data type methods enable.

Exists(XQuery, [node ref])

The XML data type's Exists method enables you to check the contents of an XML document for the existence of elements or attributes using an XQuery expression. (More information about the XQuery language is presented in the next section.) The following listing shows how to use the XML data type's Exists method:

```
SELECT * FROM MyXMLDocs
WHERE MyXmlDoc.exist('declare namespace xd=http://MyXMLDocSchema
/xd:MyXMLDoc[xd:DocumentID eq "1"]') = 1
```

The first parameter of the XML Exists method is required and takes an XQuery expression. The second parameter is optional and specifies a node reference within the XML document. Here the XQuery tests for a DocumentID element equal to a value of 1. A namespace is declared because the MyXMLDoc column has an associated schema. The Exists method can return the value of TRUE (1) if the XQuery expressions returns a node, FALSE (0) if the expression doesn't return an XML node, or NULL if the XML data type instance is null. You can see the results of the XML Exists method here:

```
DocID       MyXmlDoc
----------- --------------------------------------------------------
1               <MyXMLDocxmlns="http://MyXMLDocSchema"><DocumentID>1
</DocumentID> <DocumentBody>"My text"</DocumentBody></MyXMLDoc>
(1 row(s) affected)
```

Modify(XML DML)

As you might guess, the XML data type's Modify method enables you to modify a stored XML document. You can use the Modify method either to update the entire XML document or to update just a selected part of the document. You can see an example of using the Modify method in the following listing:

```
UPDATE MyXMLDocs
SET MyXMLDoc.modify('declare namespace xd=http://MyXMLDocSchema
  replace value of  (/xd:MyXMLDoc/xd:DocumentBody)[1] with "My New Body"')
WHERE DocID = 1
```

The XML data type's Modify method uses an XML Data Modification Language (XML DML) statement as its parameter. XML DML is a Microsoft extension to the XQuery language that enables modification of XML documents. The XQuery dialect supports the Replace value of, Insert, and Delete XML DML statements. In this example, since the MyXMLDoc XML column is typed, the XML DML statement must specify the namespace for the schema. Next, you can see where the Replace value of XML DML command is used to replace the value of the DocumentBody element with the new value of "My New Body" for the row where the relational DocID column is equal to one. The replace value of clause must identify only a single node, or it will fail. Therefore the first node is identified using the [1] notation.

NOTE

While this example illustrates performing a replace operation, the Modify method also supports insert and delete operations.

Query(XQuery, [node ref])

The XML data type's Query method can retrieve either the entire contents of an XML document or a selected section of the XML document. You can see an example of using the Query method in the following listing:

```
SELECT DocID, MyXMLDoc.query('declare namespace xd=http://MyXMLDocSchema
  /xd:MyXMLDoc/xd:DocumentBody') AS Body
FROM MyXMLDocs
```

This XQuery expression returns the values from the XML document's DocumentBody element. Again, the namespace is specified because the MyXMLDoc Data type has an associated schema named MyXMLDocSchema. In this example, you can see how SQL Server 2005 easily integrates relational column data with XML data. Here, DocID comes from a relational column, while the DocumentBody element is queried out of the XML column. The following listing shows the results of the XQuery:

```
DocID  Body
------ -----------------------------------------------------------------------------
1      <xd:DocumentBody xmlns:xd="http://MyXMLDocSchema">My New Body</xd:DocumentBody>
2      <xd:DocumentBody xmlns:xd="http://MyXMLDocSchema">"My 2nd text"</xd:DocumentBody>

(2 row(s) affected)
```

Value(XQuery, [node ref])

The Value method enables the extraction of scalar values from an XML data type. You can see an example of how the XML data type's Value method is used in the following listing:

```
SELECT MyXMLDoc.value('declare namespace xd=http://MyXMLDocSchema
    (/xd:MyXMLDoc/xd:DocumentID)[1]', 'int') AS ID
FROM MyXMLDocs
```

Unlike the other XML data type methods, the XML Value method requires two parameters. The first parameter is an XQuery expression, and the second parameter specifies the SQL data type that will hold the scalar value returned by the Value method. This example returns all of the values contained in the DocumentID element and converts them to the int data type, as shown in the following results:

```
ID
-----------
1
2

(2 row(s) affected)
```

XQuery Support

In the previous section you saw how XQuery is used in the new XML data type's methods. XQuery is based on the XPath language created by the W3C (www.w3c.org) for querying XML data. XQuery extends the XPath language by adding the ability to update data as well as support for better iteration and sorting of results. At the time of this writing, the XQuery language used by SQL Server 2005 is an early implementation based on a working draft of the XQuery standard submitted to the W3C, so it's possible that some implementation details could change before SQL Server 2005 is officially released. A description of the XQuery language is beyond the scope of this book, but for more details about the W3C XQuery standard you can refer to http://www.w3.org/XML/Query. The SQL Server 2005 Books Online also has an introduction to the XQuery language.

XML Indexes

The XML data type supports a maximum of 2GB of storage, which is quite large. The size of the XML data and its usage can have a big impact on the performance the system can achieve while querying the XML data. To improve the performance of XML queries, SQL Server 2005 provides the ability to create indexes over the columns that have the XML data type.

Primary XML Indexes

In order to create an XML index on an XML data type column, a clustered primary key must exist for the table. In addition, if you need to change the primary key for the table you must first delete the XML index. An XML index covers all the elements in the XML column, and you can have only one XML index per column. Because XML indexes use the same namespace as regular SQL Server relational indexes, XML indexes cannot have the same name as an existing index. XML indexes can be created only on XML data types in a table. They cannot be created on columns in views or on XML data type variables. A primary XML index consists of a persistent shredded representation of the data in the XML column. The code to create a primary XML index is shown in the following listing:

```
CREATE PRIMARY XML INDEX MyXMLDocsIdx ON MyXMLDocs(MyXMLDoc)
```

This example shows the creation of a primary XML index named MyXMLDocsIdx. This index is created on the MyXMLDoc XML data type column in the MyXMLDocs table. Just like regular SQL Server indexes, XML indexes can be viewed by querying the sys.indexes view.

```
SELECT * FROM sys.indexes WHERE name = 'MyXMLDocsIdx'
```

Secondary XML Indexes

In addition to the primary index, you can also build secondary XML indexes. Secondary indexes are built on one of the following document attributes:

▶ **Path** The document path is used to build the index.

▶ **Value** The document values are used to built the index

▶ **Property** The documents properties are used to build the index

Secondary indexes are always partitioned in the same way as the primary XML index. The following listing shows the creation of a secondary-path XML index:

```
CREATE XML INDEX My2ndXMLDocsIdx ON MyXMLDocs(MyXMLDoc)
 USING XML INDEX MyXMLDocsIdx FOR PATH
```

FOR XML Enhancements

The FOR XML clause was first introduced to the T-SQL SELECT statement in SQL
Server 2000. It has been enhanced in SQL Server 2005. Some of the new capabilities
that are found in the FOR XML support in SQL Server 2005 include support for the
XML data type, user-defined data types, the timestamp data type, and enhanced support
for string data. In addition, the FOR XML enhancements also include support for a
new Type directive, nested FOR XML queries, and inline XSD schema generation.

Type Directive

When XML data types are returned using the FOR XML clauses' Type directive,
they are not serialized. Instead the results are returned as an XML data type. You can
see an example of using the FOR XML clause with the XML Type directive here:

```
SELECT DocID, MyXMLDoc FROM MyXMLDocs
  WHERE DocID=1 FOR XML AUTO, TYPE
```

This query returns the relational DocID column along with the MyXMLDoc XML
data type column. It uses the FOR XML AUTO clause to return the results as XML.
The TYPE directive specifies that the results will be returned as an XML data type.
You can see the results of using the Type directive here:

```
<MyXMLDocs DocID="1">
  <MyXMLDoc>
    <MyXMLDoc xmlns="MyXMLDocSchema">
      <DocumentID>1</DocumentID>
      <DocumentBody>My New Body</DocumentBody>
    </MyXMLDoc>
  </MyXMLDoc>
</MyXMLDocs>
```

NOTE

*The Type directive returns the XML data type as a continuous stream. I added the formatting to the
previous listing to make it more readable.*

Nested FOR XML Queries

SQL Server 2000 was limited to using the FOR XML clause in the top level of a query. Subqueries couldn't make use of the FOR XML clause. SQL Server 2005 adds the ability to use nested FOR XML queries. Nested queries are useful for returning multiple items where there is a parent-child relationship. One example of this type of relationship might be order header and order details records; another might be product categories and subcategories. You can see an example of using a nested FOR XML clause in the following listing:

```
SELECT DocID, MyXMLDoc,
  (SELECT MyXMLDoc
    FROM  MyXMLDocs2
    WHERE MyXMLDocs2.DocID = MyXMLDocs.DocID
    FOR XML AUTO, TYPE)
FROM MyXMLDocs Where DocID = 2 FOR XML AUTO, TYPE
```

In this example the outer query on table MyXMLDocs is combined with a subquery on the table MyXMLDocs2 (for this example, a simple duplicate of the MyXMLDocs table). The important thing to notice in this listing is SQL Server 2005's ability to use the FOR XML clause in the subquery. In this case the subquery is using the Type directive to return the results as a native XML data type. If the Type directive were not used, then the results would be returned as an nvarchar data type and the XML data would be entitized. You can see the results of the nested FOR XML query shown in the listing that follows:

```
<MyXMLDocs DocID="2">
  <MyXMLDoc>
    <MyXMLDoc xmlns="MyXMLDocSchema">
      <DocumentID>1</DocumentID>
      <DocumentBody>&quot;My text&quot;</DocumentBody>
    </MyXMLDoc>
  </MyXMLDoc>
</MyXMLDocs>
```

> **NOTE**
>
> *I added the formatting to the previous listing to make it more readable.*

Inline XSD Schema Generation

Another new feature in SQL Server 2005's FOR XML support is the ability to generate an XSD schema by adding the XMLSCHEMA directive to the FOR XML clause. You can see an example of using the new XMLSCHEMA directive in the following listing:

```
SELECT MyXMLDoc FROM MyXMLDocs WHERE DocID=1 FOR XML AUTO, XMLSCHEMA
```

In this case, because the XMLSCHEMA directive has been added to the FOR XML clause the query will generate and return the schema that defines the specific XML column along with the XML result from the selected column. The XMLSCHEMA directive works only with the FOR XML AUTO and FOR XML RAW modes. It cannot be used with the FOR XML EXPLICIT mode. If the XMLSCHEMA directive is used with a nested query, it can be used only at the top level of the query. The XSD schema that's generated from this query is shown in the following listing:

```
<xsd:import namespace="http://MyXMLDocSchema" />
<xsd:element name="MyXMLDocs">
  <xsd:complexType>
    <xsd:sequence>
      <xsd:element name="MyXMLDoc" minOccurs="0">
        <xsd:complexType sqltypes:xmlSchemaCollection="[tecadb].[dbo].[MyXMLDocSchema]">
          <xsd:complexContent>
            <xsd:restriction base="sqltypes:xml">
              <xsd:sequence>
                <xsd:any processContents="strict" namespace="http://MyXMLDocSchema" />
              </xsd:sequence>
            </xsd:restriction>
          </xsd:complexContent>
        </xsd:complexType>
      </xsd:element>
    </xsd:sequence>
  </xsd:complexType>
</xsd:element>
</xsd:schema>
<MyXMLDocs xmlns="urn:schemas-microsoft-com:sql:SqlRowSet1">
  <MyXMLDoc>
    <MyXMLDoc xmlns="http://MyXMLDocSchema">
      <DocumentID>1</DocumentID>
      <DocumentBody>My New Body</DocumentBody>
    </MyXMLDoc>
  </MyXMLDoc>
</MyXMLDocs>
```

The XMLSCHEMA directive can return multiple schemas, but it always returns at least two: one schema is returned for the SqlTypes namespace, and a second schema is returned that describes the results of the FOR XML query results. In the preceding listing you can see the schema description of the XML data type column beginning at: <xsd:element name="MyXMLDocs">. Next, the XML results can be seen at the line starting with <MyXMLDocs xmlns="urn:schemas-microsoft-com:sql:SqlRowSet1">.

OPENXML Enhancements

The FOR XML clause is great for retrieving XML from the SQL Server 2005 database. The FOR XML clause essentially creates an XML document from relational data. The OPENXML keyword is the counterpart to the FOR XML clause. The OPENXML function provides a relational rowset over an XML document. To use SQL Server's OPENXML functionality, you must first call the sp_xml_preparedocument stored procedure, which parses the XML document using the XML Document Object Model (DOM) and returns a handle to OPENXML. OPENXML then provides a rowset view of the parsed XML document. When you are finished working with the document, you then call the sp_xml_removedocument stored procedure to release the system resources consumed by OPENXML and the XML DOM. You can see an overview of this process in Figure 7-1.

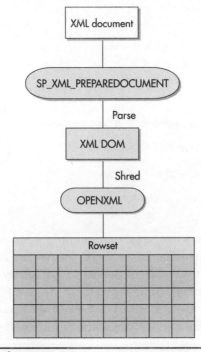

Figure 7-1   *An overview of OPENXML*

With SQL Server 2005 the OPENXML support has been extended to include support for the new XML data type, and the new user-defined data type. The following example shows how you can use OPENXML in conjunction with a WITH clause in conjunction with the new XML data type:

```
DECLARE @hdocument int
DECLARE @doc varchar(1000)
SET @doc ='<MyXMLDoc>
     <DocumentID>1</DocumentID>
     <DocumentBody>"OPENXML Example"</DocumentBody>
   </MyXMLDoc>'
EXEC sp_xml_preparedocument @hdocument OUTPUT, @doc
SELECT * FROM OPENXML (@hdocument, '/MyXMLDoc', 10)
  WITH (DocumentID  varchar(4),
        DocumentBody varchar(50))
EXEC sp_xml_removedocument @hdocument
```

At the top of this listing you can see where two variables are declared. The @hdocument variable will be used to store the XML document handle returned by the sp_xml_preparedocument stored procedure, while the @doc variable will contain the sample XML document itself. Next, the sp_xml_preparedocument stored procedure is executed and passed the two variables. The sp_xml_preparedocument stored procedure uses XML DOM to parse the XML document and then returns a handle to the parsed document in the @hdocument variable. That document handle is then passed to the OPENXML keyword used in the SELECT statement.

The first parameter used by OPENXML is the document handle contained in the @hdocument variable. The second parameter is an XPath pattern that specifies the nodes in the XML document that will construct the relational rowset. The third parameter specifies the type of XML-to-relational mapping that will be performed. The value of 2 indicates that element-centric mapping will be used. A value of 1 would indicate that attribute-centric mapping would be performed. The WITH clause provides the format of the rowset that's returned. In this example, the WITH clause specifies that the returned rowset will consist of two varchar columns named DocumentID and DocumentBody. While this example shows the rowset names matching the XML elements, that's not a requirement. Finally, the sp_xml_removedocument stored procedure is executed to release the system resources.

This SELECT statement using the OPENXML feature will return a rowset that consists of the element values from the XML document. You can see the results of using OPENXML in the following listing:

```
DocumentID DocumentBody
---------- --------------------------------------------------
1          "OPENXML Example"
(1 row(s) affected)
```

XML Bulk Load

One of the first things that you'll probably want to do to take advantage of the new XML data type is to load your XML documents into XML columns from disk. The new XML bulk load features make that task quite easy. This feature provides a high-speed mechanism for loading XML documents into SQL Server columns. You can see an example of using XML bulk load in the following listing:

```
INSERT into MyXMLDocs(MyXMLDoc) SELECT * FROM OPENROWSET
   (Bulk 'c:\temp\MyXMLDoc.xml', SINGLE_CLOB) as x
```

In this example the INSERT statement is used to insert the results of the SELECT * FROM OPENROWSET statement into the MyXMLDoc column in the MyXMLDocs table. The OPENROWSET function uses the Bulk rowset provider for OPENROWSET to read data in from the file 'C:\temp\MyXMLDoc.xml'. You can see the contents of the MyXMLDoc.xml file in the following listing:

```
<MyXMLDoc xmlns="http://MyXMLDocSchema">
        <DocumentID>3</DocumentID>
        <DocumentBody>"The Third Body"</DocumentBody>
</MyXMLDoc>
```

If you execute this command from the SQL Server Management Studio, you need to remember that this will be executed on the SQL Server system, and therefore the file and path references must be found on the local server system. The SINGLE_CLOB argument specifies that the data from the file will be inserted into a single row. If you omit the SINGLE_CLOB argument, then the data from the file can be inserted into multiple rows. By default, the Bulk provider for the OPENROWSET function will split the rows on the Carriage Return character, which is the default row delimiter. Alternatively, you can specify the field and row delimiters using the optional FIELDTERMINATOR and ROWTERMINATOR arguments of the OPENROWSET function.

Native HTTP SOAP Access

Another new XML-related feature found in SQL Server 2005 is native HTTP SOAP support. This new feature enables SQL Server to directly respond to the HTTP/SOAP requests that are issued by web services without requiring an IIS system to act as an intermediary. Using the native HTTP SOAP support, you can create web services that are capable of executing T-SQL batches, stored procedures, and user-defined scalar functions. To ensure a high level of default security, native HTTP access is turned off by default. However, you can enable HTTP support by first creating an HTTP endpoint. You can see an example of the code to create an HTTP endpoint in the following listing:

```
CREATE ENDPOINT MyHTTPEndpoint
STATE = STARTED
AS HTTP(
    PATH = '/sql',
    AUTHENTICATION = (INTEGRATED ),
    PORTS = ( CLEAR ),
    SITE = 'server'
    )
FOR SOAP (
    WEBMETHOD 'http://tempUri.org/'.'GetProductName'
             (name='AdventureWorks.dbo.GetProductName',
              schema=STANDARD ),
    BATCHES = ENABLED,
    WSDL = DEFAULT,
    DATABASE = 'AdventureWorks',
    NAMESPACE = 'http://AdventureWorks/Products'
    )
```

This example illustrates creating an HTTP endpoint named MyHTTPEndPoint for the stored procedure named GetProductName in the sample AdventureWorks database. Once the HTTP endpoint is created, it can be accessed via a SOAP request issued by an application. You can use the ALTER ENDPOINT and DROP ENDPOINT DDL statements to manage SQL Server's HTTP endpoints. The new HTTP endpoints are also able to provide data stream encryption using SSL. More information about SQL Server's new HTTP support can be found in Chapter 2.

The follow command shows how to list the HTTP endpoints that have been created:

```
select * from sys.http_endpoints
```

XML Enhancements for Analysis Server

While the majority of the XML enhancements in SQL Server 2005 have been implemented for the relational database engine, Analysis Services has also received several important new XML-related features, the most important of which is the new XML for Analysis Services also known as XMLA. In this section you'll learn more about the new XML for Analysis Services feature.

XML for Analysis Services

XML for Analysis Services is an API that provides data access to Analysis Services data sources that reside on the web. XML for Analysis Services is modeled after OLE DB in that it is intended to provide a universal data access model for any multidimensional data source. However, unlike COM-based OLE DB, XML for Analysis Services is built on the XML-based SOAP protocol. Also unlike OLE DB, which was built with the client/server model in mind, XML for Analysis Services is optimized for use on the web.

XML for Analysis Services provides two publicly accessible methods: the Discover method and the Execute method. As its name implies, the Discover method gets information about a data source. The Discover method can list information about the available data sources, the data source providers, and the metadata that is available. The Execute method enables an application to run commands against XML for Analysis Services data sources.

System XML Catalog Views

SQL Server 2005 stores information about the XML that's used in the server in a number of new system views. Table 7-1 briefly describes the new system XML views.

XML Catalog View	Description
sys.xml_attributes	This view provides a row for each stored XML attribute.
sys.xml_components	This view provides a row for each component of an XML schema.
sys.xml_component_placements	This view provides a row for each placement of an XML component.
sys.xml_elements	This view provides a row for each XML component that is an XML element.
sys.xml_facets	This view provides a row for each facet (restriction) of an XML type.
sys.xml_model_groups	This view provides a list of all the XML component that are part of a Model-Group.
sys.xml_namespaces	This view provides a row for each XSD-defined namespace.
sys.xml_types	This view provides a row for each XML component that is an XML type.
sys.xml_wildcards	This view provides a row for each XML attribute or element wildcard.
sys.xml_wildcard_namespaces	This view provides a row for each XML wildcard namespace.

Table 7-1   *SQL Server 2005 XML Catalog Views*

Business Intelligence Features

CHAPTER

8

Reporting Services

IN THIS CHAPTER:

Reporting Services Architecture

Reporting Services Components

Report Authoring

One of the most important enhancements found in SQL Server 2005 is the new Reporting Services subsystem. Reporting Services was first introduced as an add-on to SQL Server 2000 and filled an important hole in the SQL Server product line. Since its introduction, SQL Server has always been one of the easiest relational database platforms to implement, and this ease of use has made it incredibly popular for department-level implementations as well as a database platform for small- and medium-sized businesses. Once SQL Server was installed, however, if you wanted to begin retrieving information from the database by generating reports, then you needed to go out and get another product with built-in reporting capabilities in order to output that data as a viewable or printed report. SQL Server had no built-in tools that were capable of generating reports—the most common and expected output from a relational database system. To get some initial reports out of SQL Server, many companies started using desktop reporting tools like Microsoft Access, but in the end most medium- and larger-sized organizations wound up adopting more powerful third-party reporting products such as Business Object's Crystal Reports.

The introduction of Reporting Services with SQL Server 2000 changed all of that. Reporting Services provides an out-of-the-box reporting solution that goes far beyond the capabilities of simple reporting solutions like Access. Reporting Services is an enterprise-capable reporting system that not only provides the ability to graphically design reports but also enables you to securely deploy those reports across the enterprise rendered in a variety of different formats including web-based HTML reports, Windows-based rich client reports, and reports rendered for mobile devices. SQL Server 2005 Reporting Services continues to evolve into the new standard for SQL Server enterprise reporting. In the first part of this chapter, you'll get an overview of the architecture and system components used by SQL Server 2005's Reporting Services. Then in the second part of this chapter, I'll dig in deeper and give you a look at how you design and deploy reports using Reporting Services.

Reporting Services Architecture

SQL Server 2005's Reporting Services isn't just a report design tool. Instead, it's a reporting platform that not only enables the creation of reports but also stores report definitions, provides secure access to reports, renders reports in a variety of different output formats, schedules report delivery using either a push or pull delivery mechanism, and enables the deployment of those reports.

Reporting Services is an optionally installed component that requires the presence of IIS (Internet Information Services) in order to be installed. If IIS is not present on the system running the installation, the option to install Reporting Services will not be present on SQL Server 2005's installation dialogs. While Reporting Services can be installed on the same server system as the SQL Server database engine, for improved scalability it's usually better to install Reporting Services on a separate server.

NOTE

Reporting Services is licensed as a part of SQL Server 2005 and does not require any separate licensing for use on a single system. However, it does require an additional license if you implement it on a separate system.

SQL Server 2005 Reporting Services is more than just a single application. It's a server-based subsystem that's designed to enable the creation, management, and deployment of reports across the enterprise. Reporting Services can be used to create tabular, graphical, and freeform reports that can be viewed and managed using a web-based connection. These reports can run against a SQL Server 2005 database as well as any OLE DB- or ODBC-compliant database sources. You can see an overview of the Reporting Service architecture in Figure 8-1.

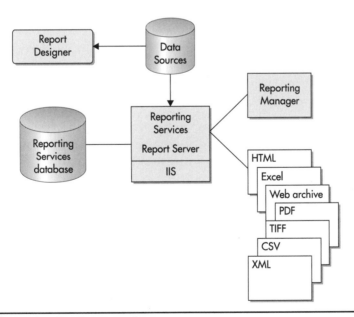

Figure 8-1   *Reporting Services overview*

As you can see in Figure 8-1, Reporting Services reports are created using the Report Designer. The Reporting Services Report Designer has a fully graphical design surface and interface program that enables you to interactively design and test reports. Unlike the banded report designer that's part of the familiar Microsoft Access program, the Reporting Services Report Designer is completly unbanded, giving it a much greater degree of flexibility. A banded report designer restricts specific areas of the report designer for predefined uses; for example, the top portion of the page is always the heading, the middle portion of the page is for the report body, and the bottom part of the page is for the reporting footer. While many reports follow this style, you don't have the flexibility to do anything else. The Reporting Services Report Designer's unbanded layout gives you a much greater degree of freedom; for example, you can easily lay out your report in four quadrants of the page, each section using its own formatting and data. A much more detailed look at the Reporting Services Report Designer is presented in the second part of this chapter.

After a report is designed using the Report Designer, the report definitions are stored in the ReportServer database. Reporting Services reports are stored in a new XML-based data format called Report Design Layout (RDL). By default, these RDL definitions are stored in SQL Server 2005's ReportServer database. In addition to the report's RDL specifications, the ReportServer database also stores information about a report's security and destination.

The Reporting Services Report Server, the core component in the Reporting Services architecture, is an ASP.NET application that runs on top of Windows Internet Information Server (IIS). The primary responsibility of the Report Server is to process the stored report definition files and then render reports in the appropriate format for the specified delivery mechanism. In addition to standard printed reports the Reporting Services Report Server can render reports in the following different output formats:

▶   HTML
▶   Excel
▶   Web archive
▶   PDF
▶   TIFF
▶   CSV
▶   XML

Reporting Services is managed using the Report Manager. The Report Manager is a web-based application that enables the DBA or reporting administrator to control the security and overall management attributes of the reports created using Reporting Services. This includes specifying who can create and change a report as well as who can run a given report. The Report Manager can also set up both push and pull delivery schedules for Reporting Services reports.

In the next section, you get a more in-depth look at the functionality provided by each of these components.

Reporting Services Components

SQL Server 2005's new Reporting Services system consists of a variety of interrelated components. In this section, you'll get a closer look at each of those components, beginning with the part that has the most visibility: the Report Designer.

Report Designer

The Reporting Services Report Designer enables you to visually design reports as well as control their deployment. Unlike the Reporting Services add-on for SQL Server 2000, which required Visual Studio in order to design reports, SQL Server 2005's Reporting Services provides the Report Designer as part of the Business Intelligence Development Studio. To start the Report Designer, you first open up SQL Server 2005's Business Intelligence Studio and then select the File | New | Project | Report Project option to create a new Report Services project. Then, to open the Report Designer, you select the Project | Add New Item | Report option. You can see an example of the Reporting Services Report Designer in Figure 8-2.

Toolbox

The Toolbox window in the Reporting Services Report Designer is shown on the left side of the screen in Figure 8-2. The Toolbox is used to drag and drop components onto their respective design surfaces.

Report Controls   The Report Design Toolbox contains the following controls:

▶ **Textbox**   The Textbox control enables you to display textual data on your report. The textbox can be placed anywhere on the report and can contain column data, labels, and calculated fields.

▶ **Line**   The Line control enables you to draw a line on the report layout.

▶ **Table**   The Table control enables you to bind a table to the report layout.

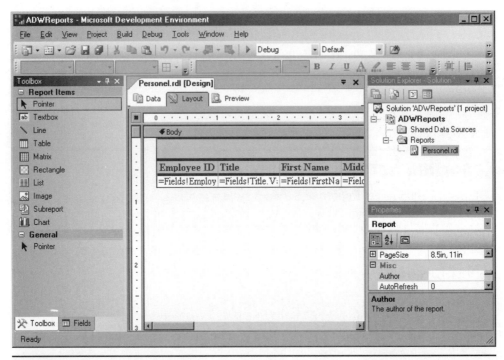

Figure 8-2   *Reporting Services Report Designer*

► **Matrix**   You can use the Matrix control to display a grid on the report layout. You can bind the Matrix control to the report's dataset.

► **Rectangle**   The Rectangle control is primarily used as a container for other report elements. It can also be used as a graphical element by the Line control.

► **List**   The List control enables you to place a list on your report layout. The list can be bound to fields in your dataset.

► **Image**   The Image control enables you to bind binary images to the report layout. The supported formats are: bmp, jpg, gif, and png.

► **Subreport**   The Subreport control is used to link a section of the report to another previously defined report. The Subreport can either be a stand-alone report or be expressly designed to run within another report.

► **Chart**   The Chart control draws a chart on the report layout. The Chart control can be bound to the report's dataset and supports a large number of different chart types, including: columns, bar, line, pie, scatter, bubble, area, doughnut, radar, stock, and polar.

Design Surface

In the center of the screen in Figure 8-2, you can see the Report Designer's Design Surface. The Report Designer's Design Surface is where you create the layout of your report. The Design Surface presents three tabs: Data, Layout, and Preview. To create a report, you must first define a dataset, and you can do that using the Data tab. The dataset is built by specifying the database connection either by manually entering the appropriate connection string or by filling in the prompts displayed in the Data Link dialog. Once the connection is set up, you then define your query either by entering the SQL statement or by using the graphical Query Designer. The Query Designer enables you to visually build a SQL query by dragging and dropping tables and then selecting the desired columns and visually defining any required join and row selection criteria. Once the query has been designed, a graphical query builder representation of that query will be shown on the Data tab.

The Layout tab is where you design your report. You design the report by dragging and dropping items from the Toolbox onto the Layout pane and then moving and resizing them. As you can see in Figure 8-2, the Layout pane shows all of the Reporting Services controls that have been added to the report as well as their bindings.

The Preview tab allows you to preview what the rendered report will look like. When you click the Preview tab, the Report Designer will execute the report and display it in the Preview tab. The Preview doesn't allow you to make changes to the way the report looks. In order to change the report, you need to use the Layout tab.

Solution Explorer

You can see the Report Designer's Solution Explorer in the upper right-hand corner of Figure 8-2. The Solution Explorer provides a hierarchical tree view of the different projects and files that are included in a Business Intelligence Development Studio solution. The top item in the Solution Explorer hierarchy is the solution name. In Figure 8-2, you can see the solution is called ADWReports. Under the solution, you can have one or more projects. In Figure 8-2, you can see that in this example the solution has one Reporting Services project, called reports, and that under that project is a report named Personel.rdl. Each Report Services project can contain multiple reports.

Properties

You can see the Report Designer's Properties window in the bottom-right corner of Figure 8-2. The Properties window can be used to set the attributes of the report layout items at design time.

Fields

The Report Designer also provides a Fields window that shows the contents of the dataset that's in use. You can drag and drop fields listed in the Fields window onto the Report Designer's design surface to include them in the report. You can see the Fields window in the upper-left corner of Figure 8-3.

You can alternate between the Fields window and the Toolbox by clicking the appropriate tab shown at the bottom of the Fields window.

Output

The Report Designer also provides an Output window that shows the results of building and deploying reports. After a report is designed, it must be built and then deployed before it can be used. The Build process creates a .NET assembly, while the Deploy process takes that assembly and installs it in the ReportServer database. The result of these actions is shown in the Output window that you can see in the bottom of Figure 8-3.

OLAP Report Designer

Much as the Reporting Services Report Designer enables you to design reports for relational databases, the OLAP Report Designer enables you to design reports for

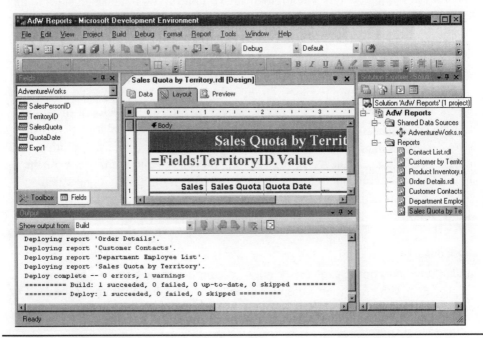

Figure 8-3   *Report Designer Fields Window*

Analysis Services databases. Depending upon the type of data source that you select, the Report Designer will automatically open either as the relational Report Designer just described or as the OLAP Report Designer. If the data source that you choose is an ODBC, OLE DB, or Native SQL Client data source, then the relational Report Designer that was shown earlier in Figure 8-3 will be opened. If the data source that you choose is a Microsoft SQL Server for Analysis Services data source, then the new OLAP Report Designer that's shown in Figure 8-4 will be opened.

The OLAP Report Designer is optimized for building reports based on Analysis Services cubes. Instead of showing tables and columns, the designer shows you the cubes metadata that you can use to build your reports.

Metadata

On the left side of Figure 8-4, you can see the OLAP Report Designer's Metadata window. The Metadata window lists all of the cube's attributes. At the top of the list, you'll find the cube's measures, followed by the KPIs and then all of the different dimensions. You can drag and drop fields listed in the Fields window onto the Dimensions and Measures panes.

Dimensions Pane

Shown in the upper-right portion of Figure 8-4, the Dimensions pane is used to specify all of the dimensions that are to be used in the report. To add a dimension to

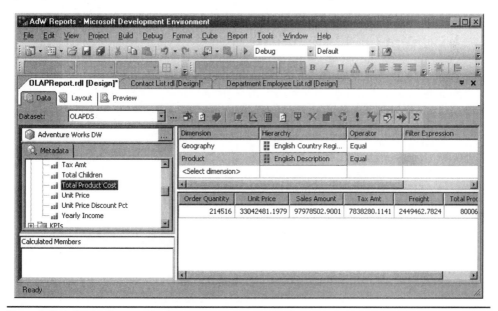

Figure 8-4   *OLAP Report Designer*

the Dimensions pane, you simply drag the desired dimension for the Metadata window and drop it onto the Dimensions pane.

Measures Pane

The OLAP Report Designer's Measures pane is shown in the bottom portion of Figure 8-4. You use the Measures pane very much as you do the Dimensions pane, by dragging and dropping measures from the Metadata window into the Measures pane. The OLAP Report Designer automatically builds the headers across the top of the Measures pane and fills in the rest of the pane with the appropriate data values from the cube.

Report Server

The Report Server is the primary rendering and distribution engine for Reporting Services. The Report Server consumes the Report Definition Layout (RDL) files that are created by the Report Designer and renders the report into the desired output format. In addition to rendering reports, the Report Server also handles the security and distribution of the reports. Figure 8-5 presents an overview of the functionality provided by the Reporting Services Report Server.

The Report Server is an ASP.NET-based application and exposes an HTTP SOAP endpoint that's used to manage and access the server. The Report Server is the heart of SQL Server 2005's Reporting Services and handles all of the essential report generation and distribution tasks. When a user requests a report or a report is deployed to an end user, the Report Server checks the report's security attributes to ensure that the user has permissions to both the report itself as well as the database objects that are used by the report. If the user has the required permissions, then the Report Server will retrieve the report definition from the ReportServer database and render the report according to the format specified in the RDL. As the report is rendered, the Report Server will access all of the required data sources, retrieve the data, and build the report. Once the report has been created, the Report Server

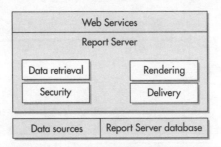

Figure 8-5   *Report Server overview*

handles distributing the report to all of its predefined delivery targets. The Report Server caches the retrieved results in an intermediate format for a predefined amount of time. This caching is a terrific feature for scalability, as it enables repeated requests for the report to be processed very quickly. When the reports are cached, all of the required data retrieval and rendering steps have already been completed and the Report Server simply needs to distribute the cached report to the end user.

Report Delivery

One of the key points in creating your reporting solution is to define how the reports will be delivered to the end users. Report Server is responsible for the delivery of reports and supports pull-style on-demand reports as well as push-style and subscription-based delivery options.

▶ **On-demand delivery**   Reporting Services provides two types of on-demand report delivery: URL-based report access and web services–based report access. With URL access, the end user either directly enters a URL into the browser or clicks a link to access the Report Server. Any required parameters are passed in as part of the URL. Report Server will render the report in HTML format in the user's browser. End users can also access reports by issuing SOAP requests to the Reporting Services Report Server. In this scenario, the user would typically select an option from their application that actually submits the SOAP request. One advantage to this method is that SOAP provides discovery methods that enable the application to dynamically discover any required report parameters. As you'll see in the next section, Reporting Services SOAP access isn't limited to just delivering reports. It also provides full access to the Reporting Services management functions.

▶ **Subscription delivery**   In addition to pull-style report delivery, Reporting Services also supports push-style subscription delivery. In contrast to pull report delivery, where the user initiates the report generation, with subscription-based push-style report delivery, the Report Server engine delivers reports to end users according to a predefined schedule. Subscriptions can be based on times or can be data driven. For instance, you can configure Report Server to deliver a given report or set of reports at the end of the day, week, or month. To deliver reports on a timed schedule, Reporting Services uses the SQL Agent. Data-driven subscriptions are different from regular subscription in that data-driven subscriptions acquire their subscription information at run time. Data-driven subscriptions are designed to handle situations where the report recipients can change between different runs of the report. Both on-demand and subscription-based delivery mechanisms share the same report output options.

Report Manager

As its name suggests, the Report Manager is the primary tool for managing Reporting Services reporting solutions. The Report Manager is an ASP.NET web-based application and is accessed by pointing your web browser to http://<servername>/Reports. You can see the Report Manager in Figure 8-6.

If you've used Sharepoint, then you'll no doubt notice a distinct similarity between the Reporting Services Report Manager and a Sharepoint site. Both share a very similar look and feel. The Report Manager enables you to view and manage all of the reports that have been deployed to the Report Server. You can edit the data sources and connection strings used by the reports and modify the various report properties. In addition, the Report Manager enables the Reporting Services Administrator to set up the security and subscriptions for the reports that can be accessed using Reporting Services.

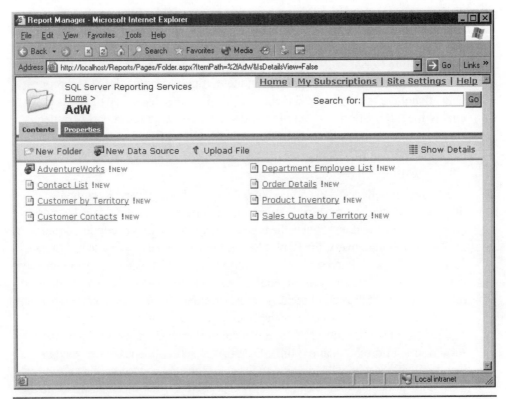

Figure 8-6   *Reporting Services Report Manager*

Report Builder End User Reporting Client

For an enhanced end-user reporting experience, Reporting Services will also include Report Builder which is based on the ActiveViews technology. Microsoft acquired the Report Builder technology in 2004 from the company ActiveViews. The inclusion of Report Builder gives SQL Server 2005 a web-based report authoring an end-user query tool. Report Builder directly addresses the problem of unending user report requests by providing a tool that enables end users to author their own reports. Report Builder is based on Microsoft's .NET framework and has been designed from the outset to be completely integrated with Reporting Services. The Report Builder end-user reporting tool is simple to use; the details of the reports can be viewed directly in the Report Builder window as the report is being created. After the Report Builder reports have been authored, they can be deployed in a browser just like any other Reporting Services report.

Report Authoring

In the first section of this chapter, you learned about the various components that make up SQL Server 2005's Reporting Services. In the second half of this chapter, you'll get a more detailed look at steps required to design and deploy a simple report.

Development Stages

The process for developing a Reporting Services application begins with using the Report Designer to define the report's data sources and layout. Next, you need to build and deploy the report to the Report Server. Finally, you need to make the report available to end users by either embedding the report within an application or adding subscriptions for the report.

Designing the Reporting Solution

In creating reporting solutions using Reporting Services, you first select a dataset that defines the data that will be used in the report, and then you lay out the individual data fields on the report. To handle stock reports that are presented in a tabular or matrix format, Microsoft has provided a Report Design Wizard that steps you through the process of creating a data source and laying out the report.

Building and Deploying the Reporting Solution

Once the report has been designed, you need to build the report and then deploy it to the Report Server. Building the report creates a .NET assembly that will run the report. Deploying the report essentially takes this assembly and copies it to the Reporting Services Report Server. While you can perform this manually, the Report Designer has built-in options to both build and deploy reports to the Report Server.

Making the Report Available to End Users

After the report has been deployed to the Report Server, you can then make the report available to end users via several different mechanisms. You can allow access to the reports by embedding them in an application, via their URLs, or by creating a subscription that will push the report to the end user. Report subscriptions can be set up to be delivered at a certain time, or they can be data driven.

Now that you have an overview of the Reporting Services development process, the next section will take you through the steps of developing and deploying a simple report using SQL Server 2005's Reporting Services.

Creating a Reporting Services Report

You can begin using the Report Designer either by starting the Report Wizard and using it to create your initial report or by starting off with a blank design surface and then adding your own report definition elements. In either case, defining a dataset is the first thing you need to create a report. In this example, I'll show you how you can quickly build a report using the Report Wizard.

To build a Reporting Services application, first open the Business Intelligence Development Studio and then select the File | New | Project option to display the New Project dialog that's shown in Figure 8-7.

To create a new Reporting Services report using the Report Wizard, first select the Business Intelligence Projects option from the Project Types list. Then, in the Templates list shown in the right side of the screen, select the Report Project Wizard option. Then fill in the boxes at the bottom of the dialog. In the Name text box, enter the name of the current project. The Location box specifies where the report project's source files will reside. The Solution Name box allows you to name the Reporting Services solution. Here, you can see that the value AdWReports is used as the name of the project and the solution. Clicking OK starts the Report Wizard Welcome dialog that's shown in Figure 8-8.

The Report Wizard Welcome dialog gives you an overview of the steps that the Report Wizard follows during the creation of a report. You first select a data source, then design a query, then select the type of report that you want, and finally specify the formatting for the report. Clicking Next displays the Select The Data Source dialog you can see in Figure 8-9.

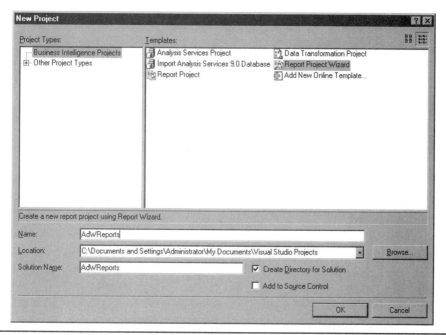

Figure 8-7   *Creating a new report: New Project*

Figure 8-8   *The Report Wizard Welcome dialog*

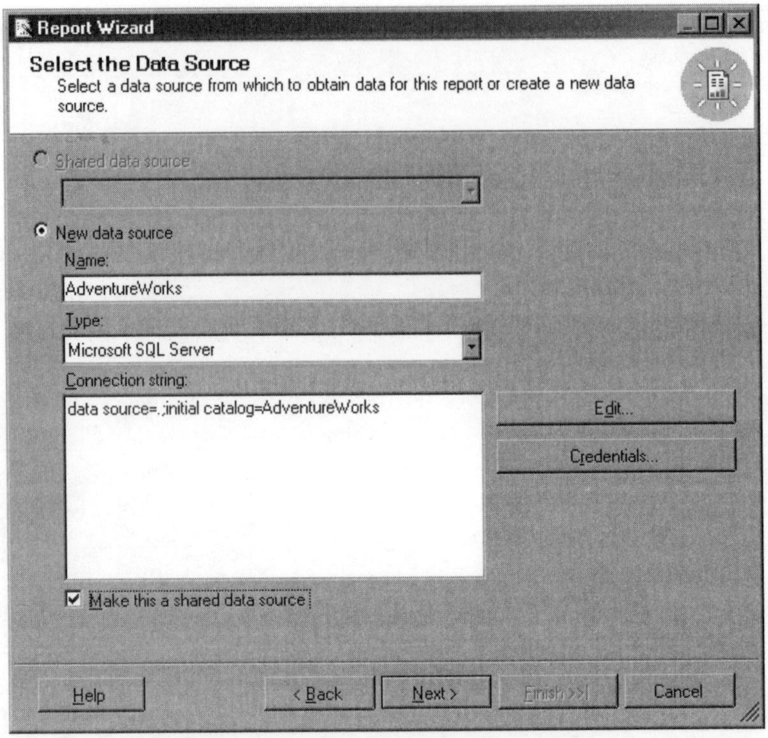

Figure 8-9 *Select the Data Source*

The Select the Data Source dialog allows you to define your connection to the database. To create the Data Source, first give it a name. The name can be anything you choose. It just serves to identify the data source. Next, use the Type drop-down to select the type of database system that the data source will use. The default value is Microsoft SQL Server, but you can also choose OLE DB, Microsoft SQL Server Analysis Services, Oracle, or ODBC. Next, in the Connection String box input the connection string that's required to connect to the target database. If you're unfamiliar with the connection string values, you can click Edit to display the Data Link dialog, which will step you through the creation of the Data Source. Then make this a shared data source check box at the bottom of the screen allows you to share the data source with other reports. You can choose either to create a shared data source, which can be used by several different reports, or to create a data source that will be used only by the report that you are currently creating. If you plan to create several reports that all come out of the same database, creating a shared data source is a good idea, as it can be freely used by all of the reports in your solution and will make it unnecessary to create a unique data source for each report. Clicking Next displays the Design the Query dialog.

From the Design the Query dialog, you can manually enter a SQL statement that will define the dataset used by the report, or else you can click the Query Builder button to display the Query Builder shown in Figure 8-10.

The Query Builder is an interactive query design tool that enables you to build SQL queries without needing to be a SQL expert. However, to effectively use the Query Design tool you still need to have a good basic knowledge of your database's design and scheme. You can select tables from your database by right-clicking in the top portion of the Query Builder and then selecting Add Table from the pop-up menu to display the Add Tables dialog. There you can select one or more tables (multiple tables are selected by holding down the CTRL key and clicking the desired table). The Query Builder will automatically detect any relationships between the tables based on like column names and data types and will draw links between the tables visually showing the relationships.

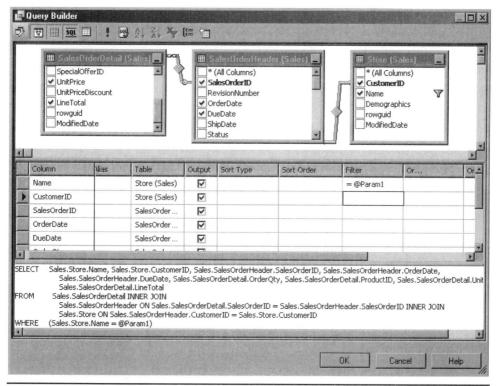

Figure 8-10   *Query Builder*

After selecting the tables, you then select the desired columns from each table by putting a check in the check box that precedes the column name. As you might have guessed, checking the * (All Columns) entry will automatically select all of the columns from the table. As you interactively select the tables and columns and define the relationships between the tables, the Query Designer automatically builds the SQL statement that you can see at the bottom of Figure 8-10.

It's easy to overlook the fact that the Query Builder can also be used to build parameterized queries where the end user supplies a value to the query at run time. To build a parameterized query using the Query Builder, you simply type a question mark into the Filter column that's in the row of the database column name that you want to use with a parameter. The Query Builder will automatically convert the question mark character to the =@Param value that you can see in the middle of Figure 8-10.

You can test the query by clicking the exclamation icon (!) shown in the toolbar. After you've completed designing the query, you can save the query and continue by clicking OK. The SQL statement that was created by the Query Builder will be written into the Design The Query dialog. Clicking Next displays the Select The Report Type dialog that you can see in Figure 8-11.

Figure 8-11   *Select the report type*

While the Report Designer allows you an incredible degree of flexibility in designing reports, the Report Wizard is more restrictive in the type of reports that it will build for you. The Report Wizard will generate either of two different types of reports: a tabular-style report or a matrix-style report.

NOTE

While the styles of reports are limited, the Report Wizard makes a great starting point for building a base report that you can later customize in the Report Designer.

The Tabular report follows your traditional report layout where headers are presented at the top of the page and the detail information is listed below in the body of the report. The Matrix report style presents a crosstab style report where there are headers across the top of the page and down the left-hand side of the page. In Figure 8-10, you can see that the tabular style of report is selected. If you look closely at the bottom of the dialog, you'll notice the Finish button. Clicking Finish allows you to quickly complete the report formatting by selecting all of the default values. Clicking Next displays the Design The Table dialog that is shown in Figure 8-12.

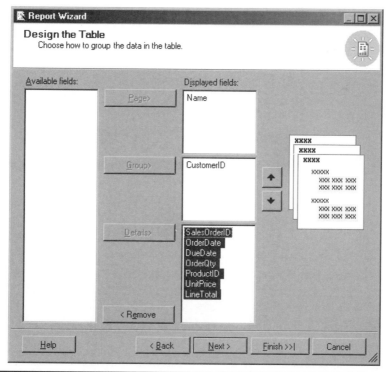

Figure 8-12   *Design the table*

Initially, all of the available columns from the query are shown in the Available Fields list that you can see in the left side of Figure 8-12. From that list of available fields, you can selectively drag fields to the area of the report where you want them to appear. If you want a field to be displayed in the page header, you drag it to the Page section shown in the upper-right side of the screen. If you want a field to be used for group totals, you drag it to the Group section. And if you want a field to be a data field, you drag it to the Details section. In Figure 8-12, you can see that the Name field is used as the page header; the CustomerID field is used as the group header; and the SalesOrderID, OrderDate, DueDate, OrderQty, ProductID, UnitPrice, and LineTotal fields are used in the details area. Once you have laid out the fields that will be used in the report, clicking Next displays the next Report Wizard dialog that you can see in Figure 8-13.

The Choose The Table Style dialog allows you to select the general design of the report that will be generated by Reporting Services. The different table styles are similar, but each style uses a different color scheme and slightly different formatting. In Figure 8-13, you can see that the Corporate style was selected. The Choose The

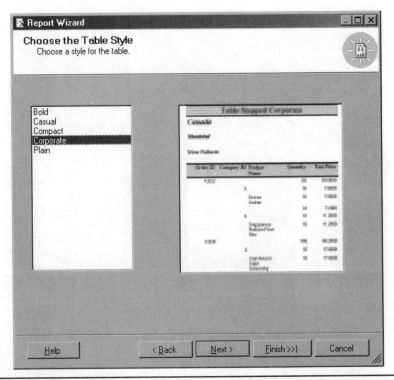

Figure 8-13   *Choose the table style*

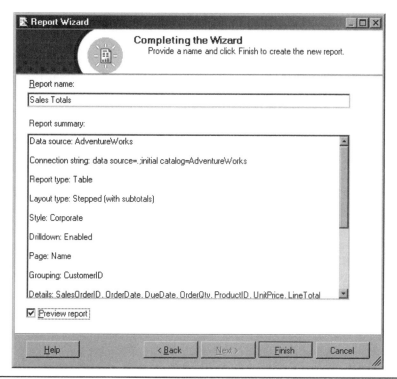

Figure 8-14   *Completing the wizard*

Table Style dialog is the final report creation dialog that's displayed by Report Wizard. Clicking Next displays the Completing The Wizard screen that you can see in Figure 8-14.

The Completing The Wizard dialog allows you to review all of the selections that were made in the previous wizard dialogs. At this point, you can either use the Back button to page back and made corrections to the report specifications, or you can click Finish to generate the report. Selecting the Preview check box will render the report for you to view in the Report Designer's Preview window. After the report is generated, it's added to the Reporting Services solution shown in the Business Intelligence Development Studio.

Deploying a Reporting Services Report

After the report has been created, the next step in creating a Reporting Services application is to build the report and deploy it to the Report Server. Building the report

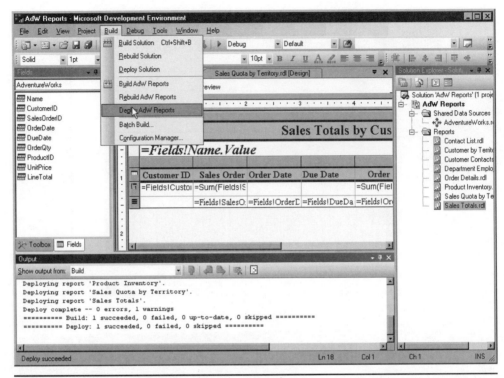

Figure 8-15 *Deploying the Reporting Services solution*

creates a .NET DLL assembly, and deploying the report copies that assembly to the Reporting Services Report Server. You can deploy reporting solutions from the Report Designer by selecting the Build | Deploy Reports option that you can see in Figure 8-15.

If you select one of the deployment options and the report has been changed, the Report Designer will automatically build the report before it is deployed. The output from the build and deployment processes is shown in the Output window that you can see in the bottom of Figure 8-15. Any errors or problems will be listed in the window. Likewise, if the report deployment succeeds, then the success message is listed in the Output window.

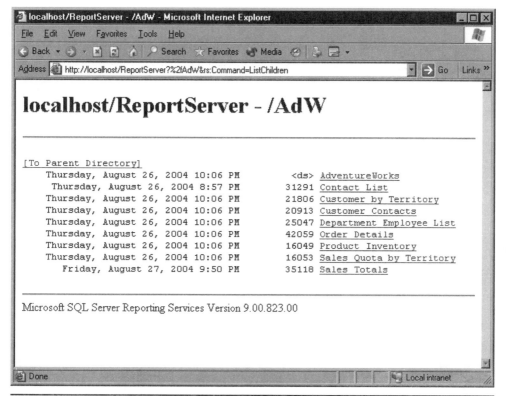

Figure 8-16 *Accessing Reporting Services reports from a URL*

Running a Reporting Services Report

Reporting Services reports can be run by accessing their URL or by embedding them in your applications. You can access and run Reporting Services reports by pointing your browser to the http://<servername>/ReportServer URL, where all of the Reporting Services reports are listed. Figure 8-16 shows the ReportServer web page.

The ReportServer URL lists all of the reports that have been deployed to the Report Server. Each different solution is stored in its own subdirectory. To test the Reports that

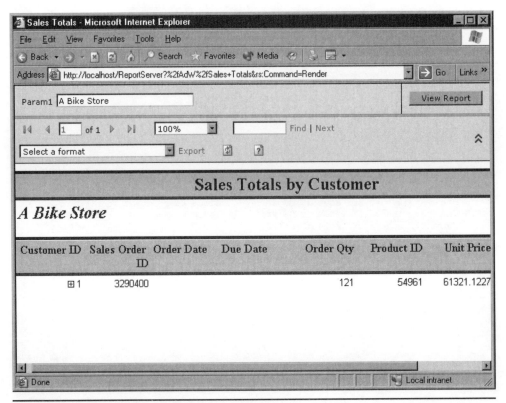

Figure 8-17   *Running Reporting Services reports*

have been deployed, simply click the link and the Report Server will render the report inside the browser. Figure 8-17 shows the example report in the browser.

The report that's rendered in the browser follows the format that was set up in the report design phase. Since this report uses parameters, the param1 field is displayed at the top of the screen. The end user needs to enter a value into this field and then click the View Report button to render the report. In Figure 8-17, you can see that the value of A Bike Store was entered for the replaceable parameter.

In addition, because this report was generated using the drill-down option, a plus sign is displayed in front of the detail line shown on the report. Clicking the plus sign (+) displays the row detail lines that go into that top-level summary line. In this example, clicking the plus sign (+) expands the display, as Figure 8-18 illustrates.

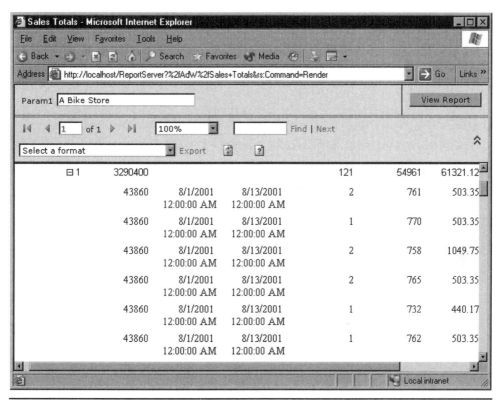

Figure 8-18   *Drilling down into the report*

In Figure 8-18, you can see the details that went into the summary line shown in the previous figure. Clicking the minus sign (–) retracts the detail display and shows the summary line.

Running the reports directly from the Reporting Services URL is great for testing, but when your application goes live, you'll want to embed the report URL in your application or access the Report Server via web services calls.

Integration Services

Data Transformation Services (DTS) has been one of the most useful and popular SQL Server utilities since its introduction with SQL Server 7. DTS was originally conceived to be a tool used to perform data extraction, transformation, and loading (ETL) for OLAP Services data warehouses. However, Microsoft quickly realized its usefulness and made DTS the primary tool for importing and exporting data from SQL Server's relational databases as well as a BI ETL tool. Besides being much easier to use than the old command-line bcp (Bulk Copy Program) tool it replaced, DTS took a big step beyond being a mere data transfer program by providing the ability to transform the data as it transferred it between source and destination endpoints.

DTS offered both a user-friendly wizard designed to perform simple data transfers as well as a graphical designer for more sophisticated data transfer and transformation operations. The SQL Server 7 and 2000 versions of DTS supported 100 percent of OLE DB for the source and target database. This means that although DTS was a part of SQL Server, it could actually be used to transfer data between any two OLE DB data sources without requiring that SQL Server be either the data source or destination. For instance, in addition to being able to import and export data from SQL Server databases, DTS could also be used to transfer data between other database systems such as Access, Oracle, and DB2 without involving SQL Server at all. This kind of flexibility made DTS a very powerful and useful database transfer tool.

However, as cool and useful as DTS was, it still had some rather important limitations. To be enterprise ready, DTS needed better scalability. Plus, DTS packages were not easily transportable between systems. In other words, a DTS package that was designed to perform a transfer from SQL Server system A could not be easily reused to perform that same transfer from system B. In addition to these deployment limitations, the earlier versions of DTS lacked robust error handling and logging, and they had limited manageability.

With SQL Server 2005 Microsoft completely revamped DTS and rewrote it from the ground up. Reflecting its all new nature, Microsoft renamed DTS to Integration Services. Microsoft's goal for SQL Server 2005's Integration Services was to make it an enterprise ETL platform for Windows on a par with any of the stand-alone enterprise-level BI ETL products. To those ends, Microsoft wrote the all-new Integration Services using managed .NET code, giving it a more robust foundation. In the process, Microsoft completely redesigned Integration Servces, giving it an all-new architecture, providing better support for programmability and improved run-time performance. The new Integration Services features a new graphical designer and a greatly enhanced selection of data transfer tasks and transformations. Integration Services, like the old DTS, supports 100 percent of the source and target destination, meaning it can independently connect to both the source and destination data sources with no need that either data source be a SQL Server system,. In this chapter you'll learn about the new features found in SQL Server 2005's Integration Services. First, you'll get a look inside the new Integration Services architecture and then take a guided tour of the new Integration Services tools and components.

New Integration Services Architecture

The new Integration Services architecture is divided into two main sections: the Data Transformation Pipeline (DTP) and the Data Transformation Runtime (DTR). Microsoft split Integration Services into two different pieces mainly to make a clear delineation between data flow and work flow. In the previous versions of DTS, the data flow engine was stronger than the work flow capabilities. This new division essentially makes the work flow portion of Integration Services a first-class component on the same level as the data flow component. The new DTP essentially replaces the old DTS Data Pump that was used in the SQL Server 7 and 2000 versions of DTS. Its primary function is to handle the data flow between the source and target destinations. The DTR is basically a job execution environment that controls the work flow that's used in an Integration Services package. Each of these components is implemented using its own DLL as well as its own distinct object model that you can program against. In Figure 9-1 you can see an overview of the new Integration Services architecture.

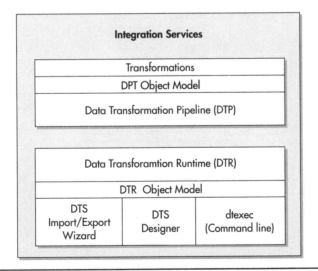

Figure 9-1   *Integration Services architecture*

The new Integration Services DTP and DTR are discussed in more detail in the following sections. More information about the new Integration Services tool set is also presented later in this chapter.

Data Transformation Pipeline (DTP)

The DTP takes care of the data flow and transformations that take place as rows are moved between the data source and the data target. DTP uses data adapters to connect to the source and destination data sources. As you can see in Figure 9-1, the DTP engine is accessed using the DTP Pipeline object model. This object model is the API that is used by both the built-in transformations supplied by Microsoft and any user-created custom transformations. Transformations move and optionally manipulate row data as they move data from the source columns to the destination columns. You can get a more detailed look at the new DTP architecture in Figure 9-2.

The DTP uses data adapters to connect data source and destination endpoints. As their names suggest, source data adapters connect to the source of the data and provide the input for Integration Services packages. Destination data adapters connect to the data target and output the data. SQL Server 2005 provides a number of source and

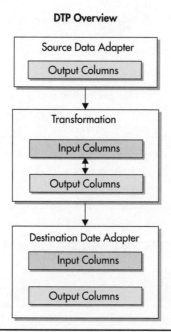

Figure 9-2 *Data Transformation Pipeline components*

destination data adapters. Out of the box, SQL Server 2005's Integration Services comes with a number of built-in source and destination adapters, including adapters for SQL Server, flat files, and other OLE DB–compliant data sources. More information about the specific data adapters that are supported is presented in the section "Integration Services Package Components" later in this chapter.

While the job of the data adapters is to make connections to the data's source and destination endpoints, the job of the Integration Services transformations is to move and optionally manipulate the data as it's moved between the source and destination endpoints. Integration Services transformation can be as simple as a one-to-one mapping between the source columns and the target columns, or it can be much more complex, performing such tasks as selectively moving columns between the source and target, creating new target columns using one-to-many mappings, or computing derived columns. SQL Server 2005's Integration Services comes with a substantial number of built-in transformations which are listing in the section "Integration Services Components" later in the chapter. In addition to these built-in transformations, you can build your own custom transformations by taking advantage of the DTP object model API.

Data Transformation Runtime (DTR)

The DTR consists of the DTR engine and the DTR components. DTR components are objects that enable you to govern Integration Services' execution. The DTR components are used to build work flows, containers that provide structured operations, tasks that provide data transfer and transformation functionality, and constraints that control the sequence of a work flow in a package. You can see an overview of the new DTR architecture in Figure 9-3.

The primary DTR components are containers and tasks. *Tasks* are collections of DTR components; each task is composed of data sources and target destinations as

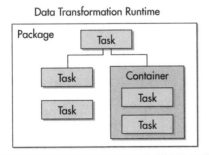

Figure 9-3 *Data Transformation Runtime overview*

well as data transformations. *Containers* are used to organize and structure related tasks. These containers and tasks are grouped together to form packages. The Integration Services *package* is the physical unit that groups together all of the functions that will be performed in a given transfer operation. Packages are executed by the DTR to perform data transfers. Integration Services packages can be easily rerun or even moved to a different system and executed stand-alone. More information about the specific components that make up the DTR is presented in the section "Integration Services Package Components" later in this chapter.

The primary purpose of the DTR engine is to control the execution of Integration Services packages. The DTR controls the work flow of the tasks contained in a Integration Services package. In addition, the DTR engine stores package layout; runs packages; and provides debugging, logging, and event handling services. The DTR engine also enables you to manage connections and access Integration Services package variables.

The DTR is accessed using the DTR object framework. The DTR run-time object framework is the API that supports the Integration Services Import/Export Wizard and the Integration Services Designer in addition to the command-line dtexec tool. Both the Import/Export Wizard and the Designer are used to create packages. The DTR engine is written in C++, and its API is exposed using both a native C++ API as well as a .NET assembly that enables it to be accessible to managed .NET applications. Programs that use the DTR object model can automate the creation and execution of Integration Services packages.

Integration Services Package Components

Integration Services packages are organized collections of DTP and DTR components. The package is the unit of execution for a Integration Services transfer operation. In other words, to use Integration Services to perform data transfers and ETL operations, you must create a package that contains all of the DTP components that define the source target and destinations for the data and the transformations that will take place, as well as the DTR components that define the work flow or sequence of actions that will be performed by the Integration Services package. Once the package has been created, you execute the package to perform the data transfer. You can see an overview of a sample Integration Services package shown in Figure 9-4.

Integration Services packages can be created using the set of tools provided with SQL Server 2005, or they can be created programmatically using the DTR API. Integration Services packages can be saved either in SQL Server's msdb database or as XML files that reside in the file systems. You can get a preview of the Integration

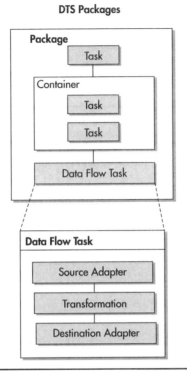

Figure 9-4   *Integration Services package overview*

Services design tools in the section "Integration Services Tools" that is presented later in this chapter.

Integration Services Package Features

Not surprisingly, the new Integration Services architecture adds some significant new capabilities to Integration Services that make it a more robust enterprise data transformation tool. Next, let's look at some of the major enhancements that this new version of Integration Services brings to the table.

Setting Run-Time Properties of Integration Services Packages

One of the major limitations of the earlier versions of Integration Services was the fact that packages were essentially tied to a given source and destination. That meant that it was really difficult to take a given package and easily reuse it on a different server, even if that server supported the same databases. While it was possible to use global variables and other complex workarounds to get around this limitation, these workarounds weren't the most graceful or robust solutions to the problem. The new SQL Server 2005 Integration Services enables one package to handle multiple source and destination endpoints. You can use this feature to set package properties at run time from parameters files, the Registry, or XML documents.

Logging

The original Integration Services also didn't support any built-in logging capabilities. Logging the operation of packages is particularly useful for auditing and troubleshooting. While you could add them yourself, this required development work on your part. The new SQL Server 2005 Integration Services provides built-in logging options for packages, tasks, and transformations.

Checkpoint Restart

Another great new feature in SQL Server 2005's Integration Services is support for checkpoints and restarts within Integration Services packages. This new feature enables different checkpoints to be associated with multiple steps in complex Integration Services packages. Thus if a package fails that's using checkpoints, the entire package doesn't need to be rerun from the very beginning. Instead, the package can be restarted at the first unsuccessful checkpoint. For long-running packages, this can be a huge time saver, as the entire package doesn't need to be reprocessed. Instead, the Integration Services package can resume processing where it left off. When combined with event handling, this can be a powerful tool for automatically managing your Integration Services jobs.

Variables

Support for variables is another new feature found in SQL Server 2005 Integration Services. With SQL Server 7 and SQL Server 2000, DTS packages supported variables for use in transformation scripts but didn't support package-scoped variables. This lack of global variables made it difficult to reuse DTS packages on multiple databases and on multiple servers. To be sure, there were workarounds, but since DTS packages were not designed to be used in this fashion, these workarounds were somewhat complex and not particularly robust. With SQL Server 2005 the new Integration Services design provides support for package, task, and event-level variables, greatly increasing the flexibility of Integration Services packages and also significantly facilitating the reuse of Integration Services packages. As their name implies, package-scoped variables can be seen by all of the components in the Integration Services package. Task-scoped variables can be seen and accessed by the components of that particular task but not by any other components that are part of that Integration Services package. One example usage of a package-scoped Integration Services variable might be to contain the name of the current SQL Server system, allowing the package to be easily run on another system by substituting that system's server name into the Integration Services variable at run time.

System Variables   All Integration Services packages have a number of built-in system variables that represent different aspects of a Integration Services package. Table 9-1 lists the new Integration Services System variables.

System Variable	Description
BreakpointTargetDescription	Contains a description of the break point
Cancel	Indicates that execution should be canceled
CountDone	Contains the transfer progress counter
CreationDate	Contains the package creation date
CreatorComputerName	Contains the name of the computer used to create the package
CreatorName	Contains the name of the user who created the package
CustomEventDescription	Describes a custom event
CustomEventInfo	Contains custom event information
CustomEventName	Contains a custom event name
CustomEventValue	Contains the custom event value
CustonEventGUID	Contains the custom event's GUID
ErrorCode	Contains an error code
ErrorDescription	Contains an error description
ExecutionInstanceGuid	Contains a GUID identifying the current package instance
ExecutionStatus	Contains the package's execution status
LocaleId	Contains the Locale identification code
MachineName	Contains the current machine name
MaxCount	Contains the maximum number of items to be transferred
PackageId	Contains the current package identification
PackageName	Contains the current package name
PercentComplete	Contains the transfer progress status

Table 9-1   *Integration Services System Variables*

System Variable	Description
ProgressCountHigh	Contains the transfer progress high count
ProgressCountLow	Contains the transfer progress low count
ProgressDescription	Contains a transfer progress description
ProgressEvent	Contains a transfer progress event identification
Propagate	Indicates if an event can be propagated
SourceDescription	Contains an event source description
SourceID	Contains an event source identification
SourceName	Contains an event source name
StartTime	Contains the package's execution start time
TaskID	Contains a task identification
TaskName	Contains a task name
UserName	Contains the name of the user running the package
VersionBuild	Contains the package's build number
VersionComment	Contains the package's description
VersionGUID	Contains the package's GUID
VersionMajor	Contains the package's major version number
VersionMinor	Contains the package's minor version number

Table 9-1   *Integration Services System Variables* (continued)

Complex Flow Control

SQL Server 2005's Integration Services also supports complex flow control. Within each Integration Services package you can specify the path that will be taken if a given operation succeeds or fails. For instance, if an operation succeeds you can set up your Integration Services package to proceed along with the next subsequent action. Otherwise, if the operation fails you can take an alternative action. More information about the new error flow feature is presented in the following section. You can also set up the control flow in such a way that multiple tasks can be executed in parallel, or you can force tasks to execute sequentially by specifying that the next task will not be executed until the current task has completed. You can also use a new Integration Services construct known as a *container* to group together related Integration Services tasks. Each container can have its own internal control flow and variables. There are also multiple looping structures that enable you to set up repeated actions. There's a For Each Loop container that is capable of iterating over a group of objects, taking action on those objects on every iterations. In addition, there's a For Loop container that can evaluate an expression and conditionally perform repeated actions. More information about all of the available tasks is presented later in this chapter.

Error Flows   One of the big new features with SQL Server 2005 Integration Services is its ability to support error flows. The new Error Flows feature essentially enables you to add error handling to your Integration Services packages. With the new Error flows feature, when a Integration Services transform encounters rows that produce error conditions, instead of halting the process with an error, Integration Services can route the problem row according to the error flow that has been set up. For instance, the error flow may indicate that the row is simply written out to a log file, or it can also direct the package into a task that performs much more sophisticated error routines that can even manipulate the data and place the row back into the pipeline for reprocessing.

Immediate Mode and Project Mode

Similar to the way that SQL Server 2000 DTS worked, where DTS had both a wizard interface that was primarily designed to execute ad hoc data transfers and a DTS Designer that was used to build more complex DTS packages, SQL Server 2005's Integration Services supports both an *immediate* mode and a *project* mode. To use Integration Services in the immediate mode, you can run the Integration Services Import/Export Wizard from the menu. The Integration Services Import/Export Wizard can be used to build, execute, and optionally save Integration Services packages that perform simple transfers. SQL Server 2005's new Integration Services Import/Export Wizard looks and acts much like the version found in SQL Server 2000.

While immediate mode is useful for quick one-time data transfer operations, the project mode is useful for building more sophisticated Integration Services packages using the Business Intelligence Development Studio. The Business Intelligence Development Studio contains an all-new Integration Services Designer that supports an entirely new set of Data Flow, Control Flow, and Event handlers that can be used to build Integration Services packages. The new Integration Services Designer also provides full support for debugging Integration Services packages. You can see the new Integration Services Designer in more detail in the section "Integration Services Tools" later in this chapter.

Digital Signing of Integration Services Packages

Using a method much like the digital signing feature found that's available for Microsoft .NET applications, Integration Services packages can now be signed as well. This enables you to verify the authenticity of a package when it is executed.

Packages can be digitally signed during the design process using the Integration Services Designer. Once a package had been digitally signed, that package is read-only and can no longer be modified.

Data Adapters

The DTP uses data adapters to connect data source and destination endpoints. As their names suggest, source data adapters connect to the source of the data and provide the input for Integration Services packages. Destination data adapters connect to the data target and output the data. SQL Server 2005's provides a number of source and destination data adapters. Table 9-2 lists the set of built-in data adapters that are supplied with SQL Server 2005.

Containers

Containers are a new construct that Microsoft has added to SQL Server 2005's Integration Services. The primary purpose for Integration Services containers is to add structure and flow control to your Integration Services packages. Containers group together related tasks and are designed to be used to execute repeated tasks or to provide scope for variables. SQL Server 2005 Integration Services supports the types of containers shown in Table 9-3.

Tasks

The Integration Services tasks are the most basic elements of the Integration Services package. The Integration Services task essentially defines an action that will be performed. These actions range from copying files, executing T-SQL

Data Adapter	Description
Flat File Destination Adapter	A file system adapter that writes text-delimited data to a file
Flat File Source Adapter	A file system adapter that reads text-delimited data from a file
OLE DB Destination Adapter	An OLE DB provider that writes data to an OLE consumer
OLE DB Source Adapter	An OLE DB consumer that reads data from an OLE DB provider
Raw File Destination Adapter	A file system adapter that writes data to a file
Raw File Source Adapter	A file system adapter that reads data from a file
SQL Server Destination Adapter	A SQL Server adapter that's used to write data to a table or view
Web Service Source Adapter	A Web Service adapter that reads data from an XML web service

Table 9-2   *Built-in Data Adapters*

Container	Description
Package Container	A collection of package elements
Foreach Loop Container	Provides iterative control flow in a package
For Loop Container	Provides support for repeated actions in a package
Sequence Container	Groups related tasks and containers in package
TaskHost Container	Provides services to a task
Container Properties	Holds values that are common to the container
Container Collections	A collection of containers

Table 9-3   *Integration Services Container Types*

statements, and running scripts, to performing FTP transfers and running data mining models. Multiple related tasks can be grouped into containers. Table 9-4 presents the tasks that are included in SQL Server 2005's Integration Services.

Task	Description
ActiveX Script Task	Executes an ActiveX script that performs a specified action
Analysis Services Execute DDL Task	Executes T-SQL DDL statements
Analysis Services Processing Task	Processes Analysis Services objects
Bulk Insert Task	Inserts data from a text file into a table
Data Flow Task	Copies and transforms data between data sources
Data Mining Query Task	Executes data mining queries
Execute Package Task	Executes other packages
Execute Process Task	Executes a program or script
Execute SQL Task	Executes T-SQL statements
File System Task	Executes actions on the file system
File Transfer Protocol Task	Executes FTP data transfers
Message Queue Task	Sends and receives messages from MSMQ data queues
Script Task	Executes scripts written in VB.NET using the Microsoft Visual Studio for Applications (VSA) environment.
Send Mail Task	Sends an e-mail message
XML Task	Accesses data in XML documents

Table 9-4   *Integration Services Tasks*

Transformations

Integration Services transformations control what happens to the data as it's moved from the source data adapter to the destination data adapter. SQL Server 2005 supports both a number of built-in transformations and user-defined custom transformations. You can create custom transformations using the API provided by the DTP object model. SQL Server 2005's Integration Services provides an extensive list of built-in standard transformations, as shown in Table 9-5.

Transformation	Description
Aggregate Transformation	Performs aggregations
Allocation Transformation	Spreads the value of an input column across multiple output columns
Character Map Transformation	Applies string functions to character data
Conditional Split Transformation	Evaluates data and routes it to different outputs
Copy/Map Transformation	Creates new output columns by copying input columns
Data Mining Model Accuracy Transformation	Calculates the accuracy of data mining models
Data Mining Model Training Transformation	Trains data mining models
Data Mining Query Transformation	Runs data mining prediction queries
Data Conversion Transformation	Converts the data type of an input column to a different output data type
Derived Column Transformation	Creates an output column from the results of expressions
Dimension Processing Transformation	Processes OLAP cube dimensions
File Extractor Transformation	Reads data from a package's data flow and writes that data to file
File Injector Transformation	Reads data from a file and adds that data to a package's data flow
Fuzzy Grouping Transformation	Standardizes values in input column data
Fuzzy Lookup Transformation	Looks up values in a reference table using fuzzy matching
Logged Lineage Transformation	Provides environment information to the package's data flow
Lookup Transformation	Looks up values in a reference table using exact matching
Merge Transformation	Merges two sorted datasets
Merge Join Transformation	Joins two datasets using a FULL, LEFT, or INNER join
Multicast Transformation	Distributes input data to multiple outputs
Partition Processing Transformation	Processes OLAP partitions
Pivot Transformation	Pivots the input data according to an input column value
Row Count Transformation	Counts the input rows and stores the count in a variable

Table 9-5   *Built-in Standard Transformations*

Transformation	Description
Sampling Transformation	Creates a representative sampling of the input dataset
Script Transformation	Executes a script to transform the input
Slowly Changing Dimension Transformation	Coordinates updating and insert rows into OLAP dimensions
Sort Transformation	Sorts input data and copies the sorted data to the transformation output
Surrogate Key Transformation	Provides additional custom properties to the Integration Services package
Union All Transformation	Merges multiple datasets
UnPivot Transformation	Unpivots input data according to an input column value

Table 9-5   *Built-in Standard Transformations* (continued)

Event Handling

The ability to raise and handle events is another new feature found SQL Server 2005 Integration Services. Event handling enables Integration Services packages to respond to events that are raised at run time by containers and tasks. Events can be fired by the Integration Services package elements to signal a number of different states, including error conditions, when a task has started, when a task completes, or a change in variable status. Table 9-6 lists the Integration Services Event Handlers.

Event Handler	Description
OnCustomerEvent	Raised on demand by a task or package
OnError	Raised by a task or container on an error
OnExecStatusChanged	Raised by a task or container when its execution status changes
OnPostExecute	Raised by a task or container after it has run
OnPostValidate	Raised by a task after it has been validated
OnPreExecute	Raised by a task or container before it has run
OnPreValidate	Raised by a task before it has been validated
OnProgress	Raised by a task or container when a specified progress metric has been met
OnQueryCancel	Raised by a task or container to determine if it [ok] should stop running
OnTaskFailed	Raised by a task when it fails
OnVariableValueChanged	Optionally raised by a variable when its value changes
OnWarning	Raised by a task or container when a warning is generated

Table 9-6   *Integration Services Event Handlers*

Log Provider	Description
The Text File log provider	Writes log entries to ASCII text files using a comma-separated value (CSV) format using a default file extension of .log
The SQL Profiler log provider	Writes SQL trace data to a trace file using a default file extension of .trc
The SQL Server log provider	Writes log entries to the sysdtslog90 table in a SQL Server database
The Windows Event log provider	Writes entries to the Windows Application
The XML File log provider	Writes log files to an XML file using a default file extension of .xml

Table 9-7   *Log Providers*

Log Providers

Log providers are another completely new feature that Microsoft has added to Integration Services packages. As their name suggests, Integration Services log providers enable you to add logging to your packages, containers, and tasks. Logging is used to record error information or other important run-time or status information. Table 9-7 lists the log providers that Microsoft ships with SQL Server 2005.

Integration Services Tools

Reflecting its totally new architecture, the Integration Services tool set has been completely revamped and sports an entirely new look. While there are some similarities in some of the simpler tools—the Integration Services Import/Export Wizard, for instance, which is used to perform ad hoc data transfer operations—the more sophisticated tools such as the Integration Services Designer are completely different. Whether you're a DTS expert or a novice DTS user, SQL Server 2005's Integration Services will require you to learn how to use the new tools from the ground up. In this section you'll gain an overview of the new Integration Services tools and utilities that come with SQL Server 2005.

SQL Server 2005's Integration Services toolset is divided into two basic areas: tools that are used to create and execute Integration Services packages, and tools that are used to work with existing DTS packages. The Integration Services Designer tools include the basic Integration Services Import/Export Wizard and the more advanced Designer. As you'll see next, the Integration Services Designer reflects the architectural separation of control flow and data flow by providing separate editors for designing package data flow and control flow. The Integration Services Designer provides a graphical representation of the work flow that occurs inside a Integration Services package. The new Integration Services Designer provides enterprise-level features such as source control to facilitate multideveloper environments. There are also built-in package deployment and debugging tools, including the ability to set and monitor breakpoints within a package. You can also use the Integration Services Designer to monitor a package's execution—its overall progress and the outcome of individual tasks and transformations. The Integration Services package tools include a Package Migration Wizard that is designed to migrate SQL Server 7 and SQL Server 2000 packages to the new SQL Server 2005 format. There is also a Integration Services Package Installer Wizard that creates installation programs for Integration Services packages, making it easier to deploy these packages to remote systems. In addition, there is a Integration Services Package Execution utility that enables you to execute Integration Services packages from the command line; this is a handy tool for incorporating Integration Services transfer as part of your management scripts.

Integration Services Design Tools

Here you get a closer look at the new Integration Services design tools. First, you'll see the Integration Services Import/Export Wizard. Next, you'll get a more detailed look at the new Integration Services Designer.

Integration Services Import/Export Wizard

The Integration Services Import/Export Wizard is SQL Server 2005's first entry point into the new Integration Services. Like its predecessors found in SQL Server 7 and SQL Server 2000, the SQL Server 2005 Integration Services Import/Export Wizard provides a series of dialogs that lead you through the process of selecting the data source, the destination, and the objects that will be transferred. The Integration Services Import/Export Wizard also allows you to optionally save and execute the Integration Services package. You can start the Integration Services Import/Export Wizard by select the Integration Services Import/Export option from the SQL Server menu or by entering **dtswizard** at the command line. Saving the packages generated with the Integration Services Import/Export Wizard and then editing them in the Integration Services Designer is a great way to learn more about Integration Services— especially if you're just getting started with Integration Services or if you're transitioning to the new SQL Server 2005 Integration Services from one of the earlier versions. You can see the new Integration Services Import/Export Wizard in Figure 9-5.

The Integration Services Import/Export Wizard first leads you through the process of choosing a data source. In the Data Source drop-down, you select the provider that you want to use. Depending on the provider that you select, the options for the rest of the screen change. If you select the Microsoft OLE DB Provider for SQL Server, you will see a screen like the one shown in Figure 9-5, where you then select

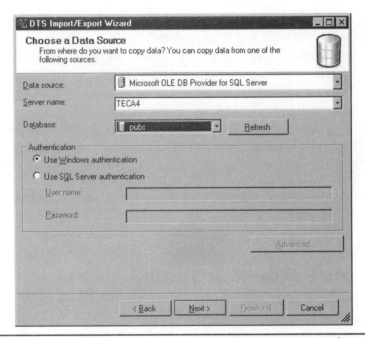

Figure 9-5 *Integration Services Import/Export Wizard—Data Source Selection*

the server that you want to connect to followed by the database and the type of authentication that you need to use. Clicking Next leads you through the subsequent wizard dialogs. The next dialog allows you to select the data destination, which is essentially identical to the data source dialog except that it defines where the data will be transferred to.

NOTE

While the SQL Server 2005 Integration Services Wizard does provide the same basic functionality as the Integration Services Import/Export Wizard that was included in SQL Server 7 and 2000, the new version lacks the ability to perform custom data mappings as well as the ability to input custom data transformation scripts. In order to use these more advanced capabilities, you need to use the Integration Services Designer.

After you select the data source and destination, the wizard prompts you to optionally save and execute the Integration Services package. As each task in the package executes, the transfer window is dynamically updated, showing the Integration Services package's transfer progress. When the Integration Services package has been successfully executed, the Integration Services Import/Export Wizard will display the dialog that you can see in Figure 9-6.

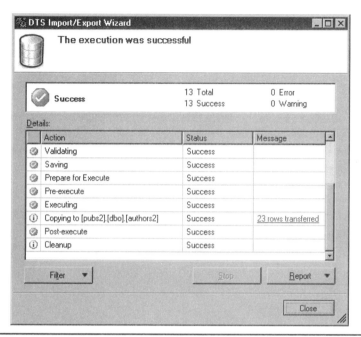

Figure 9-6   *Integration Services Import/Export Wizard—Package Execution*

Integration Services Designer

While the Integration Services Import/Export Wizard is useful for simple ad hoc transfers, extraction, transformation, and loading (ETL) tasks require significantly more sophistication and power than the Integration Services wizard exposes. By their nature, ETL tasks are far more than just simple data transfers from one destination to another. Instead, they often combine data from multiple sources, manipulate the data, map values to new columns, create columns from calculated values, and provide a variety of data cleanup and verification tasks. These more demanding capabilities are outside the scope of the simple Integration Services Import/Export Wizard. That's where the new Integration Services Designer comes into play. The Integration Services Designer is a set of graphical tools that you can use to build, execute, and debug Integration Services packages. You can use the Integration Services Designer to open up simple Integration Services packages that were created using the wizard, or you can use it to create very powerful and robust data transfer and transformation solutions.

The Integration Services Designer is started from the Business Intelligence Development Studio by selecting File | New | Project to open the New Project dialog.

Then to create a new Integration Services project, you select Business Intelligence Projects from the Project Types list and then Data Transformation Project from the list of Templates, as is shown in Figure 9-7.

> **NOTE**
> *Don't be confused by the fact that the Integration Services Designer is started from the Business Intelligence Development Studio. It is not limited to just Analysis Services projects. The Integration Services Designer and the projects developed in the Business Intelligence Development Studio are fully capable of working with relational and other types of data and are not limited to analysis service data.*

Once you've created the project, you can open the Integration Services Designer by right-clicking Packages in the Solution Explorer window that's displayed on the right portion of the screen. Then select the New Package option to start the Integration Services Designer. When the Integration Services Designer first starts, you're presented with a blank design surface that looks nothing like the earlier Integration Services Designers, so getting started can be a bit of a challenge.

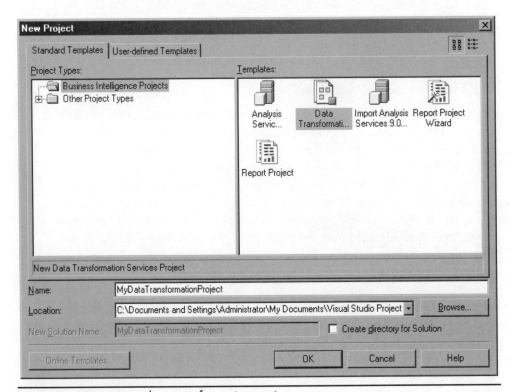

Figure 9-7   *Opening a data transformation project*

New Control Flow Designer   While you can approach using the Integration Services Designer in a couple of different ways, the easiest method is probably to begin with the Control Flow tab and then open the Control Flow Toolbox. After the Toolbox is displayed, click the Data Flow task and then drag it to the design surface. The Integration Services Designer's Control Flow surface will appear as shown in Figure 9-8.

At this point the Integration Services package is pretty simple, as it consists of a single Data Flow task. Obviously you could make this package much more complex by adding additional tasks from the Control Flow toolbox and even organizing multiple related tasks into containers.

New Data Flow Designer   At this point the package knows that it is going to perform a data transfer operation, but it doesn't know what it's going to transfer or where the data is coming from or going to. After adding the Data Flow task, the next step is to define the actual data flows. To define the data flows, you double-click the Data Flow task to display the Data Flow tab. Initially, the Data Flow tab will be blank. To add data source and data destination connections, open the Data Flow Toolbox on the left side of the IDE and then drag and drop an OLE DB Source data flow item and an OLE DB Destination data flow item onto the Data Flow Design surface. In

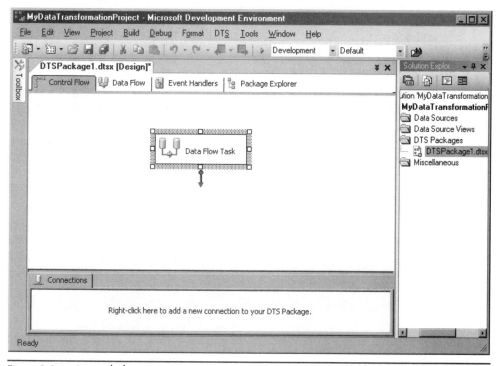

Figure 9-8   *Control Flow Designer*

addition, you can add a Flat File Destination that can be used to output any error rows to an ASCII log file.

Now you've told Integration Services that you're transferring data from one OLE DB source to another OLE DB destination, but you still need to define the source and destination connections. In addition, you need to set up a connection for the flat file error flow. Basically, every data flow source or destination needs an accompanying connection, which essentially provides the specific details about the connection's endpoint. Because this example uses three Data Flow Items, three different connections are needed: two OLE DB connections and one Flat File connection. To define those connections, you can right-click in the Connection pane shown at the bottom of the Integration Services Designer, which displays a pop-up menu enabling you to select the type of connection that you want to create. Selecting the connection type from the pop-up menu displays the Connection Manager. In Figure 9-9 you can see the Connection Manager being used to create a new OLE DB connection.

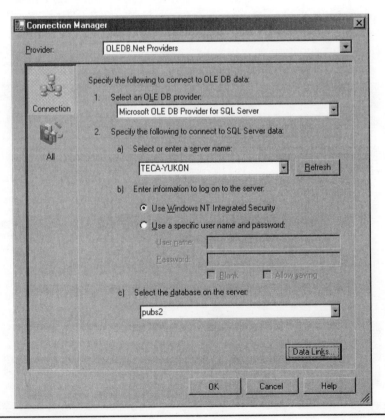

Figure 9-9   *Connection Manager*

Once the connections are created, you need to associate each connection to the appropriate data flow item. To link a connection to a data flow item, you right-click the data flow item, select either the Edit or the Advanced Edit option from the context menu, and then select the connection from the drop-down list of connections displayed in the Edit dialog. As you define each connection, you specify the column mapping and any other transformations that will be performed. When you complete the configuration, the Integration Services Designer's Data Flow tab will appear something like the one shown in Figure 9-10.

In the middle of the Data Flow Design tab you can see the OLE DB Source, OLE DB Destination, and Flat File Destination data flow items. A straight green arrow data flow connects the OLE DB Source to the OLE DB Destination, and a bent red arrow error flow connects the OLE DB Source to the Flat File Destination. The connections for each of these items are shown in the Connections pane at the bottom of the display.

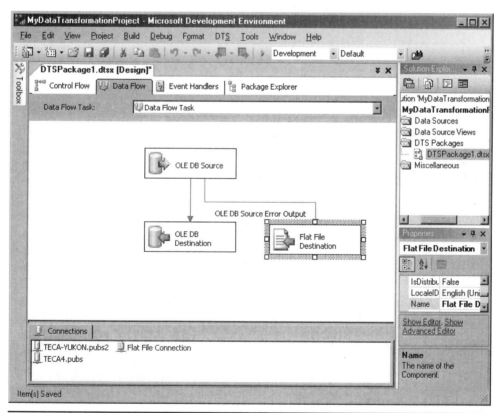

Figure 9-10   *Data Flow Designer*

Graphical Presentation of Package Execution   Once all of the data flows and connections have been defined, the package can be run by clicking the green run arrow on the toolbar or by selecting the Start option from the Debug menu. Before running the package, you can optionally define breakpoints in the package by selecting an item followed by the New Breakpoint option from the Debug menu. When the package is run, the Watch and Call Stack windows are automatically opened and the currently executing Data Flow Item turns green. You can see the result of running the sample package in Figure 9-11.

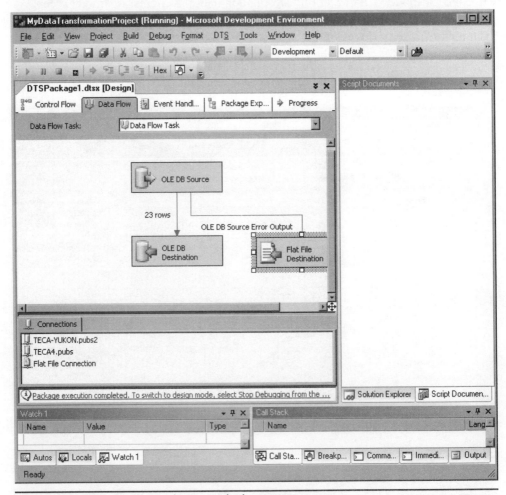

Figure 9-11   *Running the package inside the Designer*

New Package Explorer   Another new feature that is found on the Integration Services Designer is the Package Explorer. The Package Explorer provides a hierarchical tree view of the Integration Services Package that's displayed in the designer. The Package Explorer is illustrated in Figure 9-12.

At the top level you can see the package name, and each of the package's components is listed beneath the package. Clicking the plus sign in front of each component displays the actual items. It's worth noting that the Package Explorer is not just a view-only tool. From the Explorer view, you can delete items as well as edit their properties. However, you can't add new items. That can be done only in the design surface.

Configuration   The new Integration Services configurations feature was designed to make it easier for you to deploy Integration Services packages. The new configurations feature enables you to dynamically update a package to run in a different environment. For instance, connections require connection strings, and these connection strings are

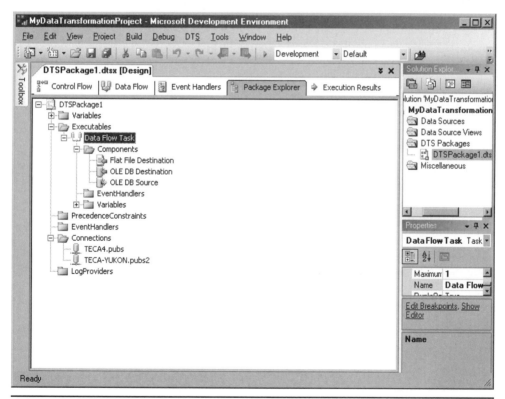

Figure 9-12   *The Package Explorer*

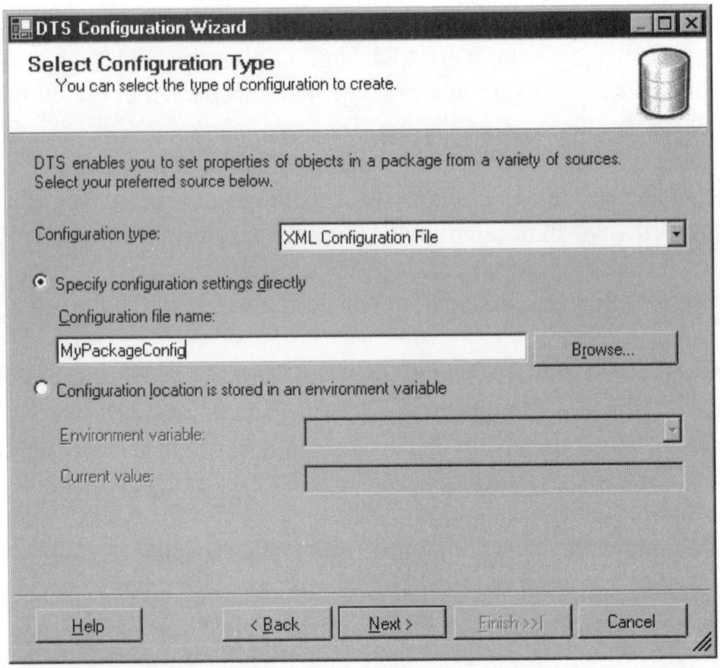

Figure 9-13   *Configuration Wizard*

often suitable only to a given environment. Configurations enable you to dynamically update these types of site/server-specific values when the package is deployed. You can create configurations using the Configuration Wizard. You can start the Configuration Wizard using the Integration Services | Configurations menu option to display the Package Configurations Organization dialog, where you can click Add to start the Configuration Wizard. You can see the Configuration Wizard in Figure 9-13.

Although this section was able to touch on only a fraction of the capability found in the SQL Server 2005's new Integration Services, hopefully this section has given you a feel for how the Integration Services Designer works.

Integration Services Packaging Tools

The last section of this chapter will introduce you to some the other package management utilities that are provided with SQL Server 2005. A Package Migration

Wizard is provided to assist you in converting your existing Integration Services packages into SQL Server 2005's new package format. There's also a Package Management utility that enables you to work with existing Integration Services packages. In addition, a new command-line tool enables you to run packages from the command line.

Package Migration Wizard

Considering the complete architectural change and the adoption of the .NET Framework, it should come as no surprise that DTS packages built for SQL Server 7 and SQL Server 2000 must be migrated to the new format before they can be modified.

NOTE

Existing DTS Packages built for SQL Server 2000 can be run against SQL Server 2005. They can also be included in new SQL Server 2005 Integration Services package solutions. They just can't be modified unless they are first migrated to the new format.

SQL Server 2005's Package Migration Wizard will migrate existing Integration Services packages into the SQL Server 2005 Integration Services package format. The Package Migration Wizard attempts to take existing Integration Services package elements like tasks, precedence, constraints, and variables and convert them into the equivalent SQL Server 2005 package items. The Package Migration Wizard can handle the Microsoft-supplied DTS package components, but it cannot convert custom tasks. Custom tasks maintain their old structure and are encapsulated as a subpackage that is linked to the migrated package. Scripts can be another problem issue for the Package Migration Wizard. While most ActiveX transformation scripts can be converted to the new ActiveX Script task, existing scripts that reference the old DTS object model cannot be converted.

Integration Services Package Management Utility

Another command-line tool that's provided with SQL Server 2005's Integration Services is the Package Management Utility. You can run the Package Management Utility by entering **dtutil** on the command line. The dtutil tool enables you to access packages that are stored in SQL Server's msdb database. It can also be used to copy, delete, and sign existing packages.

Integration Services Package Execution Utilities

Two additional utilities can be used to execute packages: dtexec and dtexecui. As you might surmise from their names, the dtexec tool is run from the command line, while the dtexecui tool displays a graphical user interface that enables you to load and run Integration Services packages. One notable aspect of the dtexec tool is the fact that for enhanced security it can be run using encrypted arguments. The dtexecui tool can be used to generate a text file that contains the commands and parameters required to run the dtexec command line tool (including the option to generate encrypted arguments). You can see the dtexecui tool in Figure 9-14.

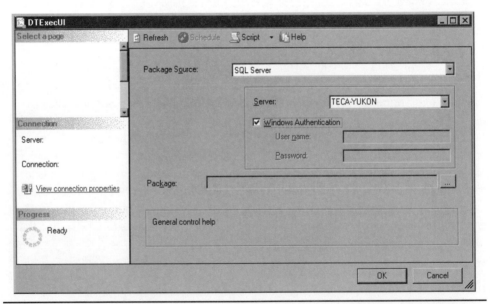

Figure 9-14 *The dtexecui tool*

Analysis Services

S ince the release of SQL Server 7 and OLAP services, SQL Server has been the clear leader in the business intelligence (BI) market. SQL Server 7 and its successor SQL Server 2000 ushered BI from being a niche technology into the computing mainstream. Now BI is one of the hottest market segments in the IT world, and for good reason. One of the primary reasons behind the rapid growth of BI is the fact that it enables an organization to get more information and value from the information resources than before. This has become a vital factor over the past several years, as many companies have experienced IT belt-tightening in recent times. Doing more with the resources that you already have enables IT to provide increased strategic value to the business organization.

BI enables a business to get more meaningful information out of the operational data that it currently uses in its line of business applications. By taking the operational data from their order entry, shipping, and sales applications, OLAP, data warehousing, and data mining technologies enable businesses to accumulate and aggregate important pieces of information in ways that are not possible with pure relational data access techniques. The end result uncovers more meaningful information about your business and the important factors that influence it. There's no free lunch, and BI is no exception to this rule. The road toward BI isn't free—personnel and training issues as well as technology issues need to be addressed—but in the long run, the costs can be justified. Being able to get more meaningful information out of your operational data can help transform IT into a core strategic advantage for your business.

In the past year the term BI has grown beyond the traditional interpretation, where BI was essentially synonymous with OLAP. Now BI has broadened to include all technologies that enable the business to provide decision-making information. With SQL Server 2005, Microsoft has certainly adopted this broader definition of BI. BI has taken a major role in SQL Server 2005. More than just OLAP and analysis, BI includes other information tools such as Integration Services and Reporting Services. Chapters 8 and 9 covered the new features in Integration Services and Reporting Services in more detail. In this chapter you'll get an overview of SQL Server 2005's new Analysis Services features.

BI has been a huge emphasis in this release of SQL Server, and there are so many new features that an entire book could be devoted to explaining them all. In this chapter I'll point out the most important new features in SQL Server 2005 Analysis Services. The first part of this chapter will provide a brief overview of OLAP and the role of Analysis Services. Next, you'll see the most important new features found in the Analysis Services Engine and you'll also get an introduction to Microsoft's new Unified Dimensional Model. The section after that covers the new Analysis Services Management and Development features. Finally, this chapter will present the new data mining algorithms that Microsoft has added to Analysis Services.

Analysis Services Overview

Analysis Services and its predecessor OLAP services were originally designed as a reporting solution for the data contained in a data warehouse or data mart. The information stored in a data warehouse is not typically relational data but rather summary data that's usually derived from a relational data store. This summary data is stored using a scheme that's optimized for flexible and fast ad hoc reporting. These data warehousing schemas are stored as either snowflake or star schemas. The data in a data warehouse or data mart is processed using *online analytical processing (OLAP)* technology. Unlike relational technology, which derives results by reading and joining data when the query is issued, OLAP is optimized to navigate the summary data to quickly return results. Improved query performance is the reason behind the emergence of OLAP. For example, to come up with the local, regional, national, and worldwide sales totals for a given organization, a relational query might have to process hundreds of thousands or even millions of rows—a process that could be quite lengthy even on the fastest of systems. In contrast, OLAP, because it works primarily on summary information, might need to read only two or three data points in order to come up with the same answer. Obviously, this results in a huge performance gain. OLAP's much faster performance enables ad hoc querying and processing of data that just isn't feasible using traditional means of relational data access.

Rather than working with sets of related tables, OLAP technologies work with *cubes,* consisting of dimensions and measures. A *dimension* is a descriptive category. For instance, a dimension might be a geographical location or a product type. A *measure* is a quantitative value such as sales dollars, inventory amount, or total expenses. Aggregates derived from the original data source are stored in each cube cell. This method of organizing data makes it easy to filter data as well as making subsequent queries fast and efficient. However, there is a trade-off. While OLAP aggregates are a key to the query performance attainable in data warehouse queries, the cost of storing the aggregate data is disk storage. In fact, the number of aggregates can easily exceed the number of original detail rows. In addition, line-of-business applications do not typically natively store their data in OLAP databases. Instead, the data to load a data warehouse is usually extracted from relational databases and loaded to the OLAP database in a process called *extraction, transformation, and loading (ETL).*

OLAP Storage Types

Three primary methods are used to store the dimensional data used in data warehousing: multidimensional OLAP (MOLAP), relational OLAP (ROLAP), and hybrid OLAP (HOLAP). Each of these methods has its own characteristic data storage requirements and data retrieval speed. SQL Server 2005 supports all of these methods.

MOLAP

Multidimensional OLAP (MOLAP) stores dimension and fact data in a persistent data store using compressed indexes. Aggregates are stored to facilitate fast data access. MOLAP query engines are usually proprietary and optimized for the storage format used by the MOLAP data store. MOLAP offers faster query processing than ROLAP and usually requires less storage. However, it doesn't scale as well and requires a separate database for storage.

ROLAP

Relational OLAP (ROLAP) stores aggregates in relational database tables. ROLAP use of the relational databases allows it to take advantage of existing database resources, plus it allows ROLAP applications to scale well. However, ROLAP's use of tables to store aggregates usually requires more disk storage than MOLAP, and it is generally not as fast.

HOLAP

As its name suggests, *hybrid OLAP (HOLAP)* is a cross between MOLAP and ROLAP. Like ROLAP, HOLAP leaves the primary data stored in the source database. Like MOLAP, HOLAP stores aggregates in a persistent data store that's separate from the primary relational database. This mix allows HOLAP to offer the advantages of both MOLAP and ROLAP. However, unlike MOLAP and ROLAP, which follow well-defined standards, HOLAP has no uniform implementation.

With a basic understanding of OLAP terminology behind us, let's take a look at some of the new enhancements in SQL Server 2005's Analysis Services.

Analysis Services Engine Enhancements

One of the primary areas of enhancements with Analysis Services has been in the Analysis Services engine itself. Many of these enhancements address limitations that were present in the SQL Server 2000 version of Analysis Services, and others have brought the product forward into totally new areas of functionality.

Multiple Instance Support

With SQL Server 2000, Analysis Services did not provide multiple instance support even though the relational database engine was able to support up to 16 instances. Multiple instance support is especially useful for application service providers (ASP) when multiple customers each maintain their own database instances that are all located on a shared server. Earlier versions of Analysis Services could not really be deployed in these situations. With SQL Server 2005, Analysis Services now provides support for up to 50 instances per server. Instances of SQL Server 2005 Analysis Services can also be set up to run side-by-side with previous versions of Analysis Services.

Failover Clustering Support

SQL Server 2005 has extended its support for failover clustering to Analysis Services. SQL Server 2000 Analysis Services did not support failover clustering for Analysis Services out of the box. The SQL Server 2005 Analysis Services installation process is cluster aware and can seamlessly install Analysis Services on cluster nodes. With SQL Server 2005, failover clustering is now aware of Analysis Services, and SQL Server Agent and Notification Services make failover clustering a complete server-level availability solution.

Integration with the .NET Framework

Just like the SQL Server 2005 relational database engine is integrated with the .NET Framework, Analysis Services also provides .NET integration. The new Analysis Services .NET integration enables full support for XML and Simple Object Access Protocol (SOAP) support as well as support for creating stored procedures and triggers in .NET languages such as Visual Basic and C#.

Unified Dimensional Model

One of the biggest changes for Analysis Services in SQL Server 2005 is the introduction of the new unified dimensional model. UDM, which can be viewed as the next evolutionary step in OLAP processing beyond cubes, promises to provide a unified reporting model by combining the best of OLAP and relational reporting. With previous technologies, some relationally based reports such as orders and invoices were very difficult to produce using OLAP tools. Likewise, the high-performance ad hoc query style of reporting that OLAP supports cannot be well adapted to relational reporting. The UDM provides a common ground that can handle both of these very different types of requirements. You can see a high-level overview of the relationship between applications and the UDM in Figure 10-1.

In SQL Server 2005 the cube is essentially the external representation of the UDM. While a cube is still presented to the reporting application under the covers, the mechanism for accessing the data is quite different. The UDM contains metadata that

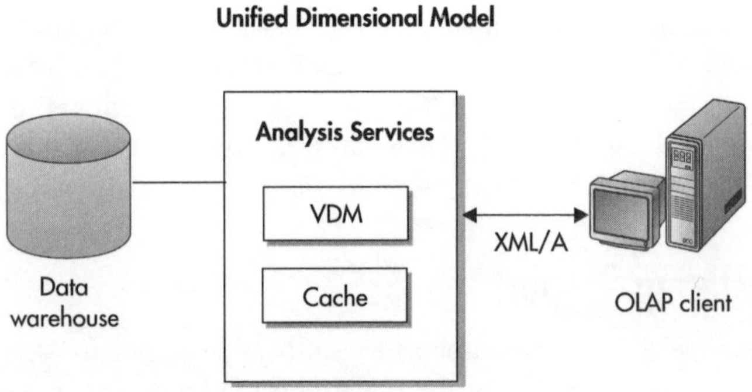

Unified Dimensional Model

Figure 10-1   *The unified dimensional model*

enables a number of capabilities that are not possessed by the MOLAP, ROLAP or HOLAP cubes that were present in SQL Server 2000 Analysis Services. In SQL Server 2005, OLAP applications connect to Analysis Services using XMLA and query the UDM, which can be built directly over both analytical and relational data sources.

Proactive Caching

The UDM can automatically cache data, providing very fast MOLAP-style data access without the accompanying need to explicitly define MOLAP storage. Using slider style controls you can control the latency and lifespan of the data in the cache. A setting of zero latency means that all of the data will be cached as MOLAP data. The data lafttime slider controls how long the data will live in the cache. You can specify that lifetimes of varing intervals such as daily, weekly or monthly and when the interval expired the cache will be cleared. Under the covers the proactive cache uses an on disk structure that's similar to a MOLAP cube.

Proactive caching really addresses the cube deployment pain points that were present in SQL Server 2000 Analysis services. With SQL Server 2000 Analysis Services a cube need to be processed (populated with data) before it could be deployed. For large data sets this processing time could be lengthy. Proactive caching solved this problem by enabling you to deploy cubes before they are processed. The cube is automatically populated as requests are made for the data.

Trigger Support

The addition of trigger support in SQL Server 2005 Analysis Services is another long-anticipated enhancement. Like their relational database counterparts, Analysis Services triggers can fire stored procedures when a specific database action occurs.

Analysis Services triggers run synchronously, which means that the job that fired the trigger is blocked until the triggered stored procedure has executed.

Trace Support

Another important new enhancement for SQL Server 2005's Analysis Services is support for tracing. Trace events are asynchronous and are used to monitor system performance and troubleshoot problems.

Scripting Support

SQL Server 2005's Analysis Services now supports the creation of Analysis Services databases and objects via scripting. SQL Server 2005 provides the new XML-based Object Definition Language (ODL), which can be used to create, modify, and delete Analysis Services database objects. ODL can also initiate such server actions as cube processing and comparing database versions. More information about ODL is presented later in this chapter.

Localization Enhancements

Another major enhancement in the Analysis Services engine is improved localization support. SQL Server 2005's Analysis Services engine is able to store object information in multiple languages. This allows Analysis Services applications to display both cube metadata and business data in the end user's native language. The Analysis Services engine also supports default language settings for client applications. This enables multilingual client applications to automatically use the appropriate language to display object information.

Orphaned Fact Table Row Support

Another limitation of SQL Server 2000 Analysis Services that SQL Server 2005 addresses is the problem of orphaned rows. SQL Server 2000 Analysis Services ignored rows that had an undefined member for a dimension. This resulted in a mismatch of the cube totals when compared with the data from the data source. Analysis Services in SQL Server 2005 allows you to specify how the Analysis Services engine handles fact table rows that have missing dimension information. You can choose either to continue to ignore the missing information or to force Analysis Services to create an Unknown dimension member for a fact table row that is missing dimension information.

Analysis Services Management Enhancements

The management tools for Analysis Services have completely changed in SQL Server 2005. In the SQL Server 2000 release, Analysis Services was managed using the Analysis Manager. With SQL Server 2005, the old Analysis Manager is gone. It's been replaced by the SQL Server Computer Manager and the SQL Server Management Studio.

SQL Server Computer Manager

The SQL Server Computer Manager is the tool to use to start and stop the Analysis Services service. You access by right-clicking My Computer and then selecting the Manage option from the pop-up menu. To start and stop Analysis Services, expand the Services and Applications node and then the SQL Computer Manager node. The display will look like the one shown in Figure 10-2.

Right-click the Analysis Services (MSSQLSERVER) service entry shown in the right pane to stop, start, and pause the Analysis Services service. More information about the SQL Server Computer Manager is presented in Chapter 2.

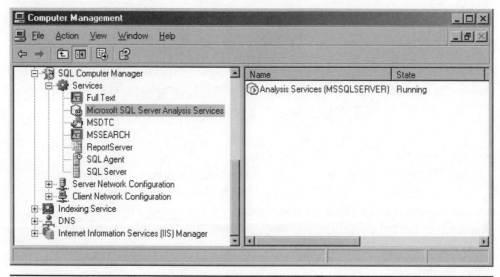

Figure 10-2 *SQL Server Computer Manager*

SQL Server Management Studio

The SQL Server Management Studio is the primary management tool for both SQL Server and Analysis Services. You can use the SQL Server Management Studio to perform a number of different management functions. It can create Analysis Services databases, plus it can script and deploy Analysis Server databases. You can use SQL Server Management Studio to set permissions for Analysis Services objects as well as to monitor the end-user access to Analysis Services.

Multidimensional Expression (MDX) Query Editor

In addition to these management functions, SQL Server Management Studio includes the Multidimensional Expression (MDX) Editor, which you can use to write and execute ad hoc queries and build Analysis Services objects using scripts. You can see the new MDX editor in Figure 10-3.

As you can see in Figure 10-3, SQL Server 2005's new MDX editor provides full support for color-coded keywords and an output window containing the MDX query

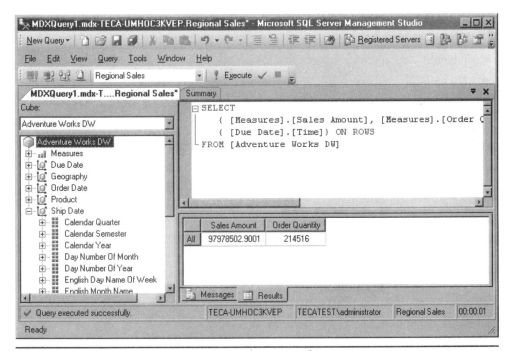

Figure 10-3   *SQL Server Management Studio MDX Editor*

results. There's also an integrated cube metadata browser that you can see in left side of the figure. More information about the SQL Server Management Studio is presented in Chapter 2.

Security

Security has been a major push for Microsoft in the past couple of years, and Analysis Services is no exception to this initiative. Analysis Services for SQL Server 2005 has over 100 security enhancements some of the most important of which are listed in the following section.

Security by Default

Analysis Services is designed to be secure by default. First, the service is installed to run with least privileges, reducing your company's exposure if the system is compromised. Next, when the product is first installed, all of the security options are turned on by default. Likewise, all features that might expose the system to threats are turned off by default. This includes

- ▶ Disabling HTTP access
- ▶ Disabling anonymous connections
- ▶ Disabling stored procedures
- ▶ Disabling Openrowset queries

If they are needed, all of these features can easily be turned on by the administrator, but they are turned off out of the box.

Encryption

Encryption is also used to enhance the security in Analysis Services for SQL Server 2005. Encryption is now present in several different areas. First, the communications channel between the client application and the server can be encrypted and the server can be configured to access only encrypted connections. The local cubes can be encrypted, plus the Analysis Services backup files can also optionally be encrypted.

Fine-Grained Administrative Privileges

The introduction of fine-grained administrative privileges is another security-related enhancement of Analysis Services in SQL Server 2005. With SQL Server 2000, you needed to be a member of the OLAP Administrators group in order to make changes to the Analysis Services database and configuration. The new administrative privileges in SQL Server 2005 Analysis Services enable you to create different administrators for each database. There are new permissions to read metadata, as well as another permission that enables an account to just process cubes.

Backup and Restore Enhancements

Analysis Services backup and restore have also been improved in SQL Server 2005. The new backup improvements include removal of the 2GB backup limit, the ability to compress and encrypt the backup, and the ability to easily restore a backup to a different instance of Analysis Services.

Removal of the 2GB Backup Limit

SQL Server 2000 Analysis Services backups were limited to backup files of less than 2GB. That limit has been lifted in SQL Server 2005, and Analysis Services' backup supports files up the NTFS limit of 16TB.

Ability to Compress and Encrypt the Backup

Analysis Services 2005's backup is now able to both compress and encrypt the files that are backed up. These options will add some time to the window required to perform the backup but will result in a smaller and more secure backup. You also have the option of skipping the backup of security information.

Ability to Easily Restore the Backup to a Different Instance

SQL Server 2005 Analysis Services supports the ability to back up Analysis Services databases just as you can relational SQL Server databases and restore them to a different instance of Analysis Services. This makes moving Analysis Services databases between servers very easy.

Development Enhancements

Analysis Services has undergone a number of development enhancements with the SQL Server 2005 release. The Business Intelligence Development Studio has replaced the Analysis Manager as the primary development tool. In addition, Analysis Services is now accessed using an entirely new protocol, XML for Analysis (XMLA), and there are two completely new .NET object frameworks: one for management, Analysis Management Objects (AMO), and the other for applications development, ADO MD.NET.

Business Intelligence Development Studio

The new Business Intelligence Development Studio is the primary tool for developing Analysis Services applications. With SQL Server 2005 there's a clear delineation between Analysis Services Management and the development of Analysis Services databases. While the SQL Server Management Studio is used to manage Analysis Services, the Business Intelligence Development Studio is used to develop Analysis Services solutions. Like the SQL Server Management Studio, the Business Intelligence Development Studio is based on the Visual Studio shell. More information about the Business Intelligence Development Studio is presented in Chapter 2.

Online and Offline Modes

Unlike the previous version of the Analysis Manager, which always worked in a connected mode, the new Business Intelligence Development Studio functions in both online and offline modes. By default, the Business Intelligence Development Studio works in an offline mode. In this mode the Business Intelligence Development Studio is not connected to the Analysis Services server and all of the changes and objects that you define reside within the development environment until you choose to deploy the project. When the project is deployed, the Business Intelligence Development Studio creates and executes an AMO deployment script. You can track the progress of this script in the output pane shown at the bottom of the Business Intelligence Development Studio window.

In contrast, online mode works much like the old Analysis Manager, where saving the changes that you make in the Business Intelligence Development Studio immediately updates the Analysis Services database on the server. You can switch from offline mode to online mode by selecting the File | Connect To Analysis Services Database option on the Business Intelligence Development Studio menu.

Data Sources and Data Source Views

The first step in creating new SQL Server 2005 Analysis Services projects is selecting the data source and creating a data source view. Very much like a relational data source, the Analysis Services data source essentially defines the server and the database where the data originates as well as encapsulating the authentication information. You define a data source by right-clicking the Data Source node in the Solution

Explorer window and then selecting the New Data Source option to start the Data Source Wizard, which guides you through the process of selecting the desired server and database. Analysis Services supports database connections to SQL Server, Oracle, DB2, and Teradata databases.

After the data source is created, you define a data source view to define the fact and dimension tables that you want to use to build your cube. To create a new data source view, you right-click the Data Source View node in the Solution Explorer window and then select the New Data Source View option. This starts the Data Source View Wizard. The first step in the wizard allows you to select the appropriate data source. After selecting the data source, you then select the fact and dimension tables using the Select Tables And Views dialog that you can see in Figure 10-4.

The Data Source View Wizard's Select Tables And Views dialog enables you to optionally filter the list to show a subset of the available database, which can be handy when dealing with large numbers of tables. To select tables and views, double-click them in the left-hand column. This action populates the Included Objects list that

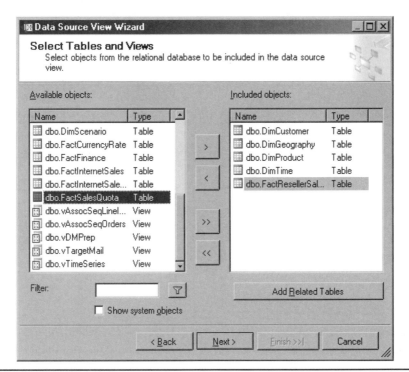

Figure 10-4 *Creating a data source view*

you can see in the right side of the figure. When you finish the Data Source View Wizard, the Data Source View Designer, shown in Figure 10-5, is automatically started.

The data source view is essentially an abstraction of one or more underlying data sources, and the Data Source View Designer enables you to customize the information that goes into the data source view. Using the Data Source View Designer, you can customize a number of different aspects and control how the data is presented. For instance, you can define and change database relationships, rename the tables, and create calculated columns. The changes that are made to the data source view are not propagated back to the underlying data sources. They reside only in the data source view.

Cube Wizard

To help you design your cubes, Analysis Services has an all-new Cube Wizard. After you've created your data sources and data source views, you run the Cube Wizard by right-clicking the Cube node in the Solution Explorer window and then selecting the

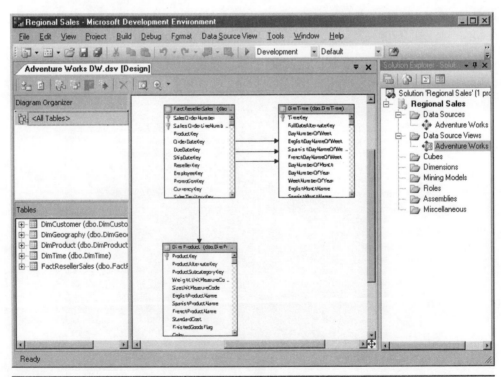

Figure 10-5   *Data Source View Designer*

New Cube option from the pop-up menu. This starts the Analysis Services 2005 Cube Wizard, which you can see in Figure 10-6.

The Cube Wizard in SQL Server 2005 is much more powerful that the Cube Wizard in the version of Analysis Services that was part of SQL Server 2000. The SQL Server 2005 Cube Wizard enables you to build a cube either in bottom-up fashion by selecting the data source and data source view that you defined or in top-down fashion by first designing the cube and its metadata. In the bottom-up scenario, the new IntelliCube feature will analyze the tables that were selected and automatically suggest fact and dimension tables to match their schema attributes. Alternatively, to build the cube in top-down fashion, you can select the Build The Cube Without A Data Source option. In this scenario, you manually define all of the cube's attributes. You can see the results of the IntelliCube's table selection in Figure 10-7.

IntelliCube does a pretty good job of automatically selecting the appropriate fact and dimension tables, but it's not perfect and you can freely change the table classifications that IntelliCube generates. After selecting the desired tables, the

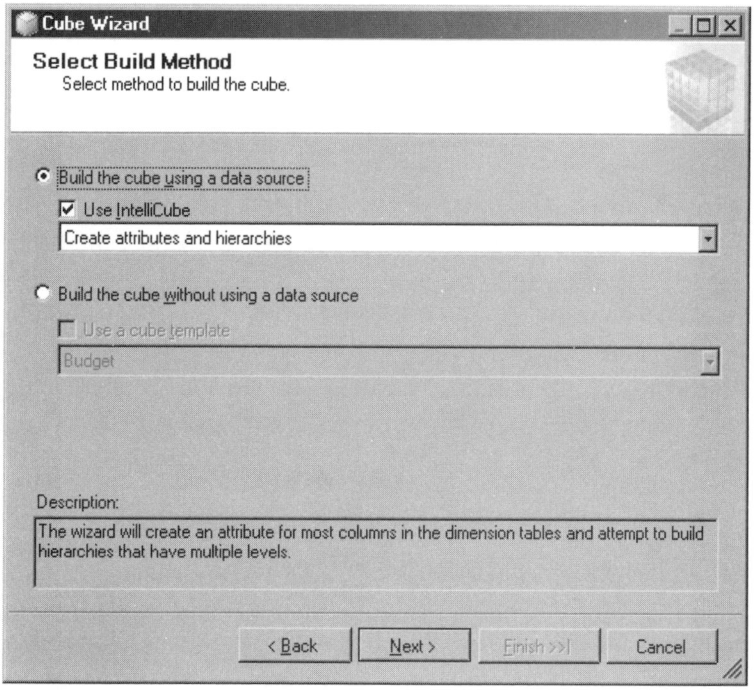

Figure 10-6 *Cube Wizard*

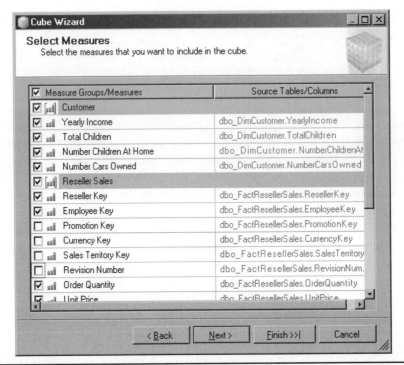

Figure 10-7   *Identify Fact and Dimension Tables*

Cube Wizard guides you through the process of selecting the measures for the cube. Basically, IntelliCube picks all of the numeric columns as possible measures. You can then select the columns that you want to use. You can see the Cube Wizard's Select Measures dialog in Figure 10-8.

After the fact and dimension tables have been selected and the appropriate measures have been defined, the Cube Wizard samples the data looking for possible relationships and creating data hierarchies.

Cube Editor

Once the Cube Wizard is finished, the Cube Editor is automatically displayed. The Analysis Services 2005 Cube Editor is significantly enhanced and offers a great deal of functionality beyond the features provided in the previous versions of Analysis Services. You can see the Cube Editor in Figure 10-9.

Figure 10-8   *Select Measures*

The SQL Server 2005 Analysis Services Cube Editor provides nine separate tabs, and each tab enables you to work with a different aspect of the cube. The nine cube views provided by the Cube Editor are

- ▶ **Cube Builder**   Works with the cube measures
- ▶ **Dimensions**   Works with the cube dimensions
- ▶ **Calculations**   Works with calculations for the cube
- ▶ **KPIs**   Works with Key Performance Indicators for the cube
- ▶ **Actions**   Works with cube actions
- ▶ **Partitions**   Works with cube partitions
- ▶ **Perspectives**   Works with views of the cube
- ▶ **Translations**   Defines optional transitions for the cube
- ▶ **Browser**   Enables you to browse the deployed cube

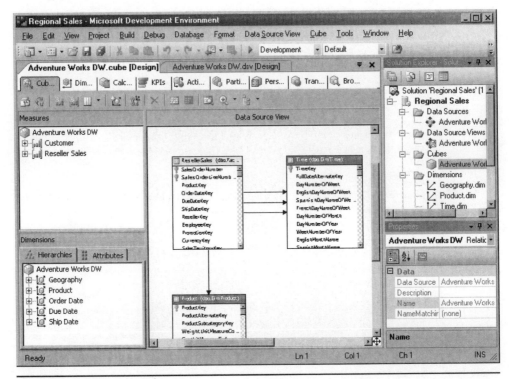

Figure 10-9   *The Cube Editor*

After the project has been defined, you can select the Build | Deploy Solution option to build the cube on the Analysis Services server. The project options control whether the cube will be processed after it is deployed to the server. By default, the cube will be processed when it is initially deployed.

Cube Browser

Once the cube has been deployed and processed, you can view and navigate through the cube's dimensions and measures using the Cube Editor's built-in browser. You can see an example of the Cube Browser in Figure 10-10.

The Cube Browser is built using the Office Web Component (OWC). You use the Cube Browser by dragging and dropping dimensions from the cube's attributes shown on the left side of the screen onto the OWC's row and column axes shown in the middle of the screen. Then you select the desired measures and drop them into

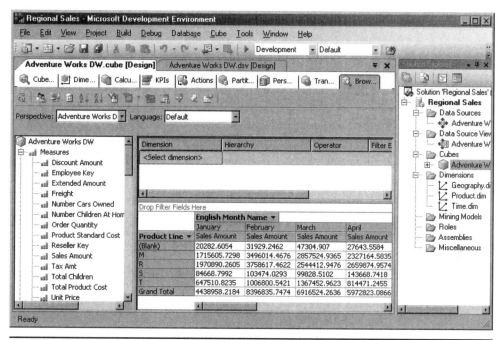

Figure 10-10   *The Cube Browser*

the data field. The Cube Browser automatically retrieves the data and displays it in the browser window.

Profiler

With SQL Server 2005, Analysis Services is no longer a black box server. SQL Server 2000 Analysis Services and SQL Server 7 OLAP Services didn't really provide any way for the administrator to see what the server was doing. With SQL Server 2005, the Profiler is capable of tracing all of the different functions that are running on Analysis Services just as it does for the relational SQL Server database. You start the Profiler by selecting the Profiler option from Window's Start | All Programs | Microsoft SQL Server 2005 menu. You can see the Profiler running against Analysis Services in Figure 10-11.

The Profiler is also a great tool for learning more about MDX. In addition, the Profiler is also a powerful troubleshooting tool for tracing the activities of the server. You can use the Analysis Services Profiler to capture and replay events on the server.

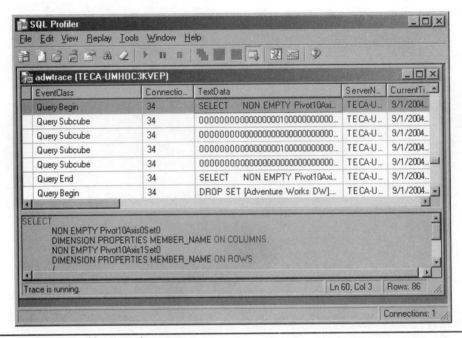

Figure 10-11   *Profiling Analysis Services*

XML for Analysis (XMLA)

XML for Analysis (XMLA) is a platform-independent protocol that's based on web services and SOAP. Microsoft SQL Server 2005 Analysis Services uses XMLA to handle all client application communications to Analysis Services. This includes both of Microsoft's own management and development tools: the SQL Server Management Studio and the Business Intelligence Development Studio. XMLA is optimized for the Internet and is designed to reduce round-trips to the server. In Figure 10-12 you can see how OLAP client and management applications use XMLA to connect to the Analysis Services platform.

XMLA supports two basic types of functions: execute requests and discover requests.

Execute Requests

As their name suggests, execute requests perform an action; they change the state of objects on the server. You can use execute requests to create, alter, and delete objects as well as process cubes.

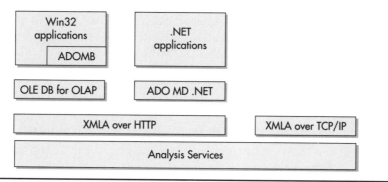

Figure 10-12   *XMLA connects clients to Analysis Services*

Discover Requests

Discover requests are used to retrieve information about objects on the server. Using discover requests, you can retrieve partition, cube, and security definitions. You can also query the system state of the server to learn about the number of connections in use as well as the resource utilization of the server.

ODL Enhancements

One of the most important management enhancements in Analysis Services for SQL Server 2005 is the new Object Definition Language (ODL). ODL brings the same type of scriptable object creation capabilities to Analysis Services that the relational SQL Server has always had. Analysis Services ODL enables you to write scripts that can automatically create all of your Analysis Services database objects. You can also use these scripts to control Analysis Services database versioning.

SQL Server 2005's new Analysis Services DDL is an open specification that's built on XML for Analysis (XMLA). Based on an open standard, Analysis Services ODL scripts can be created using any XML-aware editor.

MDX Enhancements

MDX remains the core query language for Analysis Services databases, and in SQL Server 2005 MDX has several important enhancements.

MDX Scripts

One of the biggest changes for MDX in SQL Server 2005 is the ability to group together multiple MDX statements into a script. Scripting enables multiple

MDX statements to be executed in sequence. Each MDX statement in the script is separated from the next by a semicolon.

Simplified Syntax

MDX now provides a new shorthand syntax for calculated members. The new shorthand syntax assumes the dimensions for identifying members, making it unnecessary to repeatedly explicitly specify the dimensions in your MDX statements.

Automatic Type Conversion

Automatic type conversions makes it possible to automatically convert from a member to a couple to a set and vice versa. This eliminates the need to write brackets and parentheses when specifying sets, making the MDX simpler and more readable.

Handling Missing Members

Another enhancement in SQL Server 2005 MDX is the ability to handle missing members. With SQL Server 2000, when you defined a report and one or more of the members the report used were no longer present, the report would fail. Various factors could cause this type of condition, including explicit changes to the underlying cube structure, as well as slow changes to dimensions. In SQL Server 2005's new MDX, you can use the MDXMissingMemberMode dimension property to enable a report to continue to function even when members of a dimension are missing.

Aggregation of Distinct Count Members

Adding another capability that was not present in SQL Server 2000's Analysis Services, MDX in SQL Server 2005 is now able to aggregate the contents of distinct count members.

Sets in the WHERE Clause

Using sets in the MDX WHERE clause is another important enhancement to Analysis Services in SQL Server 2005. Using sets in the MDX WHERE clause is essentially the same as using the OR keyword in the SQL WHERE clause. Sets enable the query to return the results from all of the members that are contained in the WHERE clause.

ADOMD.NET

ADOMD.NET is an all-new native .NET data provider that's designed to access multidimensional data sources. ADOMD.NET is designed to be the replacement for the older COM-based ADO MD multidimensional data access object library. Client applications built using any of the .NET languages such as Visual Basic, C#, Managed C++, or J# can use ADOMD.NET to retrieve data and metadata information from SQL Server 2005's Analysis Services. Under the covers, ADOMD.NET uses the XMLA protocol to connect to the Analysis Services server. ADOMD.NET applications can connect to Analysis Servers in two ways: XMLA over HTTP or XMLA over TCP/IP.

Analysis Services Management Objects (AMO)

Analysis Services Management Objects (AMO) is another entirely new object framework that Microsoft has introduced with SQL Server 2005. AMO is the successor to the older COM-based Decision Support Objects (DSO) that was provided with SQL Server 2000. DSO has not gone away. A version of DSO is included with SQL Server 2005 but is primarily available for backward compatibility.

AMO is built using the .NET framework and is designed exclusively to manage Analysis Services. AMO works at a higher level than XMLA, and like the other new Analysis Services object frameworks, AMO uses XMLA to communication with the Analysis Services server. Both the SQL Server Management Studio and the Business Intelligence Development Studio utilize AMO.

AMO supports secure management connections to Analysis Services. It provides support for Windows authentication as well as an encrypted communications channel between the client application and the server. AMO also optimizes the connection to the server by compressing the XML that is sent between the client and the Analysis Services server.

AMO provides several advantages over the old DSO model. First, AMO intelligently enumerates objects, giving it better performance when listing large numbers of items. AMO also provides the ability to back up and restore the system. In addition, AMO makes impact analysis available to your applications. An impact analysis enables your application to determine what Analysis Services objects will be affected by a given action. For instance, if a statement alters a cube's dimensions, it could require the cube to be reprocessed. Impact analysis helps to show you the effects of your statements.

Data Mining

Data mining allows organizations to utilize information derived from a line of business and use that information to make predictions about future business trends. Data mining predictions can help a business make better decisions about its future direction and how to make the best use of its resources. SQL Server 2000 provided two basic data mining algorithms: decision trees and clustering. To these SQL Server 2005 adds several new data mining algorithms. The data mining algorithms that are included with SQL Server 2005 are: Decision Trees, Time Series, Sequence Clustering, Naïve Bayes, and Association Rules.

Decision Trees

The Microsoft Decision Trees (DT) algorithm is designed primarily for prediction. This algorithm is used to predict continuous and discrete variables.

Times Series

The new Time Series algorithm introduces the concept of past, present, and future into the prediction business. Designed to predict the next steps of the numerical sequence, the Time Series algorithm not only selects the best predictors for a given target but also identifies the best time periods over which you should expect to notice the effect of each predicting factor.

Clustering and Sequence Clustering

The Clustering algorithm is designed to find a good cluster count for your model given the properties of the training data. Sequence clustering allows you to find clusters of sequences of data. In other words, it is order-sensitive clustering.

Naïve Bayes

The new Naïve Bayes algorithm is a predictive algorithm. Designed for very fast performance, this algorithm predicts relationships between classifications of items.

Association Rules

Designed for analyzing transactional data, the Association Rules algorithm is used to find groups of items that exist within a single transaction.

Appendixes

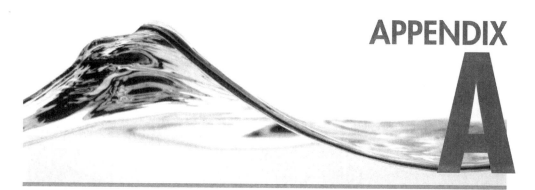

Installation
and Upgrading

IN THIS APPENDIX:

SQL Server 2005 Editions

Installing SQL Server 2005

Upgrading to SQL Server 2005

I n this appendix, you'll get an overview of the SQL Server 2005 installation and upgrade options.

SQL Server 2005 Editions

As with the previous releases of SQL Server, Microsoft provides several different editions of SQL Server 2005. Microsoft will provide the following different versions of SQL Server:

▶ **SQL Server 2005 Enterprise Edition** The Enterprise Edition provides the full feature set available in SQL Server 2005.

▶ **SQL Server 2005 Standard Edition** The Standard Edition provides the SQL Server core feature set but does not provide all of the enterprise-oriented features that support very large databases and high-end scalability.

▶ **SQL Server 2005 Developer's Edition** The Developer Edition provides the same feature set as the Enterprise Edition. However, it is not licensed for production use.

▶ **SQL Server 2005 Express** SQL Server 2005 Express is the replacement for MSDE. Like MSDE, it can be run royalty free. Unlike MSDE, it does not have a workload governor.

Installing SQL Server 2005

SQL Server 2005's installation is different than the installation process for any of the previous versions of SQL Server and addresses a number of issues that were present in the installation of the earlier versions. Unlike the earlier SQL Server installation programs, which were .EXE based, the setup program for SQL Server 2005 is standardized on Microsoft Installer (MSI) 3.0. Being MSI based makes SQL Server easier to use for unattended setups as well as for distributing the software using Microsoft Systems Management Server (SMS). The new installation program also provides one-step setup for Microsoft failover clusters.

SQL Server 2005's installation is started using the Autorun file on the CD or by running the setup.exe program. The setup.exe program greets the users with the initial splash screen that you can see in Figure A-1.

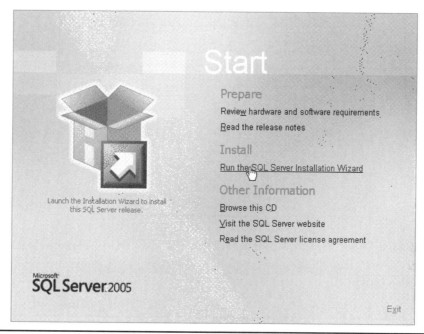

Figure A-1   *SQL Server 2005 installation splash screen*

Clicking the Run The SQL Server Installation Wizard link begins the installation by presenting the user with the End User License Agreement (EULA). After you accept the license agreement, you will see the initial installation screen shown in Figure A-2.

The SQL Server Component Update dialog checks to make sure that all of the components that are required to set up SQL Server 2005 are installed on the system. If the components are not found, they are copied to the system. This step installs the latest .NET Framework as well as copies the setup files to the local system. After all of the required setup components have been installed, clicking Finish displays the Welcome To The SQL Server Installation Wizard screen that's shown in Figure A-3.

The Welcome dialog essentially just serves to notify you that you are about to begin installing the SQL Server product. Clicking past the Welcome dialog displays the System Configuration Check dialog shown in Figure A-4.

The System Configuration Check dialog scans the system to make sure that it meets all of the requirements for installing SQL Server 2005. The installation program performs a series of system checks to make sure that the system is capable of running SQL Server 2005. As each item is checked, the installation program flags it with

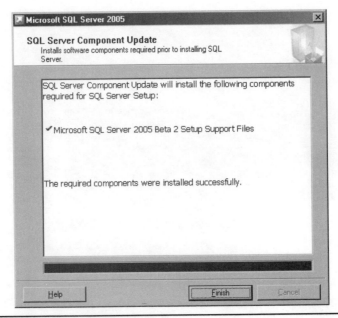

Figure A-2   *SQL Server Component Update*

Figure A-3   *Welcome to the SQL Server Installation Wizard*

Figure A-4   *System Configuration Check*

either a green check mark indicating success, a yellow warning sign indicating there is a possible problem, or a red X indicating that there is a serious error. The installation can proceed with warnings, but if there is a red X, the item must be fixed before the installation can continue. Selecting the flagged item and clicking Report can give you more information about each item. Table A-1 lists the system checks that must be passed before SQL Server 2005 can be installed.

Requirement	Description
WMI Service Requirement	The WMI Service must be installed.
MSXML Requirement	The .NET Framework Quick Fix Engineering (QFE) update must be installed.
Operating System Minimum Level Requirement	One of the following operating systems is required: Windows 2000, Windows XP, Windows Server 2003.
Operating System Minimum Service Pack Requirement	One of the following operating system service pack levels is required: Windows 2000 SP4, Windows XP SP1.

Table A-1   *System Checks*

Requirement	Description
Minimum Hardware Requirement	The minimum hardware levels required to install SQL Server 2005 follow: CPU: Intel Pentium 700 MHz. RAM: 128MB is required for SQL Server Standard and Enterprise Editions; 64MB is required for SQL Server Developer and Express Editions. Storage: A minimum of 95MB is required for SQL Server up to a maximum of 300MB, Analysis Services requires 50MB, and the Reporting Service requires 50MB.
IIS Feature Requirement	IIS must be installed in order to run Reporting Services and SQLXML applications. If IIS is not installed, installation can proceed but the Reporting Services application will not be available for installation.
Pending Reboot Requirement	Prior installation steps may require a system reboot. If so, then a system reboot must be performed.
Performance Monitor Counter Requirement	The performance counter registry keys must be able to increment properly.
Default Installation Path Permission Requirement	The user running the installation must have administrative privileges.
Internet Explorer Requirement	Internet Explorer 6.0 SP1 is required to run the Business Intelligence Development Studio.
Manifest Requirement	The setup configures the following files to use MDAC 9.0: mmc.exe, wmiprvse.exe, msftefd.exe, inetinfo.exe, dllhost.exe, w3wp.exe, and aspnet_wp.exe.

Table A-1 *System Checks* (continued)

If all of the system requirements have been met, the Continue button will be enabled. Clicking Continue displays the Registration Information dialog, which requires you to enter your name, the company name, and your 25-digit product key. After you fill in these values and click Next, the installation program will display the Components To Install dialog that you can see in Figure A-5.

The Components To Install dialog enables you to select which SQL Server 2005 components you want to install. If IIS is not present on the system, the Reporting Services option will not be available. If you're installing SQL Server 2005 on a cluster, then the Install As Virtual Server option will be enabled.

NOTE

To set up an administrative system, just select the Workstation components option.

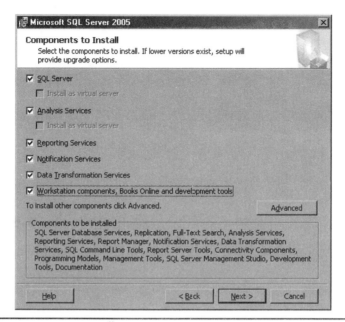

Figure A-5   *Components To Install*

While this level of component selection will be sufficient for most users, there is also a more granular feature selection dialog that gives you the ability to select exactly which components will be installed. You can display the Feature Selection dialog shown in Figure A-6 by clicking Advanced.

The Feature Selection dialog enables you to drill down into each installation component and option, excluding various features.

NOTE

By default, no sample databases or applications are installed. If you want to install the sample AdventureWorks database and/or the programming samples, then you must use the Feature Selection dialog to select the Databases And Samples option.

After you've selected the components that you want to install, click Next to display the Instance Name dialog that you can see in Figure A-7.

If this is the first time you've run through the installation program, you have the option to either set up the default instance or set up a named instance. If you've already set up a default SQL Server instance, the setup program will detect that

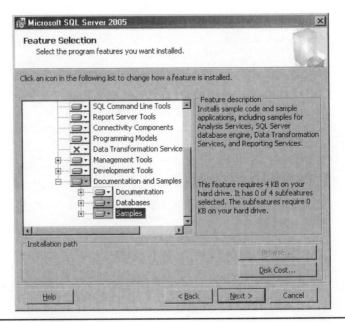

Figure A-6   *Feature Selection*

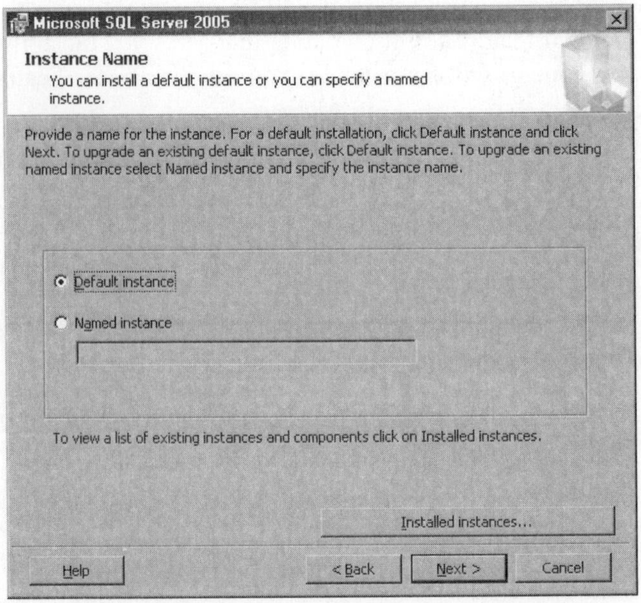

Figure A-7   *Instance Name*

instance and offer you only the option to set up a named instance. You can have up to 50 named instances on a given system. Most implementations will use only a single instance, but installation for ISPs and ASPs will often require more. If you create a named instance, each name must be 16 characters or less. Instance names are not case sensitive, but the first character of the name must be a letter. They cannot have any embedded spaces and must not contain the backslash (\\), comma (,), colon (:), single quote('), dash(-), ampersand (&), number sign (#), or at sign (@). Instance names also cannot contain the reserved words "Default" or "MSSQLServer."

NOTE

If you create a named instance, the SQL Server service name will be named as follows: MSSQLSInstanceName (where InstanceName is replaced with the instance name that you create).

After you either accept the default instance or create a named instance and click Next, the Service Account dialog that you can see in Figure A-8 is displayed.

The values in the Service Account dialog specify the user accounts used by the SQL Server service as well as the SQL Server Agent, Analysis Services, and Reporting Server. This is an important selection because it governs the permissions that each of these services runs under. By default, the Service Account dialog directs

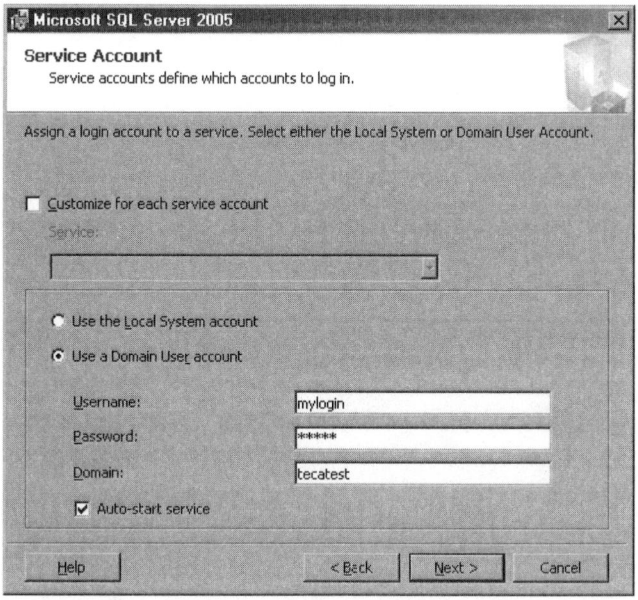

Figure A-8   *Service Account*

you to select a Domain User account for the SQL Server service. You can use the administrative account, but because of its high privilege level, that's not a great idea. You can also select the Local System account; however, this account is very powerful, having administrative-like permissions, and is limited in its ability to access network resources. Typically, you would want to create a domain user account specifically for SQL Server to run under and select this account. This gives you the ability to more granularly control the permissions that the various services possess. After you specify the service account, click Next to display the Authentication Mode dialog shown in Figure A-9.

The Authentication Mode dialog defines the type of user authentication that SQL Server 2005 will use. The default value is Windows Authentication, meaning that the Windows user accounts will also be used in SQL Server. Typically, this is what you want because it provides easier management in that only one set of login accounts needs to be managed and that set of logins is maintained by the host operating system. It is also more secure because with Windows authentication, the application does not need to pass the user ID across the network. You can also choose Mixed Mode Authentication, which means that both Windows logins and SQL Server logins can be accepted. In the case of SQL Server logins, you must manually add these logins to SQL Server, and they are maintained independently from the Windows login. After selecting the authentication mode that the server will

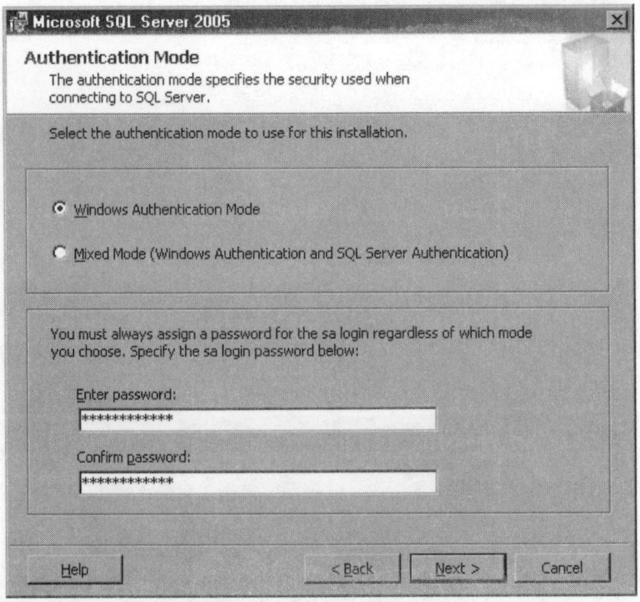

Figure A-9   *Authentication Mode*

use, you then need to select a password for the SQL Server System Administrator
(sa) login. For security reasons, you must select a non-blank password. You should
strongly consider making this a strong password that's at least eight characters
in length, containing characters, numbers, and special characters. Clicking Next
displays the Collation Settings dialog that you can see in Figure A-10.

The Collation Settings dialog enables you to specify the default sorting order that
will be used by SQL Server 2005. While the collation setting specified during the
installation sets SQL Server 2005's default collation, the collation order can also be
set for each individual database. If you choose SQL collations to install Analysis
Services, the dialog will be displayed that asks if you want to use the Latin1_General
collation for Analysis Services.

If you have chosen to install Reporting Services, clicking Next displays the
Report Server Virtual Directories dialog that you can see in Figure A-11.

The Report Server Virtual Directories dialog is displayed only if you have chosen to
install the Reporting Services component on the Components To Install dialog shown
earlier in Figure A-5. The Reporting Services Virtual Directories dialog enables you
to specify the IIS virtual directory that will be used to publish Reporting Services
reports as well as the Virtual Directory that can be used to manage Reporting Services.
If you're working with the default SQL Server instance, the names ReportingServer
and Reporting will be used. When you create a named instance, the instance name is

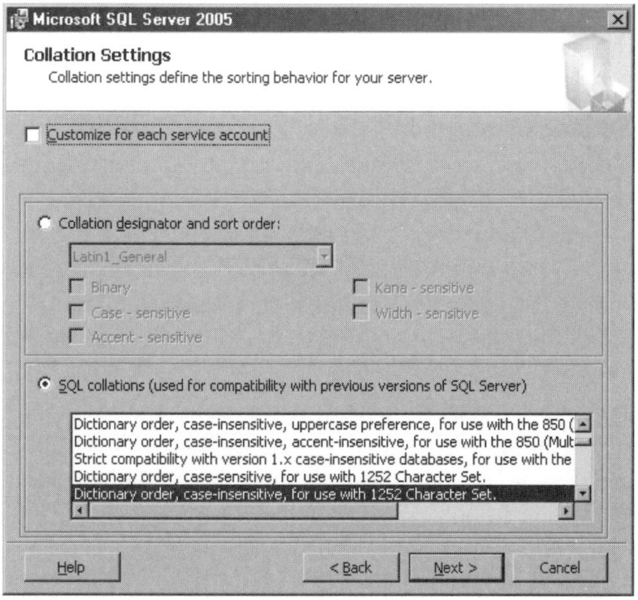

Figure A-10   *Collation Settings*

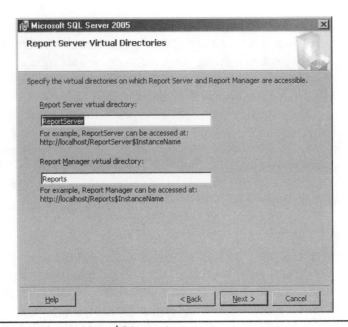

Figure A-11   *Report Server Virtual Directories*

appended to the ReportServer$ or Reporting$ constants to create the names of the publishing and management virtual directories, respectively. Once you've specified the Reporting Services virtual directory names, clicking Next displays the Report Server Database Setup dialog that you can see in Figure A-12.

The Report Server Database Setup dialog allows you to select where the SQL Server database that's used by Reporting Services will be installed. This is the database that Reporting Services will use to store its report definitions. The reports themselves can use any number of other data sources. By default, the SQL Server 2005 installation program will create the Reporting Services database in the current SQL Server instance. However, you can also choose to install the Reporting Services database in another SQL Server system. For most medium and larger organizations, separating Reporting Services out into its own server and keeping it apart from your product database is a good idea for performance reasons. The Report Server Setup dialog also enables you to specify the name that will be used for the Reporting Services database. For the default instance, the database name ReportServer will be used. If you're installing Reporting Services on a named instance, then the database name will be ReportingServer$*InstanceName,* where *InstanceName* is replaced by your SQL Server instance name. As with the virtual directory names, you can change this value. After you set the Reporting Services database options, clicking Next displays the setup screen shown in Figure A-13.

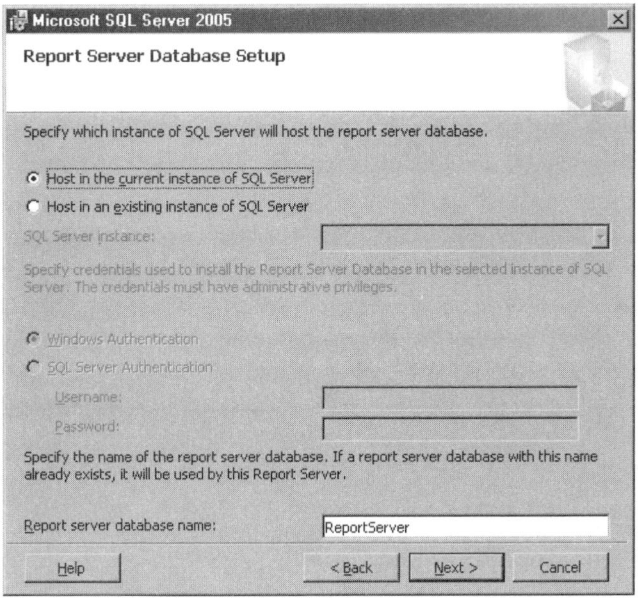

Figure A-12   *Report Server Database Setup*

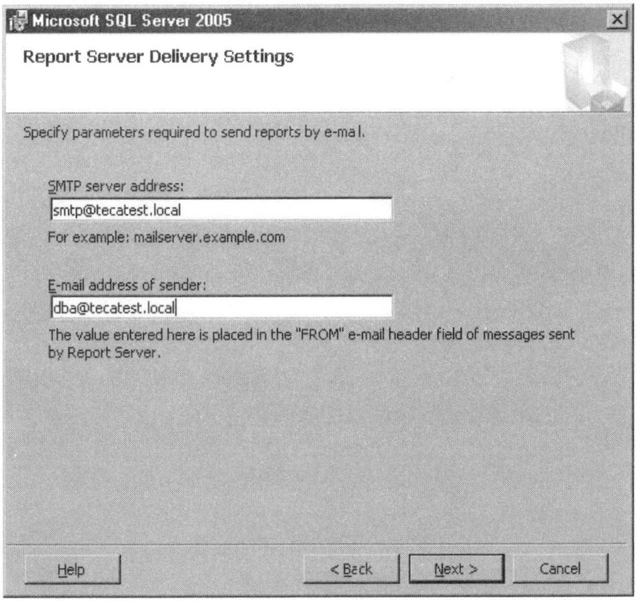

Figure A-13   *Report Server Delivery Settings*

The Reporting Services Delivery Settings dialog allows you to specify the SMTP server address that Reporting Services will use to deliver e-mail notifications and reports. It also enables you to specify the return address that Reporting Services will use when sending e-mail messages. Filling in these values is optional—you can go back and set them or change the values after the installation process has completed. Clicking Next will cause the SQL Server 2005 Error Reporting dialog to be displayed. You can see the Error Reporting dialog in Figure A-14.

Much like the Watson support that Microsoft added to Windows XP, SQL Server 2005's error reporting screen enables you to optionally report fatal SQL Server errors to Microsoft. Microsoft does not collect any personal information from these reports. They are just used to help identify and eliminate problems that may occur within SQL Server. SQL Server 2005's error reports send the following information to Microsoft:

▶ The status of SQL Server when the error occurred

▶ The operating system version

▶ The basic hardware configuration

▶ SQL Server's Digital Product ID (which is used to identify your license)

▶ The server's IP address

▶ Information from storage about the process that caused the error

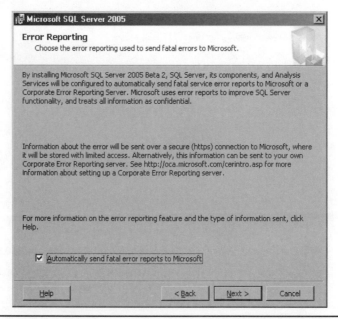

Figure A-14   *Error Reporting*

This error reporting is totally optional. While automatic error reporting is turned on by default, you can easily turn it off by unchecking the Automatically Send Fatal Error Reports To Microsoft check box. After you address the Error Reporting dialog, clicking Next displays the Ready To Install dialog that is shown in Figure A-15.

The Ready To Install dialog enables you to confirm your choices. If you need to change anything, you can use the Back button to page back through the previous installation screens. Clicking Install on the Ready To Install dialog begins the installation process for SQL Server 2005. As the installation progresses, the screen shown in Figure A-16 is displayed.

The installation progress screen displays the status of the installation. A green check indicates that a component was installed successfully. A red X indicates an error. After the installation is finished, SQL Server will be ready to use.

Verifying the Installation

You can verify the installation of SQL Server by checking to see if the necessary services are running. For help troubleshooting installation problems, you can also view the setup log file.

Figure A-15   *Ready To Install*

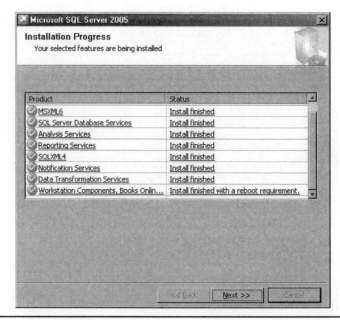

Figure A-16   *Installation Progress*

Services

Table A-2 lists the services used by SQL Server. You can see these services using the Start | Administrative Tools | Services applet.

Setup Log Files

If the installation program has failed, you can look into the SQL Server setup log files. Table A-3 lists the log files used by SQL Server 2005.

Service	Description
SQL Server (MSSQLSERVER) and/or MSSQLS*InstanceName*	The SQL Server database engine and/or a named instance of the SQL Server database engine
SQL Server Agent (MSSQLSERVER) and/or SQLAgent$*InstanceName*	The SQL Server job scheduling agent and/or a named instance of the SQL Server job scheduling agent
MSSQLServerOLAPService and/or MSOLAP$*InstanceName*	SQL Server Analysis Services and/or a named instance of SQL Server Analysis Services
ReportServer and/or ReportServer$*InstanceName*	SQL Server Reporting Services and/or a named instance of the SQL Server Reporting Services

Table A-2   *SQL Server 2005 Services*

Log File	Directory	Description
sqlstpX.log	%temp%	This file contains setup information from the Windows installer. Each run increments the value of X.
Sqlsetup<xxxx>_<machine>_support.log	%temp%	Created by setup.
SQLSetup*.txt	%sqlserver%\90\Setup\Bootstrap\LOG	SQL Server's setup bootstrap files.
sqlrunXlog.log	%temp%	Contains setup procedure information. Each run increments the value of X.
dasetup.log	%windows%	Microsoft Data Access Components setup log.
errorlog.log	%sqlserver%\mssql\log\errorlog	SQL Server error log.

Table A-3   *SQL Server 2005 Log Files*

Upgrading to SQL Server 2005

In addition to creating new installations, the SQL Server 2005 setup program can also be used to upgrade existing SQL Server 7 and SQL Server 2000 installations. However, it cannot be used to upgrade existing SQL Server 6.5 installations.

Upgrading from SQL Server 7 and 2000

The setup program supports direct upgrades from SQL Server 7 and SQL Server 2000 to SQL Server 2005. SQL Server's essential on-disk structures are the same, and the setup program can successfully perform an in-place migration for SQL Server 7 and SQL Server 2000 installations to SQL Server 2005. Table A-4 lists the supported upgrade scenarios for SQL Server 7 and SQL Server 2000.

Existing SQL Server Edition	Upgrade to SQL Server 2005 Standard Edition (32-bit & 64-bit)	Upgrade to SQL Server 2005 Enterprise Edition (32-bit & 64-bit)
MSDE 2000	Yes	No
SQL Server 7 Standard Edition	Yes	Yes
SQL Server 7 Enterprise Edition	No	Yes
SQL Server 2000 Standard Edition	Yes	Yes
SQL Server 2000 Enterprise Edition	No	Yes

Table A-4   *SQL Server 2005 Upgrade Options*

Upgrading from SQL Server 6.5 (or Earlier)

Directly upgrading from SQL Server 6.5 or any earlier edition of SQL Server to SQL Server 2005 is not supported. The on-disk structures and database storage used by SQL Server 6.5 and earlier versions are different than the on-disk structures used by SQL Server 2005. Therefore, you cannot directly perform an in-place upgrade. The only way to accomplish an in-place upgrade is indirectly, by first upgrading SQL Server 6.5 to SQL Server 2000 and then upgrading SQL Server 2000 to SQL Server 2005. However, performing two upgrades to accomplish one probably isn't the most efficient method. Assuming adequate hardware and minimum operating system levels, the setup program can be used to install a new instance of SQL Server 2005 on a system running SQL Server 6.5. However, most existing SQL Server 6.5 installations will probably be running on dated hardware, and in most cases you would want to get new hardware anyway. The bottom line is that the best way to migrate from SQL Server 6.5 to SQL Server 2005 is to perform a new installation of SQL Server 2005 on fresh hardware and then perform a manual upgrade by moving your data and database objects with DTS and recompiling your stored procedures and other user database objects.

Quick Facts

Τhis appendix presents a reference for several of SQL Server 2005's important system and database maximum limits.

Category	Capacity
Maximum addressable memory	32TB (64-bit) 64GB (32-bit using PAE)
Maximum number of processors	64 (64-bit) 32 (32-bit)
Maximum nodes for cluster	8
SQL Server instances per server	50
Locks per instance	Limited only by memory (64-bit) 2,147,483,647 (32-bit)

Table B-1 *System Maximum Limits*

Category	Capacity
Databases per server	32,767
Database size	1,048,516TB
Files per database	32,767
File groups per database	265
File size (data)	32TB
File size (log)	32TB
Objects in a database	2,147,483,647
Identifier length	128

Table B-2 *Database Maximum Limits*

Category	Capacity
Tables per database	Limited by the number of objects in a database
Rows per table	Limited by available storage
PRIMARY KEY constraints per table	1
FOREIGN KEY constraints per table	253
References per table	253
Triggers per table	Limited by the number of objects in a database
Clustered indexes per table	1
Nonclustered indexes per table	249
UNIQUE constraints per table	249 nonclustered, 1 clustered

Table B-3   *Tables*

Category	Capacity
Columns per index	16
Columns per primary key	16
Columns per foreign key	16
Columns per table	1024
Index key size	900 bytes
Bytes per character or binary column	8000
Bytes per text, ntext, or image column	2GB
Bytes per row	8060
Bytes per index	900
Bytes per primary key	900
Bytes per foreign key	900

Table B-4   *Columns*

Category	Capacity
Batch size	65,536 multiplied by the network packet size
Tables per SELECT statement	256
Bytes in source text of a stored procedure	Lesser of batch size or 250MB
Parameters per stored procedure	1024
Nested subqueries	32
Nested trigger levels	32
Columns per SELECT statement	4096
Columns per INSERT statement	1024

Table B-5   *T-SQL Maximum Limits*

Index

INTERNATIONAL CONTACT INFORMATION

AUSTRALIA
McGraw-Hill Book Company
Australia Pty. Ltd.
TEL +61-2-9900-1800
FAX +61-2-9878-8881
http://www.mcgraw-hill.com.au
books-it_sydney@mcgraw-hill.com

CANADA
McGraw-Hill Ryerson Ltd.
TEL +905-430-5000
FAX +905-430-5020
http://www.mcgraw-hill.ca

GREECE, MIDDLE EAST, & AFRICA
(Excluding South Africa)
McGraw-Hill Hellas
TEL +30-210-6560-990
TEL +30-210-6560-993
TEL +30-210-6560-994
FAX +30-210-6545-525

MEXICO (Also serving Latin America)
McGraw-Hill Interamericana Editores
S.A. de C.V.
TEL +525-1500-5108
FAX +525-117-1589
http://www.mcgraw-hill.com.mx
carlos_ruiz@mcgraw-hill.com

SINGAPORE (Serving Asia)
McGraw-Hill Book Company
TEL +65-6863-1580
FAX +65-6862-3354
http://www.mcgraw-hill.com.sg
mghasia@mcgraw-hill.com

SOUTH AFRICA
McGraw-Hill South Africa
TEL +27-11-622-7512
FAX +27-11-622-9045
robyn_swanepoel@mcgraw-hill.com

SPAIN
McGraw-Hill/
Interamericana de España, S.A.U.
TEL +34-91-180-3000
FAX +34-91-372-8513
http://www.mcgraw-hill.es
professional@mcgraw-hill.es

UNITED KINGDOM, NORTHERN, EASTERN, & CENTRAL EUROPE
McGraw-Hill Education Europe
TEL +44-1-628-502500
FAX +44-1-628-770224
http://www.mcgraw-hill.co.uk
emea_queries@mcgraw-hill.com

ALL OTHER INQUIRIES Contact:
McGraw-Hill/Osborne
TEL +1-510-420-7700
FAX +1-510-420-7703
http://www.osborne.com
omg_international@mcgraw-hill.com